TRAUMA AND RACE

TRAUMA AND RACE

A LACANIAN STUDY OF AFRICAN AMERICAN RACIAL IDENTITY

Sheldon George

BAYLOR UNIVERSITY PRESS

Cover Design and Artwork by Hannah Feldmeier

Ideas articulated in chapter 2 were first explored in the *Journal for the Psychoanalysis of Culture and Society* 6, no. 1 (Spring 2001). A version of chapter 5 appeared in *African American Review* 45, nos. 1–2 (Spring/Summer 2012). Other material throughout the book is taken from "Realism's Racial Gaze and Stephen Crane's The Monster: A Lacanian Reading." *Experiments in/of Realism*. Special issue of *Synthesis* 3 (Winter 2011): 69–86. The author is grateful to the editors of these journals for inclusion of this material.

This project was supported by a grant from the Simmons College Fund for Research and the Simmons College Completion Grant.

Library of Congress cataloging-in-publication data

George, Sheldon, 1973–
  Trauma and race : a Lacanian study of African American racial identity / Sheldon George.
  192 pages cm
  Includes bibliographical references and index.
  ISBN 978-1-60258-734-2 (hardback : alkaline paper)
1. African Americans—Race identity. 2. Slavery—United States—Psychological aspects. 3. Racism—United States—Psychological aspects. 4. Psychic trauma—Social aspects—United States. 5. Lacan, Jacques, 1901–1981—Philosophy. 6. African Americans in literature. 7. Slavery in literature. 8. Racism in literature. 9. Psychic trauma in literature. 10. American literature—African American authors—History and criticism. I. Title.
  E185.625.G46 2016
  305.896'073—dc23
                      2015014113

Dedicated to
Mathias and Sebastian

Contents

Acknowledgments

Words ever miss their mark, but sometimes they resonate with what is yet left unsaid. It is with awareness of my inability to do so adequately that I express my gratitude to all those who have made possible my writing of this book. First among my colleagues is Jean Wyatt, whose generous gift of hours of conversation about theory and whose careful reading of multiple chapters of the book challenged and sharpened my interpretation of Lacan. Jean's hand in the work of the woman who first introduced me to Lacanian theory so many years ago, Frances Restuccia, makes them both progenitors of this project. I thank Frances for modeling a rigor and dedication to clear thinking that is simply inspiring. I owe an immense debt of gratitude to Todd McGowen for his insightful feedback on this project and my broader scholarship. For their support of my work, I express particular appreciation to Annie Stopford, Lynne Layton, Naomi Morgenstern, and the members of the Boston Lacan Study Group, especially Marcos Cancado and Rolf Flor. My most gracious appreciation goes out to Lawrence Hanley, who lit the initial flame.

This book owes its existence to the kind support of my friends and colleagues in the English department at Simmons College. Pam Bromberg, Kelly Hager, and especially Lowry Pei have been careful and generous readers of my chapters. I thank Richard Wollman for his stimulating reflections on Shakespeare and deconstructive theory. Afaa Weaver has been a mentor and guide. I thank him for allowing me to hear more clearly the echoes of the unspoken past to which this theory adds its voice. Renee Bergland has been a kind patron of my scholarship, and I thank Suzanne Leonard for her inspirational support and Rachel Lacasse for her self-sacrificing generosity. I am grateful to countless students, particularly those in my graduate seminars "Toni Morrison and American Literature" and "Race and Gender in Psychoanalytic Theory," for having been early and engaged responders to the readings in this book. I offer a special thank you to Carol Harper, Andrew Maxcy, Emily Brodeur, and Cassandra Geraghty, who served as my research assistants during the writing of this book. For her painstaking indexing of the text, I extend my deepest thanks to Amy Stewart.

Without my family, this book would have little meaning. I thank my parents for their liberating vision of the possible and my brother for his dogged insistence upon the will of the individual against the impediments of conventionality. Above all, I am grateful to my wife, who secures me in the path of my desires, and my sons, who point the way to a future that is not merely fantastical. For generously bequeathing me with the gift of time and solitude that writing this book demanded, I thank my extended family, Luke, Maria, and Allen.

Introduction
Race Today, or Alterity and Jouissance

On November 23, 2012, a seventeen-year-old African American boy named Jordan Davis was shot and killed at a gas station in Jacksonville, Florida. During a verbal exchange with Davis over loud music being played by Davis and three friends, the shooter, a forty-seven-year-old white male named Michael Dunn, pulled out a handgun from his glove compartment and fired ten shots at the parked SUV that Davis occupied; three bullets struck Davis, piercing his liver and killing him, with the other seven riddling the side and back of the SUV as it drove off. In his murder trial, Dunn justified his actions as self-defense, arguing that he feared for his life. Yet Dunn's fear-induced response seems clearly excessive, begging us to question what fuels this fear that inspired him to fire ten times at a retreating vehicle. Dunn's case, which ignored a focus on racial motivations and led to both his conviction for *attempted* murder of Davis's friends and a mistrial on the charge of murder for *succeeding* in killing Davis, exacerbated national outrage about the apparent lack of value placed on the lives of young black men in America, a debate already ignited months earlier by the Florida not guilty verdict for George Zimmerman in the killing of another black teenager, Trayvon Martin. Both these cases help to demonstrate how race functions in contemporary American society. They

1

point to the need to understand race not strictly as an embodied fact but as a projected reality, the contours of which are drawn in our minds but experienced in the real world. They call for an understanding of a psychic reality that governs racial interactions.

The Dunn case in particular brings to the fore issues of psychic fantasy and racial imagining. Dunn claims that he pulled out his gun and decided to shoot first because he saw Davis pick up what he assumed to be a shotgun from the floor of the SUV. Though Dunn would later admit to police that it could have been a pipe or a broom, no weapon (or other object resembling a shotgun) was found by police. In addressing the mistrial, State Attorney Angela Corey explains, "A person in [Dunn's] position doesn't have to see something (an actual weapon), but there has to be reasonable fear"; "that," she says, "is the way Florida law reads."[1] If fear is thus sanctioned by the law as justification for the killing of others, it seems even more imperative that we understand its source.

Read from this book's Lacanian psychoanalytic perspective, Dunn's fears facilitate analysis of not just race but also the core process of othering[2] that is constitutive of racial difference. These fears point to a deeper hatred of the other that is veiled by the restrictions upon self-expression imposed by America's shifting discourses on race. Blurring the lines between self-defense and hatred, what today complicates cases such as Dunn's and Zimmerman's is our increased inability to account for racist motivations. Though African Americans remain largely convinced that race continues to be a primary factor in American life, as a result of the successes of the civil rights movement, Americans have become more conscious of the moral impropriety of racial bias. While this self-consciousness has led to more respectful treatment of African Americans, it has also allowed Americans to become more adept at a kind of self-policing that enables the expression of racially biased opinions through the screen of politically correct speech.[3] In the supposedly postracial era initiated by the presidency of Barack Obama, in which race purportedly no longer matters, it is impolite both to express racist views and to accuse others of racism. Thus the discourse of race has shifted to such arenas as culture, which recall race without naming it.

This shift is what we see particularly in the Dunn case, where rap music becomes the link of association Dunn uses to bind African Americans to "thug culture" and define them as criminals in need of violent disciplinary instruction in proper conduct. Though masked within this shift, Dunn's desire to discipline racial others subsumes his articulated motive of fear under a deeper hatred of the racial other as true inspiration for his actions. In evading direct reference to racial difference through a focus upon the boys' "behavior" and the rap music they enjoy, Dunn simultaneously divulges a hatred of the other that extends beyond race toward what Jacques Lacan calls the other's *jouissance*, or enjoyment, the very core around which, I suggest, otherness articulates itself to constitute racial difference. It is against this *jouissance* that Dunn's actions must be read, and it is this *jouissance* that explains the possibility for hatred in contemporary America to address itself at racial difference without need of acknowledging this difference.

Lacanian theory defines *jouissance* as the pleasure made available to the subject through the mediation of discourse, the pleasure availed this subject by his or her ability to ground a psychic sense of the self as coherent, autonomous, and self-controlled through use of the mechanisms of language and fantasy. Where Lacan reveals the subject to be psychically split, most noticeably between the conscious and unconscious, control over the discourses that define the self, and over the environment this self occupies, becomes a means of veiling the gap that fissures all individual subjectivity. This book identifies white racial identity as just such a discourse for white Americans, serving to ground white identity in the *jouissance* of language and fantasy. Fueling Dunn's fears and hatred is apprehension over the dwindling hegemony of this discourse. Information exposed in Dunn's trial and in letters Dunn wrote from prison help to identify his aggressive response to Davis and his friends as a form of *aggressivity*, the aggression that emerges in the subject specifically upon recognition of the fracturing of his or her self-image.[4] In Dunn's case, I would suggest, this fracturing is bound to a devaluing of the sway of his personal and racial identity, a devaluing that Dunn senses through his inability to dominate the space and interpersonal environment he occupies.

As Dunn returns to the Jacksonville neighborhood he once knew but has not lived in for a number of years, what initiates the conflict between Dunn and the teenage boys is his request that they turn down the loud music that dominates this space. Dunn experiences a frustration that seems bound to spatial restriction, as he sits parked in a spot outside of the gas station's store that positions him in such tight proximity to the boys' SUV and loud music that his own doors, rattling from the pounding bass, could only open partially. The entire incident seems to involve for Dunn a reversal in the natural order of things, a restriction upon his entitled freedoms that only gets extended by his imprisonment after the shooting. Expressing, after his arrest, his frustration and uncertainty as to whether he "should feel like [he's] a victim of reverse-discrimination or a political prisoner," Dunn is convinced that "either way" the "state of Florida is screwing [him] over."[5] Dunn remains self-assured that he is "being held, illegally," because "the blacks" are "calling the shots, in the media and the courts,"[6] despite his contradicting assertion that "the jail is full of blacks and they *all* act like thugs."[7] Dunn designates the prison he occupies with these blacks "Thugville,"[8] asking, "Why am I here?"[9] Though lamenting that it is "so sad in this day and age we're still divided by race,"[10] Dunn affirms, "I'm glad I don't live in Jacksonville, the murder capitol [*sic*] of Florida."[11] While both distancing himself from the site of the murder and absolving himself of blame for its commission, Dunn seeks to establish an exclusionary identity defined by its discreet relation to place and by this identity's disciplinary function over racial others who enter spaces he seeks to control. Dunn declares, "This may sound a bit radical, but if *more* people would arm themselves and kill these fucking idiots when they're threatening you, eventually they may take the hint and change their behavior."[12]

Correcting improper behavior is at the heart of Dunn's actions and trial. Though Dunn's disciplinary actions are addressed to black males, he speaks in a moralistic vein more acceptable even to African Americans about cultural vices. Dunn argues, "I'm really not prejudiced against race, but I have no use for certain cultures. This gangster-rap, ghetto talking thug 'culture' that certain segments of society flock to is intolerable. They espouse violence and disrespect toward women."[13] Our ability to recognize the problematic relation between rap music and the glorification of violence lends support to Dunn's suggestion that his actions are not racist. But what Dunn's remarks express is a hatred directed at rap music as a source of enjoyment, or *jouissance*, that has come to be identified with black Americans more broadly. Dunn takes part in a contemporary discourse that binds difference not to the body but to *jouissance*.

Difference may be isolated from the racial body in this manner because it is ultimately *jouissance* that grounds difference, establishing this difference through its circumscription of the fantasy object Lacan calls the object *a*. Most precisely, *jouissance* designates the pleasure that would emerge from an impossible wholeness. Lacan explains, however, that in the face of such impossibility the signifier serves as "the cause of jouissance," producing pleasure through its articulation of the fantasies of wholeness, or *being*, that compensate for subjective lack.[14] This being, lost to the subject, is defined as a psychic sense of unity, autonomy, and individuality that the subject can construct only through the signifier's isolation of the object *a*, the illusory lost object that promises to return the subject to a *jouissance*-filled state of wholeness. In American society, this fantasy object *a*, I argue, is often racial identity, supporting both difference and *jouissance*-inducing fantasies of being. Within the fantasies of the racialized subject, this object *a* of race, this "object that puts itself in the place of what cannot be glimpsed of the other" and the self, serves as the "basis of being," isolating an imaginary core self that "holds the image [of the racial body] together," granting it psychic and semantic significance for the subject.[15] Race, as object *a*, functions as what I would call after Lacan the "para-being," the "being beside," which is "substitute[ed] . . . for the being that would take flight."[16] More so than the physical body, it is racial identity as founded by this illusory core being, the racial essence distinct to each racial group, that provides structure and coherence to fantasies of difference. But where this *a* as racial core is both illusory and thus elusive, what racial fantasies ultimately isolate as proof of the other's alterity is the other's enjoyment, which is perceived as an index of this other's *jouissance*, a reification of the bliss experienced by this other through access to an illusory *a*.

In racial fantasies, the other's visible or even stylized expressions of pleasure, which are exemplified so distinctly in music, come to define the other's particular mode of *jouissance*, his or her specific manner of accessing being. This visible enjoyment helps to construct the other as bound to a distinctive *jouissance* of being that differentiates self from other and racial group from racial group. Through the group's mode of *jouissance*, its very being or core self is defined and its racial identity is solidified. Racial alterity is thus often contextualized by a fantastical sense of the incompatibility of the other's mode of *jouissance* with that of the subjective self, or that of this self's racial group; but the other's *jouissance*, bound to fantasy, actively oscillates between subjective imaginings that designate it alternately as alien and as excessive, and this *jouissance* can therefore also found what Lacan terms "jealouissance," the frustrated hatred that may spring forth from the subject upon conviction that the other "has the *a*" and accesses a bountiful bliss the subject lacks.[17] Where hatred of the other is fundamentally "addressed to being" and is essentially isolated through the *jouissance* perceived in the other's manifest enjoyment, it is toward the bountiful excesses of a visible pleasure alien to Dunn's self-identity, an unrestrained *jouissance* of being expressed in the boys' loud rap music and undisciplined behavior, that Dunn directs his hatred and aggressivity.[18]

Behavior, signaling a mode of *jouissance*, becomes the core of an otherness that Dunn would violently restrain and discipline. Echoing his interpretation of the case, Dunn's attorney, Cory Strolla, asserts to the press that "this isn't a black-and-white issue."[19] He states, "It's what [Dunn] would call a subculture thug issue. . . . And again, it doesn't go to race. It goes to how people behave and respond to situations."[20] While proclaiming, with the help of Strolla, that the incident occurred because he requested "a common courtesy" in asking the boys to turn their music down, Dunn attests that the boys responded to his request by not turning down but turning off the music; however, they then turned it back on, he says, and Davis started to curse and verbally threaten him from inside the boys' vehicle, actions Dunn himself responded to by rolling down his window and directly asking Davis, "Are you talking about me?"[21] Dunn describes the boys' behavior as "obnoxious," adding that he was "stunned and . . . horrified and just couldn't believe that things escalated the way they did over a common courtesy."[22] The boys' "obnoxious" behavior confirmed for Dunn an existing image into which he now solidly positioned them: acknowledging that he could have been "imagining" the danger he feared, Dunn explains, "You know, you hear enough news stories and you read about these things, they go through your mind"; with such stories about fearsome blacks in mind, and given "the way they behaved" in response to his request, Dunn concluded that "everybody in the car was a thug or a gangster."[23]

Though Dunn's focus on misguided behavior that is directed by a "thug culture" evades the issue of race, the excesses in *jouissance* he associates with this culture are clearly reflective of racial difference for Dunn. In his letters, Dunn conflates race and culture in the term "Black thug," which he uses to compare the "thugs in SUV" to an earlier robbery, committed "at gunpoint" by a "Black thug" against his friend's mother.[24] Aligning these two incidents, Dunn proclaims, "Eventually, we as a society will wake up and realize that we need to arm ourselves, as the government welfare programs have produced a culture of entitlement for a certain segment of our society. These fools feel entitled to live above the law and do violence at will."[25] Echoing discourse about the welfare state that has been tied to black Americans at least since the presidency of Ronald Reagan in the 1980s, Dunn espouses disciplinary violence against blacks through a focus on culture that evokes racial difference without directly naming it. What is named instead are the entitlements, the benefits, the objects of enjoyment made available to a people whose behavior must be constrained. Voicing his conviction that "armed robbery is the most common offence" of his black cellmates, Dunn expresses a "jealouissance" in which this entitlement means blacks not only have the *a* but take it from whites "at gunpoint."[26] Dunn defends himself not just against his would-be attackers but also against an entire race of people taught by a culture of entitlement to grope after the pleasures of a *jouissance* that should rightfully belong to white Americans.

In evoking a discourse about black entitlement, Dunn's case engages more far-reaching contemporary debates about the rights accorded to black Americans. These debates have played out in such matters as the Supreme Court's upholding of the University of Michigan's ban on race-based college admissions in a decision rendered in April of 2014 and in the Court's earlier overturning, in June of 2013, of a key feature of the 1965 Voting Rights Act that required states with a history of discriminatory voting practices to gain preapproval for changes to their voting laws. What is being debated in these cases is how far we have progressed as a country, given the presidency of Barack Obama and other positive social changes, and how much weight should be granted to arguments about the lingering legacies of America's racist history. But at the core of these debates, I would submit, is an effort to balance *jouissance*, to weigh what is taken away from others in attempts to establish equality for African Americans. *Trauma and Race* suggests that such a balancing act is made necessary because the racial history of America has bound African Americans discursively to excesses in *jouissance*. Though contemporary etiquette insists that these racialized individuals not be read differentially, African American identity remains open to rearticulation by a historical lineage of racial significations that, even when functioning through the vagaries of culture, has psychological import for both Americans and African Americans.

For African Americans specifically, vulnerability to dominant discourses productive of racial otherness leads also to exposure to a psychic trauma that issues from the racial past and repeats itself in the present through the agency of the signifier. I call this trauma *the trauma of slavery*, and I will define it as a continual assault on African Americans' fantasies of being. Though this trauma is bound to slavery, I will show that what slavery made manifest to black Americans was the fundamental psychic condition of the subject who, at root, is alienated from being. Where fantasy and discourse mask alienation through such concepts as racial whiteness for white Americans, this alienation confronts African Americans repeatedly through signifiers of otherness that oscillate between pinning African Americans to undeserved excesses of *jouissance* and binding them to notions of inferiority that question not just their access to being but also their very humanity. Indeed, notions of African Americans' relation to excesses of *jouissance*, which have often expressed themselves in American fantasies of African Americans' hypersexuality and pronounced physical prowess, facilitate an American readiness to receive its own portions of *jouissance* from voyeuristic observation of the athletic or entertaining black other and his or her body. At root here is an overvaluing of the black body and a minimizing of processes that bestow an individual subjectivity and sense of being upon African Americans, so that the *jouissance* of being that is allowed African Americans often serves the purpose of tying being and otherness to the body, not primarily to a subjective self.

While *jouissance* may be pinned to the black body as confirmation of an opposing racial whiteness that is productive of both a sense of superiority and fears of losing ground for numbers of white Americans, African Americans often experience through a racial identity bound to the body an inability to separate from the excesses of a racial past. These excesses, from the standpoint of African Americans, are tied to practices of exclusion and violence that traumatically breach the salubrious limits of both the body and the psyche. Here the white subject's *jouissance* becomes the instrument of African Americans' confrontation with trauma. Beyond the trauma to the body that may present itself in a particular racist act, however, *jouissance*, as a pleasure produced (in this case) through race, functions to link African Americans to a trauma of slavery, repeating through racism a primordial challenge to African Americans' sense of being. Dunn disregards his role in violently instituting such a challenge, but his conception of the possibilities opened to him in so doing allows us to recognize the striking, divergent psychic relation that is held by many African Americans to both the racial past and the future. Dunn, even while imprisoned and awaiting trial, focuses on the future, "looking forward to moving out of the south and away from the scourge [or the blacks] of this country."[27] His rather elaborate plan for after he is set free is to hire a "slimy civil-law lawyer and sue" the county of Jacksonville for "reverse-discrimination,"[28] use "the settlement" to invest in his company, and use the business profits ensured by a "rebounding economy" to "buy or build [his] dream house on the river," a "2-story house constructed in a manner where [he, a licensed pilot,] can park a sea plane underneath and then take off or land on the river."[29] Dunn's ability to dream of the transformation of catastrophe into profit starkly contrasts the relation to racial trauma confronted by many African Americans involved in, or even merely witnessing, cases such as this one. Where Dunn remains future oriented, for many African Americans, what the cases of both Dunn and Zimmerman reinforce is a long historical past of violence and trauma that extends to slavery.

We feel the weight of this traumatic past in the responses to these cases that issue not only from the outspoken African American individuals who populate the outer premises of the courts during the trials holding signs that demand justice but also in the deeply personalized responses to the Trayvon Martin case articulated even by the first black president of the United States, Barack Obama. Though Obama is well known for his emotional collectiveness and though he had rarely addressed the issue of race in America before Martin's killing, upon being asked for an impromptu comment on the case, Obama punctuates his statements with the assertion, "If I had a son, he would look like Trayvon."[30] Calling this his "main message . . . to the parents of Trayvon Martin," Obama suggests his own familial and racial ties to Martin.[31] What Obama's response displays is the manner in which racial trauma, the excesses of *jouissance* that emerge from the transgressions of others, often becomes the source of a bond that constitutes and coheres African Americans as a racial group. Obama, occupying the distance of the presidency and acknowledging his necessary legal impartiality as "the head of the executive branch," is interpellated into identification equally with a racial identity and a racial past traced in a lineage of African American suffering.[32]

In this tracing, we see a shift from past notions of racial essentialism, such that racial identity is determined by commonalities in experience, by similarities in the discursive relation to being that is established by a racism that questions one's subjective value. This shift, like the move to culture described above, defines racial similarity through *jouissance*, through a relation to modes of enjoyment and experiences of suffering that repeat across time. After the verdict on the case was issued, Obama spoke for a second time about Trayvon Martin, identifying directly with Martin's experience. He explains, "another way of saying" Trayvon Martin "could have been my son" is to say "Trayvon Martin could have been me 35 years ago."[33] In an age when race as an inherited essence is questioned and multiraciality is abundantly visible, even in Obama himself, Obama models a shift in American culture whereby increasingly race is determined through relation to a historical past, the replication of which through racism simultaneously solidifies African American racial identity and curtails those fantasies of wholeness that define for the African American subject a sense of access to the *jouissance* of being. Obama himself notes that the restrictions placed upon African Americans, the limitations in the space allotted to them in the American social sphere by such factors as "disparities in the application of our criminal laws," reinforce a sense of exclusion that helps constitute a group perspective.[34] Noting that, after the Zimmerman acquittal, "there's a lot of pain" for members of "the African American community," Obama ties this pain to the fact that the community "is looking at this issue through a set of experiences and a history that doesn't go away."[35]

Despite the ability of a figure like Michael Dunn to leave this past behind—questioning, "Where is all of this hostility coming from?"—the past continues to beckon African Americans toward deep associations with racialized identity.[36] Though many had heralded the age of Obama as occasioning the birth of a new postracial America, these cases of violence against African Americans suggest an unchanging same in the American social sphere, a repetitive, traumatic confrontation with the legacies of the racial past. Echoing Obama, Attorney General Eric Holder relates in the aftermath of the Zimmerman verdict that "some of these same issues [raised by the killing of Trayvon Martin] drove my father to sit down with me to have a conversation . . . about how, as a young black man, I should interact with the police . . . if I was ever stopped or confronted in a way that I thought was unwarranted."[37] Though Holder is convinced that his position as the first African American attorney general, serving under the first African American president, is sign that "our country has indeed changed," Holder reveals, "Trayvon's death last spring caused me to sit down to have a conversation with my own 15-year-old son, like my dad did with me."[38]

It is the recursiveness of these experiences of discrimination that becomes the source of both racial identity and trauma in contemporary

America. The ascension to primacy of African Americans like Obama and Holder has not signaled an end to racism but instead has led to what Colin Powell, secretary of state under the George W. Bush administration, has identified as a "significant shift to the right" in contemporary American politics, a politics that Powell maintains is run through with a "dark vein of intolerance."[39] Pointing to a governor who publically referred to President Obama as lazy after his poor performance in his first presidential debate with Mitt Romney and to another governor who described Obama as "shuckin' and jivin'" in his discussion of attacks in Benghazi, Libya, that led to the death of four Americans, Powell conveys that the latter description is "a racial era slave term."[40] Elaborating on the significance of the two governors' word choices, Powell states, "It may not mean anything to most Americans but to those of us who are African Americans, the second word [after lazy] is shiftless and then there's a third word that goes along with it, Birther, the whole Birther movement."[41] What Powell hints at is the way this focus on laziness recursively brings us to a focus on what I would describe as the slave's projected mode of enjoyment. Here, binding Obama's "laziness" to the slave's "shiftless" enjoyment produces a racial lineage that becomes a means of emphasizing Obama's otherness and grounding the Birthers' assertion of his un-Americanness. Though racial difference is never directly addressed in the governors' comments, Powell's observations help show how within language itself is buried the history that unravels to reproduce ready-made structures of *jouissance* that ground a racism emerging from the past to shape the present. It is this focus on a *jouissance* bound to both language and the history of slavery that will guide much of *Trauma and Race*. Through a Lacanian understanding of the function of the signifier in language, I will present slavery as a traumatic past that, by means of the signifiers of race, comes to repeat itself in the present to organize both racial relations and personal identity around a fantasy relation to being. Where this fantasy relation articulates itself through mediation of structures of *jouissance* that emanate from slavery, I read racial identity and racism as efforts to manage and manipulate the *jouissance* of being that emerges from the trauma of this past. The paradox of race as an apparatus of *jouissance*, however, is that it binds African Americans to a past in which race was used to decimate the enabling fantasies of being that enslaved blacks sought to establish for themselves.

It is this paradox that centers the analysis of this book. Critiquing the allegiance to race that many African Americans maintain today, *Trauma and Race* argues that by embracing the concept of race contemporary African Americans become psychically bound to the traumatic past of slavery. While articulating the psychic and political limitations of race in chapters 1 and 2, the book argues for a freeing up of identity that goes some way toward relieving the self from a determinative relation to the past. Using the literature of Toni Morrison and Ralph Ellison in chapters 3 and 4, I not only suggest the pathological extremes to which race urges subjects both white and African American—extremes that extend even to the point of what Lacan terms perversion and neurosis—but also present through these works models of how a traumatic relation to the past may be altered. Throughout, I suggest the urgency especially for "African Americans" to embrace a more expansive conception of the self, one that recognizes and celebrates the self as more than racial. Arguing that it is the intensity of one's adherence to racial identity that opens one up to a reliance upon the identity structures of the past that produce for African Americans a traumatic relation to being, I advocate for an identity politics that makes room for full expression of the psychic lives of those individuals who would call themselves African Americans. Where the pursuit of both racial whiteness and African American fantasies of being seek after an impossible unity meant to mask the fragmentation inherent to the psyche, what I promote is a relation to being that embraces the multiplicity of the self. It is beyond these racial fantasies of the whole self, I will suggest, that both white Americans and African Americans must come to establish a truly salutary psychic relation to the being that is stricken from all our subjectivities.

RACE AND SLAVERY
Theorizing Agencies beyond the Symbolic

The traumatic past of slavery has rooted African American identity in contradiction. Where this identity is tasked with representing a people engaged in an ongoing struggle for social equality, the concept of race itself, which grounds this identity, leaves open the African American subject to both the racism and the trauma that issues from this past. What I would like to begin to articulate in this first chapter of *Trauma and Race* is the argument that race has emerged as a precarious apparatus of being for African Americans. The central charge of race in American culture is to mediate a relation to what we may view as a transhistorical *jouissance* of the past, a traumatic excess of pleasure and pain that emanates from slavery to organize both subjective identity and the broader American social sphere. This past of slavery has produced both race and racism as modes of *jouissance*, as methods of accessing being. *Jouissance*, I would suggest, is embedded in the very signifiers of race themselves, which enable remanifestation of structures of enjoyment that bind subjects equally to concepts of race and to practices of racism. It is therefore a focus on the function of the signifier that must contextualize this study. While I most specifically address the effects of the racial signifier upon contemporary African Americans in chapter 2, what I would like to delineate here, through reference to both the history of slavery and narratives by ex-slaves themselves, is a core relation among the signifier, *jouissance*, and the past of slavery that is missed by much of the contemporary scholarship on race.

The limitation of most African American scholarly investigations of race, I argue, is their allegiance to conceptions of discourse, race, and agency that are framed not by psychoanalysis but by poststructuralist criticism. Jacques Derrida's poststructuralist argument that "centers" of meaning have "no natural [or] fixed locus" but are secured instead by discourse provides for the scholarship on race an anxiously alluring appeal.[1] The anxiety associated with this theory emerges because poststructuralism poses a challenge to the very concept of race itself, which for many African American scholars provides both a sense of identity and a route toward agency. As early as 1987 Barbara Christian, a pioneer of African American studies, articulated the rationale for resisting this theory, observing that poststructuralist critique of the center emerged "just when the literature of peoples of color . . . began to move to 'the center.' "[2] But, even when not explicitly employing poststructuralist theory, African American scholars nevertheless mirror its signature processes of decentering and discursively resignifying identity in their efforts to establish race as a "social construct." We see this, for example, in the assertion of leading African American scholar Henry Louis Gates Jr. that "precisely because 'blackness' is a socially constructed category, it must be learned through imitation," and, most important for Gates, it is therefore also open to "repetition and revision."[3] This attempt to revise race discursively is essential to African American theoretical conceptions of agency; but, like poststructuralist models, it is limited by its frequent failure to acknowledge and account for influences upon race and the racial subject that lie outside of the structure imposed by discourse.

While this focus upon discourse directs much of contemporary race theory toward analyses of what we may call after Jacques Lacan the social Symbolic, *Trauma and Race* is an attempt not only to articulate the impact of the discursive signifiers of race on the unconscious of African Americans but also to circumscribe a traumatic Real that escapes and indeed structures the agency of the signifiers of the Symbolic. Lacan speaks of the Real as the excluded center of the subject. Coining the term "extimate," Lacan defines the Real as that which simultaneously is most intimate, or internal to the subject, and excluded from symbolization.[4] This extimate Real, I suggest, is what a theoretical focus solely upon discourse misses. My work links this Real to slavery as an exclusion within the social Symbolic that yet shapes the discourse of race and indeed founds central aspects of African American and American identity. However, my interest is not so much in the history of slavery as in the ineffable experience of *jouissance*—or excessive, traumatizing pain and pleasure—that issues out of this Real past to fuel the psychic desires and fantasies of Americans. Tying this trauma to the fundamental trauma of subject formation, the traumatic elision of being that occurs with the onset of subjectivity, I read slavery as marking an upsurge of *jouissance*, such that slavery comes to signify a moment in time when the pleasures and pains associated with being are open to manipulation by white Americans. What enables such manipulation is the concept of race itself, thus constituted by slavery as an apparatus of *jouissance* that African Americans today still struggle to control and manipulate. But this precarious source of *jouissance* and being remains for African Americans an illusory object of attachment that binds them to the unbearable past. Through the function of the signifier, I argue, race enables a psychoanalytic process of repetition that once again produces for African Americans the psychic trauma of the Real.

Maintaining, therefore, that slavery has produced a historical legacy that is both discursive and psychical, I turn to Jacques Lacan's psychoanalytic theory because his fundamental assertion that the "unconscious is constituted by the effects of speech on the subject" offers a more expansive understanding of the workings of the signifier than is available in other theoretical models.[5] Though indebted to Freud for his ideas on the unconscious, much of Lacan's thinking on the signifier emerges from a rereading of the seminal work in linguistics and semiotics produced by Ferdinand de Saussure, a theorist whose thinking also influenced Derrida. However, the divergences between Lacan's and Derrida's theories offer radical implications both for how we understand the effects of the past upon African Americans and for how we conceptualize an African American agency meant to resist this past and its continuing legacy. Both Lacan and Derrida derive from Saussure the notion that signifiers have no inherent meaning[6] but instead produce meaning by operating through what Lacan calls "themes of opposition" and "functions of contrast and similitude."[7] Derrida advances this Saussurian reading by reducing signification to "absolute chance" and the "*genetic* indetermination" of the signifier, arguing that meaning only ever accumulates as a "trace," as the by-product of differential relations established between signifiers in their

"movement [along] a chain."[8] Where Lacan differs from both Saussure and
Derrida is in his understanding of the signifier as not arbitrary or indeter-
minate but contingent upon causation that is external to the Symbolic.

The concept of contingency is what brings Lacan to a notion of
trauma as structural to the functioning of the unconscious and conscious.
Lacan explains this contingency by linking it to what he calls "cause,"
which involves "impediment, failure, split."[9] Cause is the traumatic and
eruptive core around which the signifiers of consciousness ever assemble
themselves, if only in the defensive act of establishing for the subject a
protective distance from this core. In tying cause to both failure and split,
Lacan points to its extimate relation to the subject, its internal externality:
cause, as trauma, may manifest itself in a movement outward, through the
failures, slips, and stumbles of the subject as she or he unknowingly charts
a repetitive path toward a traumatic past that remains internally salient,
simultaneously enticing and terrifying; but cause manifests, finally, as an
intrusion external to the system of signifiers that structure meaning for
the subject, as an experience that splits the subject between meaning and
nonmeaning. Emerging as that which traumatically defies meaning, cause
is always "something anti-conceptual" and thus is inevitably bound to the
Real as that register of the psyche that is removed from symbolization.[10]

The cause that *Trauma and Race* demarcates is what I call the *jouissance* of slavery, a psychic experience of trauma that emerges from the past
and repeats itself in the present through the agency of the signifier. It is
the signifier that establishes the link through which this traumatic cause,
germane to the slave's experience and not to that of his or her descendant,
intrusively establishes its place in the internal lives of African Americans.
The signifier defines the category of race, allowing for a conscious association of African Americans with a chain of signifiers that links them to
the brutal historical past. This linkage confronts African Americans not
only with the terrible history itself but also with a traumatic lack that, I
will argue, was made manifest by slavery. What the signifiers of race do,
therefore, whether emanating from the racist other or whether willfully
embraced as a source of identity, is rearticulate the subject's sense of self
around an unveiled lack once defined in the racist past. Thus, I maintain,
the discursive linking of African American identity to this past becomes
the means through which the trauma of slavery is repeated in the experiences of African Americans.

From Resignification to the Barred Subject

The anticonceptual cause of which I speak, this more than historical *jouissance* of slavery, is precisely what is ignored by both Derridean poststructuralism and leading African American scholars like Henry Louis Gates Jr. and Houston Baker. At the heart of these scholars' work is a focus on the Symbolic that actively limits African American agency and identity to what we may call after Judith Butler "resignification," the effort "to lay claim" to the terms that define us "precisely because of the way these terms, as it were, lay their claim on us prior to our full knowledge."[11] Butler's Derridean approach to agency and the challenges she recognizes in it are useful for shedding light on the mirroring route embraced by African American scholars. Working, like Butler, with a conceptualization of the Symbolic as a closed system in which existent signifiers can only be resignified and recirculated, these scholars confront a particular problematic that can be articulated as the prospect of "forging a future from resources inevitably impure."[12] Without a viable methodology by which newness can enter into the Symbolic, by which something alien to the system can either be introduced into it or act upon it, the challenge these scholars come to embrace is how to rearticulate the terms of race "that [once] signaled degradation" so that they can now "signify a new and affirmative set of meanings," so that this "reversal" is not one that "retains and reiterates the abjected history of the term."[13]

It is this focus on resignification that we see, for example, in Gates' famous theory of "the signifying monkey," which defines a discursive practice of resistance that is grounded in a "formal revision" that "turns on repetition of formal structures, and their difference."[14] Disregarding the psychoanalytic notion of repetition as tied to the unconscious and Real, Gates views African American culture as involved in continual efforts to produce a "chiasmus," or what Gates articulates as a process of "repeating and simultaneously revising in one deft, discursive act."[15] Gates relies, ultimately, on a model of agency that Derrida calls after Levi-Strauss "bricolage": the process of making use of "the instruments [one] finds at [one's] disposition around [oneself], those which are already there," in one's attempt to, by "trial and error, adapt them" to a use for "which [they] had not been especially conceived."[16] Though Gates seeks to imagine a beyond of this bricolage and reach outside of the American Symbolic by asserting that African Americans must turn to their own "black vernacular tradition" itself in their efforts to " 'deconstruct,' if you will, the ideas of difference inscribed in the trope of race," Gates limits agency to language, arguing that we must "take discourse itself as our common subject."[17] Both Gates and Baker bind African American political resistance to language and thus also to the Symbolic, with Baker viewing the slave narrative and historical figures like Booker T. Washington as embracing a politics of "liberating manipulation" and "revolutionary *renaming*" that employs language as a "black defense against and revision of ancient terrors, mistaken identities, dread losses."[18] In the view of an African American theory of race shaped by the work of thinkers like Gates and Baker, this revisionary repetition has been and continues to be a means for blacks to alter the social structure of a racist Symbolic.

This effort at resignification is laudable and indeed necessary. But the problem with a theoretical focus on the Symbolic is that it does not acknowledge how what is extimate may impact upon the Symbolic and the discursive activities of the subject beyond his or her conscious volition, and neither does it offer a direct means to address the scars that may be left on the subject's psyche through the operations of racism within this Symbolic. Indeed, it may be argued that what is missed in such a focus on the Symbolic is the very psychoanalytic subject him- or herself. As Lacan states, "the subject is not the one who thinks" or speaks through discourse.[19] Lacan's work continually returns to a critique of what he calls "the I-cracy," or "myth" of "the I that masters" discourse, the myth of the "speaker" that "is identical to itself."[20] Known for his focus on the split subject, Lacan counters the I-cracy by asserting that "the point" is "to know whether, when I speak of myself, I am the same as the self of whom I speak."[21] In opposition to the speaking subject of the I-cracy, Lacan "identifies the subject with that which is originally subverted by the system of the signifier."[22] What Lacan points to is "the function of barring, the striking out of another thing" that his theory establishes as inherent in the subject's relation to the Other's signifiers.[23]

It is this process by which something essential to the subject is stricken from him or her that I propose enables an understanding of the effects of slavery upon both the slave and contemporary African Americans. Lacanian theory shows that all subjects are constituted through the Other's signifiers. More precisely, the subject, Lacan argues, can only emerge *as* a signifier. Lacan notes that because language "exists prior to each subject's entry into it," the subject is "the slave of a discourse" in which "his place is already inscribed at his birth."[24] Gaining subjectivity and meaning through those "themes of opposition" and "functions of contrast and similitude" that we have already seen are essential to the operations of the signifier, "this subject," Lacan asserts, "which, was previously nothing if not a subject coming into being—solidifies into a signifier."[25] The function Lacan ascribes to the Symbolic and its signifiers is that of producing the *aphanisis* of the subject, her or his "fading" or "disappearance" under the signifier's agency.[26] Subjectivity not only restricts the subject to the Other's preexistent universe of meaning; it also deprives the subject of access to those essential components of the self that cannot be circumscribed by signification, the unconscious and Real as the barred or stricken portions of the self that constitute the fundamental lack of subjectivity. Where Lacan's work is particularly useful is in providing a comparative framework through which we may distinguish a heightened aphanisic effect of the signifier upon the slave, a barring that often is again manifested for African Americans as an internal lack when accosted by acts of racism. Lacan argues that what each "subject has to free himself of is th[is] aphanisic effect of the . . . signifier."[27] This ethical stance fundamental to Lacanian theory coincides with my own efforts in *Trauma and Race* to imagine an agency beyond the Symbolic.

The applicability of this notion of the barred subject to a theory of African American identity and agency becomes clearer when read in relation to race theorist Hortense Spillers' essay "Mama's Baby, Papa's Maybe: An American Grammar Book." Here Spillers describes the social Symbolic as operating through the signifiers of race to restructure the very identity of African Americans. For Spillers, African Americans are subjects "embedded in bizarre axiological ground," buried under the signifiers of "a dominant Symbolic order."[28] This order was created out of a "rupture and a radically different kind of cultural continuation" that Spillers identifies as slavery.[29] Spillers finds in slavery the "total objectification" of an "entire captive community," the "dehumanizing, ungendering, and defacing" of "subjects" who come to be "taken into account as *quantities*."[30] As a result of this process of quantifying and commodifying human beings, the slave's identity adheres to "no symbolic integrity," and a restructured Symbolic unfolds as "an American Grammar" grounded in the "originating metaphors of captivity and mutilation."[31]

Particularly useful in Spillers' theory is its prescient observation of slavery's ability to conflate identity with commodity for the slave, its ability to reduce the slave to the status of a signifier with monetary exchange value.

The narratives told by the slaves themselves support such a reading. In the slave narrative of William Wells Brown, for example, Brown describes as one of the most memorable incidents of his enslavement the case of a blind child deemed worthless by his master and sold for "the small sum of *one dollar*."[32] What the slave narratives record is not just the commodification of the slave but the appropriation and rearticulation of his or her identity by the signifiers of the Other. As James Olney argues, the repeated phrase that begins most slave narratives, "I was born," is precisely an effort to establish the identity that is stricken out by the slave master's rewriting of the slave's identity, a rewriting that we see often occurs through the violent inscriptions of the master's whip.[33] Significantly, both Brown's narrative and that of Frederick Douglass start by detailing the place of their birth and then move within mere paragraphs to scenes of whippings (suffered by Brown's mother and Douglass' aunt) as conveying through "bitter experience" what it means to be a slave.[34] The narratives identify such experiences of devaluation as "the blood-stained gate, the entrance to the hell of slavery, through which" these ex-slaves were "about to pass."[35] When read alongside the testimony of ex-slaves, Spillers' work allows us to see that excessive domination by the Other's signifier is characteristic of the slave's experience. Indeed, Brown's relation to the transcribing whip and the Other's signifiers is so overwhelming that even upon gaining freedom he states, "the fact that" there was no longer anyone "to stand over me with the blood-clotted cow-hide . . . made me feel that I was not myself."[36]

This split relation to the self is what I suggest slavery establishes for the slave. What is stricken from the slave here, and is read as a blow to his or her sense of identity, is more precisely the slave's fantasies of being. Being can be understood as an illusory, lost state of wholeness and "totality" that never existed for the subject but that the subject ever pursues.[37] This fantasy of a lost wholeness is necessary because the splitting of the subject by language is inherently traumatic, constituting the Real as a psychic register of lack founded in trauma. Where it is "rupture," the division of the psyche into the conscious and the unconscious that simultaneously grants subjectivity and makes lack and "absence emerge," the subject compensates for the trauma of this loss with the "mirage" of a "false unity," a whole being or unified self capable of being refound because it existed "anterior" to the splitting initiated by language.[38] Being fantastically emerges for the subject as an illusory autonomy and state of pleasure that is displayed most visibly in the Imaginary of the mirror stage, wherein the child conflates him- or herself with the mother seen in the mirror, forming the gestalt of a single self who is misapprehended as one "whole" being. The search for this lost being propels subjectivity, constituting desire as that which directs the subject endlessly toward Symbolic substitutions that promise to fill the subject's constitutive lack. Through such illusory notions of wholeness, the final, traumatizing truth avoided by the desiring subject is that his or her status as a subject demands both a perpetual condition of lack and a reduction to the status of signifier.

What I wish to argue is that slavery and racism seek to bring about precisely a traumatic confrontation with lack and an unveiling of the subject's status as signifier. I call this confrontation the trauma of slavery, an assault directed not simply at the slave him- or herself but, more critically, at the very fantasies that sustain subjectivity. Lacan defines "fantasy" as that which employs language and the signifiers of the Symbolic to mask the traumatic lack of the subject and construct the illusions of self, the I-cracies, through which the subject compensates for a psychic sense of loss. What we see in the case of Brown, however, is the instability of such fantasies for even the freed slave. Because his subjective sense of self remains scarred by the effects of the master's whip, Brown is unable fully to recognize himself in the illusions of autonomy that freedom more readily allows. I suggest that because the slave and his African American descendants continually confront obstacles in their efforts to manipulate the discourses that define them, these racialized subjects often struggle more than is usual to maintain their safe distance from the traumatic *jouissance* of lack. My argument is that slavery and racism become traumatic because they seek to inhibit the subjectifying function of fantasy, aiming to confront African Americans with the very lack that is necessarily masked in the Lacanian subject.

Power and *Jouissance*

This interpretation of slavery and African American identity demands an appreciation for apparatuses of power, oppression, and ideology that is rarely ascribed to Lacanian theory. Specifically in *The Other Side of Psychoanalysis*, however, Lacan provides a reading of discourse, the signifier, *and* slavery that emerges precisely as a revision of the notions of power presented in the socioeconomic theories of Karl Marx. Of particular interest to us in this work is Lacan's analysis of what he calls the master's discourse. Lacan describes the master's discourse as incorporating a master signifier that serves the hegemonic function of making a Symbolic system "readable."[39] This master signifier is the "joint," the "quilting point" that "creates" any given discourse.[40] Lacan asserts that the master signifier not only "can be any signifier" but also can serve the function of "mythical support of certain societies" when it enables a belief of the master "being identical with his own signifier."[41] Racial whiteness is just such a signifier, establishing slavery as a nodal point for the myths of race that still retain levels of structural control over American society and its social Symbolic.

This view of slavery's relation to a master signifier allows us to supplement groundbreaking scholarship done by Lacanian theorist Kalpana Seshadri-Crooks on the psychoanalytic workings of race. Astutely defining whiteness as the master signifier for discourses of race, Seshadri-Crooks argues that whiteness establishes "a structure of relations, a signifying chain that through a process of inclusions and exclusions constitutes a pattern for organizing human difference."[42] Her work supports the notion that race grounds the fantasies that promise the subject access to being. Whiteness does this by using its signifying chain to establish a hierarchy in which whiteness comes to represent the pinnacle of being, or "sovereign humanness."[43] Seshadri-Crooks thus rightly reads whiteness as "the inaugural signifier of race" that "implicates us all equally in a logic of difference," but what we are able to specify through Lacan's *The Other Side of Psychoanalysis* is a differential relation to this signifier that implies for African Americans certain obstacles in the construction of those fantasies of wholeness that protect the subject from a traumatic confrontation with lack.[44] It is here that Lacan's rereading of Marx is useful. What Lacan does in *The Other Side of Psychoanalysis* is present capital and power as determinative of access to a *jouissance* of excessive pain and pleasure made available to the subject through a display of lack. Not only does Lacan tie the pursuit of being to capitalism with an assertion that Marx's "surplus-value is surplus *jouissance*," but he also supplements Marx's focus on the worker with his own focus on the slave, arguing that surplus *jouissance* is what "the slave brings" the master.[45]

In *Theories of Surplus Value* Marx observes, "Only that labour is *productive* which creates a surplus-value."[46] Marx defines "surplus value" as the monetary excess that the laborer's work or "labour-power secures for the user of labour-power," arguing that "this surplus-value can clearly only consist in the excess of labour which the labourer returns to the capitalist over and above the quantity of labour that he receives for his wages."[47]

As an expansion of Marx's theory, Lacan's surplus *jouissance* focuses not on excess capital produced through underpaid labor but on the unearned excess pleasure the master receives through the slave's work: "The work is mine, and the surplus pleasure is yours," says Lacan.[48] But where true *jouissance* is bound to an impossible wholeness that is lost with being, surplus *jouissance* most precisely designates the fantasy of being. As a term, what surplus *jouissance* ultimately conveys is the excessive, brutal abuse of the other that may emerge from the subject's determined pursuit of actions and objects that fantastically secure an impossibly complemented state of being for the subject.

Lacan argues that capitalism is always tied to a "birth of power," and what brings slavery and capitalism together in Lacan's theory is precisely his sense that power over others facilitates a control over discourse that allows the subject to mask lack.[49] A central component of Lacan's interest in capitalism is his focus on defining a historical moment when "the signifier is introduced as an apparatus of *jouissance*."[50] Lacan's discussion of capitalism and slavery is primarily a rereading of Hegel and Marx, and not a direct analysis of race-based oppression. But one cannot ignore the striking similarity in Lacan's language to Spillers' description of slavery, an institution that Spillers sees as initiated in the middle passage's attempt at "transforming *personality* into *property*" through that process by which "subjects are taken into account as *quantities*."[51] Similar to Spillers, Lacan maintains that "something changed in the master's discourse at a certain point in history"; beginning possibly with "Luther, or Calvin, or some other unknown traffic of ships around Genoa, or in the Mediterranean Sea, or anywhere else," on "a certain day surplus *jouissance* became calculable, could be counted, totalized."[52] This traffic of ships, for Lacan, identifies the historical moment when "the accumulation of capital begins" as a means of quantifying a surplus *jouissance* that exceeds the exchange value of labor.[53]

At least in antebellum America, one cannot deny the connections between the master's pleasures, a flourishing capitalist economy, and slave labor. What Lacan allows us to do is read slavery not simply as about racism, or even capitalism, but as bound most fundamentally to the master's own masking of lack through the surpluses allowed by a coordination of capital and fantasy. Showing that capitalism and power enable certain fantasies for the master, Lacan asserts that to act "the master is to think of oneself as univocal" and to, through fantasy and discourse, "mask[] the division of the subject."[54] What "essentially constitutes the master's discourse," Lacan states, "is that he commands, that he intervenes in the system of knowledge," and thereby accesses the means to hide the "truth" that, like all subjects, "the master is castrated."[55] The master submits himself to this castration through reliance upon the signifier, even in the very act of "giv[ing] an order"; but, through the signifier, something also comes "back within the master's reach."[56] Making a distinction between the *jouissance* of being, or wholeness, that is ever lost to the subject and the *jouissance* one receives from the mere fantasy of wholeness, Lacan maintains that what returns to the master is not the lost *jouissance* of which castration deprives him, but its surplus, a pleasure one may steal from the other. He explains, "something necessitates compensation . . . for what initially is a negative number," for that subtractive loss imposed upon the subject.[57] This compensation emerges as "an irruption, a falling into the field, of something not unlike *jouissance*—a surplus," a fantasy object snatched from the Symbolic and made to signify the *jouissance* of being that it can never make manifest.[58]

Lacan calls this fantasy object the *objet a*, or object *a*, arguing that the fantasy "object *a* was the place Marx revealed, uncovered, as surplus value."[59] This fantasy object, which Lacan allows us to associate with capital, may also be seen productively in American society as race. Where the master signifier, whiteness, and its accompanying discourses of race are rooted in slavery, Lacan displays that "there is a use of the signifier that we can define by starting out from the master's signifier's split" from "the body lost by the slave, which becomes nothing other than a body in which all the other signifiers are inscribed."[60] What was split from the slave through the Symbolic's transcription upon his or her body of the master's meanings and fantasies was not only the master signifier, whiteness, but also the fantasy of being that race guaranteed to the master. The fantasy object of race established whiteness hierarchically as the pinnacle of being by binding the master's being to an asserted absence of being in the slave. As Lacan shows, "the master can only dominate [the slave] through excluding" from the slave "this [surplus] *jouissance*," this fantasy of being.[61] The master's illusory supremacy lay in his ability to reinforce for the slave the Symbolic's essential function of defining the subject as a signifier while also depriving the slave of the fantasies utilized by subjects to compensate for this traumatic subjective condition.

Through discursive manipulation of the signifier whiteness, the master attempted to reduce the slave to not just a signifier with monetary exchange value but also a fantasy object with *jouissance* value. Both the abstract concept of racial whiteness and the tangible, embodied slave himself were presented in slavery as versions of the object *a*, emerging as the supports that buttressed the master's fantasies of being. By masquerading in the master's discourse as the source of a distinctive racial identity, whiteness adopted in slavery the object *a*'s core function of remanifesting being, emerging as a "semblance of being," or as what I have called the para-being that replaces the being irretrievably lost to the subject.[62] This para-being as whiteness was the fantasy possession denied the slave, the exclusionary core difference that signaled the supreme being and true humanity ascribed to the master. But, beyond the masquerade, whiteness remained only a signifier, the signifier I shall describe more fully in chapter 4 as the phallus; where the phallus is a fantasy object *a* that has achieved discursive dominance as the representative of being, presenting itself as the possession that signals a completion that defies castration, all other manifestations of the object *a* attain their own fantasy value by standing as "referent" to the phallus, whose ascendency they thus also support.[63] As phallus, I argue, whiteness ultimately functioned to designate an ascendant state of plenitude and completion that was available to the master only through a fantasy relation to the slave as object *a*. The master's proof that he possessed the illusory phallic object of whiteness was his commodified possession of the slave, whose stricken being allowed the slave to be presented not just as the fantasy object *a* but also as a visible, tangible signifier of the master's supremacy.

The process of desubjectifying the slave through his or her transformation into a representation of the object *a* was pivotal to both the notion of whiteness and the economics that supported the social structure of antebellum America. Through denying the subjective fantasies and humanity of blacks, white slaveholding Americans not only sought to transform the slave from subject into commodity but also shored up white fantasies of being, employing slaves themselves as signifiers of this being; indeed, white Americans were able to purchase and display their illusory being through the very procurement of slaves. Slaveholding became an access route to economical bliss and the surplus *jouissance* of fantasy, grounding through the slave as possessed object the hierarchy of social status in the South. The refined sophistication and vaunted pre-eminence that seemed

uniquely inherent to the southern leisure class was the surplus snatched
from the labor of the bought slave, whose very service to this class pronounced its members' gentility through the distinction implied in having
a slave courteously answer one's door, pour the right wine at the right
time, or flaunt the master's wealth and family in the slave-driven carriage
that paraded them to church and on other outings.[64] Making *jouissance*
and being calculable, a man's slave was an index of his superiority over
both the slave and his white compatriots; but as status and surplus *jouissance* were tied to slave ownership, in buying slaves an unestablished white
man could move up the social ladder, asserting not only his entitlement to
membership within the mastering race but also his status as an individual
of distinction, worthy of a position within the master *class* of slaveholding
aristocracy. As it made white men into gentlemen, so too did ownership
of slaves enable white womanhood, providing the means for, say, a poor
white woman tilling the fields to advance into the domestic sphere as a
lady lording over her own home. The slave served as the capital, the financial backing, that guaranteed these identities of plenitude. Slavery was the
foundation of an economics in which the abstract value of both a white
man's capital and his superior being were not only signified but also reified
by the subjugated body of enslaved blacks.

This effort to reify white phallic supremacy by splitting being from the
slave was so central to antebellum America and white identity that even
the third president of the United States and author of the Declaration of
Independence, Thomas Jefferson, is inspired to assert in his *Notes on the
State of Virginia* his "suspicion" that blacks are "inferior to the whites in
endowments both of body and mind."[65] Jefferson discursively contributes
to the fantasies of race that deprive the slave of being by pinning the "real
distinctions" he finds between blacks and whites not on the "condition"
(or enslavement) of blacks but on nature, arguing that skin color is both
the sign of a difference that is "fixed in nature" and the "foundation of
a greater or less share of beauty in the two races."[66] Through the visible
difference of skin color and through the hegemonic power of the master
signifier, whiteness, to organize difference, Jefferson delineates, fixes, and
ranks deeper attributes of blacks and whites, helping to solidify race as
the fantasy object *a* that guarantees a differential relation to being and
secures white phallic sovereignty. Starting with an aesthetical argument
that merely asserts his preference for the "fine mixtures of red and white"
that are "expressions of every passion" in white faces and his distaste for

"that eternal monotony, which reigns in the countenances" of blacks, Jefferson transforms aesthetics into proof of racial inferiority, suggesting that the "veil of black" not only covers "all the emotions of the other race" but also indicates an essential absence of sentiment.[67] Through his reading of the races, Jefferson fortifies the notion of the insensate slave, immune to the inherent pains and hardships of slavery, that came to center ideological justifications for the institution.[68] Finding in blacks a want of that "tender delicate mixture of sentiment and sensation" evident in his own race, Jefferson declares of blacks, "griefs are transient," "less felt," and "sooner forgotten with them."[69] Especially in an antebellum culture that praises sentimentality, emotions are proof of sentience, humanity, and subjecthood. In denying both the emotional and intellectual capabilities of blacks, Jefferson thus questions the concept of their full humanity, the very fantasies of self that center the I-cracy of human subjectivity.

However, while this discursive remaking of the slave's identity contributed to by Jefferson and others impaired the slave's ability to compensate for lack through the surplus *jouissance* of fantasy, it did not guarantee an unproblematic relation to being for white Americans. Indeed, what especially the slave master did as a result of this curtailing of a surplus *jouissance* of fantasy was let loose a terrifying psychic *jouissance* of the Real, one that, significantly, impacted both slave and master. What occurred in slavery's discursive splitting of the master signifier from the black body that was established as other to the white self was, in actuality, a process by which the psychic distinctions between self and other became blurred by a mutual approach to *jouissance*. Defining *jouissance* as fundamentally "evil," Lacan not only acknowledges that in embracing the *jouissance* that emerges from the other's pain we "move toward some cruelty," but also poses the striking question of whose cruelty is involved here, the other's "or mine"; Lacan answers his own question with the assertion that "nothing indicates they are distinct," arguing that such evil cruelty emerges "on condition that those limits which oblige me to posit myself opposite the other as my fellow man are crossed."[70] While slavery maintained racial oppositions, it breached the psychic boundaries of the self by founding *jouissance* not just on fantasy but also on access to a Real that is approached through transgressions against the other.

In his *Ethics* seminar, Lacan associates true *jouissance* precisely with transgression. Though arguing that fantasy, or what he calls the "entropy" of the signifier that must ever miss the mark of the Real, is "the sole regular point at which we have access to the nature of *jouissance*," Lacan also identifies a "*jouissance* of transgression" that is "beyond the phallus" or fantasy object of pleasure, one that emerges from violation of the limits imposed by the Symbolic regularity of moralistic and judicial laws.[71] Maintaining that prohibition is the "all-terrain vehicle" that drives the subject through what is "impassable" in the "paths to *jouissance*," Lacan asserts that "without a transgression there is no access to *jouissance*."[72] Lacan's thinking here returns to the Freudian notion that "civilization is based upon renunciation of impulse gratification" and to Freud's conclusion that "wherever the community suspends its reproaches the suppression of evil desire also ceases."[73] I read slavery as involving just such a suspension or loosening of moral restrictions, and I argue that, most especially in the South, this allows with impunity transgression of the law and emergence of the evil desires that agitate around the internal emptiness characteristic of the subject.

The slaves' narratives themselves vividly display these evil desires and the cruelty they unleash. The narratives of both Brown and Douglass depict the illicit murders of slaves subjected to the transgressive power of white masters and citizens. Douglass describes the case of a slave named Demby who runs into a creek to escape a whipping by the overseer, who gives him to the count of three to come out of the water and then proceeds with "consummate coolness" and "savage barbarity" to shoot down his "standing victim" in front of a crowd of slaves.[74] Douglass states that Demby's "mangled body sank out of sight, and blood and brains marked the water where he stood."[75] Not only was this "horrid crime" never "submitted to judicial investigation," since it was witnessed only by slaves, but in its wake, Douglass relates, its executer's "fame as an overseer went abroad."[76] Here it is through the capacity granted whites by dictates of slavery to transgress the laws of the land that the overseer accesses a means of *jouissance*, solidifying his hierarchal fantasy relation to being while also breaching the legislated limits of Symbolic activity to express evil desires to kill and destroy that otherwise would be socially curtailed. In slavery, even the law itself promotes its own transgression. As Brown observes, "Where the slave is placed by law entirely under the control of a man who claims him, body and soul, as property, what else could be expected than the most depraved social practices?"[77]

The transgressions of the master depicted by ex-slaves point to slavery's ability to unleash "the unconscious aggression" and the "frightening core of the *destrudo*" that Freud names the death drive.[78] This death drive is always "for an Other-thing" than what is "registered in the signifying chain" of the Symbolic, and it is thus marked by a "will to destruction."[79] Aimed at the Real, the subject of the destrudo pursues an annihilating path that both decimates the other and unhinges the self from those Symbolic moorings through which subjective identity and meaning are grounded. Douglass describes most directly the birth of this destructive will in his discussion of his mistress Mrs. Auld, a "woman of the kindest heart and finest feelings," whose exposure to "the fatal poison of irresponsible power" leads to the corruption of a gentle, balanced self-identity.[80] Douglass notes, "That cheerful eye, under the influence of slavery, soon became red with rage, the voice, made all of sweet accord, changed to one of harsh and horrid discord, and that angelic face gave place to that of a demon."[81] Ultimately positioning *jouissance* beyond the Symbolic, Lacan argues that *jouissance* "begins with a tickle and ends in a blaze of petrol."[82] It is this consumption of his mistress by the hellish blaze of her transgressive *jouissance* that Douglass displays to be the result of her acquisition of power over slaves. What her slaves allow her is access to that central excluded core that is "at the heart" of the subject but "beyond" him or her, the "interior or emptiness" of which the subject does not know to whom it belongs, whether "to me or to nobody."[83] Driven toward the other in pursuit of this emptiness beyond the Symbolic, Douglass' mistress travels a destructive path that leaves her only a few steps behind the lady Mrs. Hick, who Douglass relates murdered his "wife's cousin" by "mangling her person in the most horrible manner, breaking her nose and breastbone with a stick, so that the poor girl expired in a few hours afterward."[84]

Narratives such as Douglass' and Brown's allow us to see slavery as involving the approach toward a "central emptiness" where, once reached, the other's "body breaks into pieces."[85] In the subject's approach to this lack, the racial other is reduced to the condition of what Lacan calls a "part object, . . . silhouetted there, separated from us and rising up . . . in the midst of a charnel house figure."[86] When the other is the route to the self, the other disappears, not only as a living being whose subjective existence one fails to acknowledge beyond this other's relation to the fantasy object, but also as a source of the shaming gaze that tames one's transgressive desires. Lacan presents the gaze as the look from the other that "surprises" the subject "in the function of voyeur, disturbs him" in the actions through which he pursues his transgressive desires, "overwhelms him and reduces him to a feeling of shame."[87] I read slavery as an attempt at eliding the gaze that may tame the master's transgressive pursuit of the Real. What we see in Douglass' description of the overseer is precisely the failure of the gaze of the slave community witnessing the murder to establish the limits produced by shame. This breach of the limit by the overseer allows for a Symbolic restructuring of his identity and a growth in his popularity. But what we see in Douglass' Mrs. Auld is that breaching the limit strays one from the psychic path of desire and leads one not merely to a restructuring of identity but, more importantly, to the dissolving of the subjective limits that grant identity Symbolic structure. Where the gaze is "the object that presents each [subjective] desire with its universal rule, by materializing its cause, in binding to it the subject's division," slavery forestalls the shame that may materialize the fact of that subjective limitation that is castration.[88] Not only is the slave's potential position as holder of the shaming gaze jeopardized by slavery, but the return look of all Symbolic Others is deflected by the social sanctioning of transgression. Without such enabling restraints placed on *jouissance*, the subject, who is most properly a desiring subject founded upon lack, devolves into a subject merely of the drive, advancing precipitously toward a destruction of both self and other.

African American Identity and Suffering

It may be argued that central to the discursive efforts of African Americans, from ex-slaves to later social activists and scholars, is an attempt to establish firmly a shaming gaze that does not merely wince at the spectacles of white transgressions. But given the continued power of the master signifier whiteness to define the discursive field of race and restrict the agency of African Americans, not just racism but also the concept of race itself carries over into the present a signifying chain, founded in the past, that enables both an assault on African Americans' fantasies of being and a possible confrontation with lack. Here we may conjoin the signifiers of race with the scars of the slave master's whip in the formation of what Spillers terms a "phenomenon of marking and branding [that] actually 'transfers' from one generation to another, finding its various *symbolic substitutions* in an efficacy of meanings that repeat the initiating moments."[89] Lacan speaks of "the glory of the mark," the "mark on the skin" inscribed through such acts as "flagellation"; he points to this mark as producing the subject's body as an "object of *jouissance*."[90] This flagellation is tied to what Spillers describes as a translation of "the captive body" into a "potential for pornotroping," a process of objectification that we see in the actions of the slave master described by the ex-slaves.[91] Lacan states that it is "irrefutable" that this objectification is "one of the ways in which the Other enters one's world," functioning as an apparatus of *jouissance* in the manners we have already described.[92] But what is suggested most radically in Lacan's work is also a process by which this objectification may become the grounds of identity for the abjected subject. Lacan's theory helps us identify the markings of the master's whip and the *jouissance* they produce as a very source of African American identity.

Lacan associates *jouissance* with excess, not just an excess of pleasure but also an excess that turns to "displeasure," an excess that leaves one in a state of "suffering."[93] Particularly in his reading of the *fort-da* game played by Freud's grandson, however, Lacan emphasizes that it is only through the suffering of *jouissance* that the kind of narcissism found in the mirror stage's conflation of mother and child is replaced by an independent subjectivity built on lack. Lacan reads the toy reel that the child of the *fort-da* game throws over the edge of his crib when the mother leaves the room not just as a signifier but as the object *a*, that which, in signifying an unsignifiable loss, allows the subject to jump the "ditch," the central lack that the mother's disappearance creates "on the frontier of his domain."[94] This object *a*, Lacan says, is "a small part of the subject that detaches itself from him" to symbolize some act of "self-mutilation" or other cruel loss through which the subject finds the means to his or her own self-designation.[95] This object *a*, this symbol of the lost part of the self, Lacan says, is "what in the end gives the specular image of the apparatus of the ego its real support, its consistency, . . . sustained within by this lost object."[96] Lacan states that it is through this object that "*jouissance* is introduced into the dimension of the subject's being."[97] This lost object is the means through which the subject's self-identification compulsively masks and concurrently establishes resonance with the unsymbolized trauma of the Real.

Race, I propose, is an object *a* established around lack as much for African Americans as it is for whites. The function of the object *a* Lacan outlines in his reading of the *fort-da* is not only to signify loss but also to displace it through acts of repetition, to reassociate traumatic entrance into the Symbolic with a temporally and qualitatively distinct moment of trauma later experienced in the Symbolic. In place of the subject's traumatic division in language, the mother's departure from the room becomes temporally defined as the cause of the split or "*Spaltung* in the subject," which is then repetitively represented as the true source of loss that is also "overcome by the alternating game, *fort-da*."[98] I read slavery as serving the function of repetition for African Americans that Lacan here assigns to the mother's departure, as the Symbolic and temporal signifier of a traumatic loss that is more deeply psychic. Slavery comes to serve this function because it eruptively displays psychic lack. Lacan defines repetition as "the commemoration of an irruption of *jouissance*."[99] Where this irruption designates a breach inward and a splitting of the subject, I identify in slavery a simultaneous eruption or outpouring of *jouissance* that finds its Symbolic representatives across distances of time through the signifiers of race. I suggest that both these residual signifiers (even when redefined by African Americans) and the acts of racism that may grow out of them are repetitions that function in relation to the *jouissance* of this past that both displaces and displays psychic lack. Slavery's exhibition of the slave's lack and its insistence upon the master's exultant and autonomous being produced within the Symbolic a certain excess or surplus of *jouissance*, enabling discursive and power structures through which access to *jouissance* became unusually open to manipulation. Slavery thus marks a traumatic moment in which *jouissance* as both lack and excess is localized. This eruption of *jouissance* thereby positions slavery as a temporal representative of the lack that is the Lacanian Real.

It is the signifiers of race that help to both localize this lack temporally and bind it to the identity of those subjects who come to be called African Americans. The concept of race came to center African American identity because it not only augmented the signifier's essential function of striking being from the subject, actively restricting the slave's access to fantasies of self, but also presented itself as an object of contention that promised to re-establish the illusory existence of this being. As is true in the case of the child of the *fort-da*, the signifier, as designator of the object *a*, is ever a protective source of identity, and so race is often exceedingly empowering for African Americans. In slavery and beyond, it offers subjects a sense of direction, belonging, and self-worth. But race alone could guarantee neither community nor being for enslaved blacks. To truly understand the notion of being that slaves were able to construct for themselves and to appreciate the *jouissance* of suffering to which this being yet binds contemporary African Americans, we must look to the function of religion in slavery. Because efforts during slavery to resignify race were especially open to contention, enslaved blacks were slow to embrace race truly as a source of being. And so, in truth, the nascent African American identity that began to cohere in times of slavery more often employed religion both to contend against and to positively resignify race in an effort to constitute this being, thus setting the stage for an emphasis on religion in African American culture that is yet present today.

What we find in slavery is that the unity developed by enslaved blacks emerged not primarily because of a sense of their "racial" commonality but because blacks were bound together by a common *circumstance* that both accentuated existing similarities across the group and demanded this unification as a source of resistance and a means of survival.[100] More likely to recognize differences within the racial group than the masters who asserted the power to define the group, individual slaves formed alliances and group affiliations that were more nuanced than any allowed by the category of race. The slave narrative of James Albert Ukawsaw Gronniosaw, who spends much of his enslavement on a merchant ship before landing in New York City, supports this point, displaying the internal differences among slaves that prevented their easy unification around race as a source of being. Gronniosaw's inability to identify with the other slaves in his new master's household not only leads to his conviction that the "servants were all jealous, and envied [him] the regard, and favour, shewn [him] by [his] master" but also facilitates his construction of a narrative that asserts God will not save Gronniosaw's fellow blacks or "those born under every outward Disadvantage, and in Regions of the grossest Darkness and Ignorance" if they lack "knowledge of the [biblical] Truth."[101] Written after he is freed and no longer has even the common circumstance of a mutual enslavement to link him to the larger slave community, Gronniosaw's narrative seeks support not for members of this community but for his own starving family in dire need of money. Gronniosaw's narrative maintains that *through* the bondage under which members of his race still exist, the "Lord undertook to bring" Gronniosaw "out of Darkness into His marvelous light."[102] What Gronniosaw's religious rhetoric shows is that race by itself could not unify slaves or fully promise them being; functioning at times in direct opposition to race, within and beyond slave communities, it was primarily religion that made this promise.

Such a focus by slaves like Gronniosaw on religion as the source of the object *a* that grounded being must be read within the context of a broader slaveholding society that celebrated the Christian view of God as the Supreme Being, a view expressed in the biblical statement "I am the one who is," by which, Lacan notes, "God asserts his identity with

Being."[103] The object *a*, Lacan shows, is that which presents itself as not just a semblance of being but also being's "remainder."[104] From this Lacanian perspective, we may read the *a* as the source of the soul that, for the Christians to whom Gronniosaw addresses his narrative, links mankind to the true Supreme Being; this *a* functions as the divine remnant at the core of man, the spiritual essence, shaped by God's own hands, that transcends man's earthly existence. Both within man and external to man, this extimate core as object *a* is what sets man on the path of a true love of his neighbor as the self. It is the source of a kind of love that Lacan calls "soul loving," whereby subjects "love each other as the same in the Other," aiming this love at the extimate object *a* that is both absent from the self and illusorily present in the other.[105] Where Gronniosaw wishes to establish the similarity of his soul to that of his white reader's through use of his religious rhetoric, he struggles against a racism that functions to define his core self as blackened by the absence of God's light, as devoid of the soul's divine spark. This struggle emerges because the soul loving he beseeches of the white other is equally, I would argue, the root of race love, whereby individuals of the same race come to love each other as mirrored images of the self, finding in each other the same object the self pursues, the object belonging to the self that is absent from the self. This absence fuels a desire for racial unification and solidarity that stands at odds with the universalism ostensibly glorified by religious soul loving of the neighbor. I will show in chapters 2 and 3 how race comes to supplant religion as a source of this core object *a* that offers African Americans a semblance of being, but what we find in Gronniosaw's narrative is race as an impediment to any loving of the neighbor's soul. Within slavery, race both obstructed cross-racial unity and impaired creation of an extimate object *a* capable of unifying blacks intersubjectively into a group identity.

Because race was the root of slavery's assertion of the nonbeing of the slave, race had to be redefined and buttressed by religion for it to function as a source of being. Not only religion but also communal activities like group worship or singing and working together all helped to create the unified group to which this being could be assigned.[106] Establishing unity through communal activity, religion and spiritual slave songs were especially important to both the reformation of slave identity and the gradual development of notions of race as possible sources of being. Emblematic of this fact is Lawrence Levine's observation that "the single most persistent image of the slave songs is that of [African Americans as] the chosen people."[107] Through attempting to supplant the authority of the slave master with that of God, slaves sought to recast the veil of fantasy over the psychic place of lack uncovered by the institution of slavery. Religion became the source of a fantasy grounded more in the patriarchs of the Old Testament than in race, allowing for identification with heroes like Moses, Joshua, Jonah, and Noah, who were delivered from their own suffering and that of the world around them. Through such fantasies, the slave's suffering could be contextualized as proof of a unique access to being, as proof of one's divine selection for salvation. This is precisely what we see in Gronniosaw, who asserts, "I am willing, and even desirous of being counted as nothing," for "I know that . . . every trial and trouble that I've met with . . . [has] been sanctified to me."[108] Gronniosaw takes the concept of the chosen to its extreme, articulating his worthiness of financial aid from others through a demonstration of his position of distinction from all sinners, white and black. Seeking to constitute himself as a chosen *one* by rhetorically severing this religiously sanctified self from established notions of race, Gronniosaw simultaneously distances himself particularly from other blacks because he realizes that as race augments the notion itself of a group identity it also implicitly contests the fantasies religion allows.

Though these revivifying religious fantasies of being often promised salvation in this world, and not just the next, the limits of the agency they covenanted were displayed in the ability of slave masters to themselves bind race to religion in order to justify notions of white supremacy. Such biblical events as Noah's cursing of the descendants of his son Ham to forever become the servants of all other men were significant to this process. Through this story, whites could not only promote the association of blacks with Ham, whose name "is a vulgarization of Cham," or ch'm, the Hebrew word for black, but also present black skin as the sign of a servitude and cursed suffering that was divinely sanctioned.[109] This suffering, bound to race, is merely the obverse of that constructed in the rhetoric of Gronniosaw. What we see through such contention over race and suffering is that African Americans encounter continuous obstacles in the construction of their fantasy of being through reliance upon the apparatus of race. Because race as object *a* today still remains discursively tied to the trauma it attempted to compensate for in slavery, African American identity ever circles this traumatic past, defined by a suffering that the concept of racial identity alternately attempts to alleviate and traumatically unfurls.

As Lacan notes, "There is nothing more difficult than separating a word from discourse. . . . As soon as you begin at this level, the whole discourse comes running after you."[110] Still able to function as a stigma for African Americans, what the word "race" marks is a fantasy difference that not only discursively justified the master's brutal and traumatic scarring of the slave's flesh and psyche but also still today repeats its long historical function of signifying the lack of some quality needed to make African Americans the equals of whites. It is therefore no surprise that the process initiated by slaves of forming for blacks a protective group identity demanded the unifying function of music and communal activities like religious worship, and could not rely solely upon the efforts to resignify race that we see praised by African American academics like Gates and Baker. As scholars such as Ron Eyerman have demonstrated, African American racial identity could only be truly solidified as a discursive concept after slavery ended, at the moment post-Reconstruction when an emerging black middle class and intelligentsia had finally attained sufficient levels of agency over discourse to employ race in calls for political unity.[111] While most African American scholarship repeats endlessly this early attempt by the intelligentsia and the slaves themselves to resignify and politically redeploy race, *Trauma and Race* suggests a need finally to advance beyond mere resignification. What resignification today entails is an ambivalent scholarly desire to maintain race that is actively facilitated by conceptualizations of agency and identity as discursive, a desire to uphold race while also depriving it of a lethal essentialism that is often the core of racism. This ambivalence suggests race's position not only as a fantasy object, or object *a*, but also as a Symbolic remnant, as a link— often willfully preserved by scholars—to the traumatic Real of slavery's *jouissance*. By contrast, *Trauma and Race* seeks to articulate a notion of agency and identity that distances itself from both race and the traumatic past it incorporates.

CONSERVING RACE, CONSERVING TRAUMA
The Legacy of W. E. B. Du Bois

In chapter 1, I presented slavery as constituting for African Americans a *jouissance* of the past that repeats itself in the present. Through a focus on the work of the renowned African American scholar W. E. B. Du Bois, I will now describe how racial identity facilitates an unconscious link to this traumatic past. Grounding my reading of this link on a Lacanian definition of trauma and viewing trauma as structural both to the operations of the signifier and to subjective self-identification, I will demonstrate how this past still urges at a psychic level the allegiance to race of not only contemporary African Americans but also contemporary African American scholars. Where I have argued that in slavery African Americans most often relied upon religion, and not race, to constitute for themselves an essential semblance of being, I point to Du Bois as an important nexus in efforts to shift from religion to race as determinant of the fantasies of being that organize African American identity around the trauma of slavery.

In the late nineteenth century Du Bois starts to articulate the notion that establishing and maintaining a racialized identity is a political urgency for African Americans. Recognizing the centrality of the church as "the first distinct voluntary organization of Negroes," Du Bois maintains that "the Negro church came before the Negro home" and "stands to-day as the fullest, broadest expression of organized Negro life"; yet it is Du Bois' contention that "the Negro church must become differentiated" from the home and other personal and political aspects of Negro life.[1] Du Bois finds the church incapable, ultimately, of protecting African Americans from moral and social decay "born of Reconstruction," which has left the Negro only with the limited "defense of deception and flattery, of cajoling and lying."[2] Instead of religious organizations, argues Du Bois, "we need race organizations: Negro colleges, Negro newspapers, Negro business organizations," and, above all, a "Negro Academy" that gathers "about it the talented, unselfish men and the pure and noble-minded women" of the race to "determine by careful conference and thoughtful interchange of opinion the broad lines of policy and action for the American Negro."[3] Most emphatically in his 1897 essay "The Conservation of Races," Du Bois argues that to achieve social equality African Americans must conserve the concept of race forged in slavery and "maintain their race identity."[4]

In promoting racial identity, Du Bois begins to articulate the central assertion still made today by many African Americans: that African Americans should maintain the concept of race as an essential means to fight politically against racism. Echoing this sentiment, contemporary African American critic Lucius Outlaw argues that because of "continuing legacies of invidious ethnocentrism and racism" in America, justice cannot be "achieved practically without giving consideration to raciality and ethnicity."[5] My own reading of race and trauma, however, complicates this political justification for racial identity. As Anthony Appiah's critique of Du Bois in his book chapter "Illusions of Race" implies, it is not only the political utility of race that causes African Americans to use and conserve this concept; often, it is also a compelling attachment to the concept itself. Appiah reveals that whether Du Bois was able to use the concept of race to escape "racism, [Du Bois] never completed the escape from race" itself.[6] Appiah cannot identify the influence that produces in African Americans like Du Bois this attachment to race that clearly exceeds race's political utility. What I propose, however, is that the conservation of race by African Americans often masks an effort to conserve the trauma of America's racial history and shore up a personal sense of being fortified by the apparatus of race.

The Allure of Race

The debate that has developed between Appiah and Outlaw over Du Bois' relationship to race allows us some insight into how both Du Bois and contemporary African Americans like Outlaw seek to conserve the *jouissance* of the traumatic past. The debate centers on what Appiah identifies as Du Bois' irrational inability to give up the socially accepted biological conception of race in spite of Du Bois' avowed efforts to replace it with a sociohistorical conception. Outlaw responds to Appiah in defense of Du Bois, arguing that, whereas Appiah reads Du Bois as essentially presenting a biological definition of race, Du Bois is more properly read as combining both a sociohistorical and a biological conception. Outlaw allies Du Bois with "natural philosophers of the seventeenth, eighteenth, and nineteenth centuries" who define race as a "*cluster* concept that draws together under a single word" references to "biological, cultural and geographical factors"; the properties this concept describes are to be taken "disjunctively," says Outlaw, so that possession of "at least one of the properties" identifies an individual as a member of the race.[7] Outlaw echoes Du Bois in acknowledging the inability of race to define precisely its referent, but for Outlaw this does not imply that "all racial classification is thereby inappropriate."[8] Where race fails to serve the purpose of "characterizing persons into or in terms of biologically constituted groupings," Outlaw argues, "it might well just mean that an additional racial or sub-racial category may be needed for such persons."[9]

What we find in both Du Bois and Outlaw, I suggest, is an effort to conserve race beyond its referential value and an attachment to race that extends beyond the logic of these individuals' arguments. Part of the reason for this adherence to race is a dogged belief that, despite the conceded lack of scientific basis for race, this concept does indeed have some perceivable referential value. Du Bois himself argues that a "scientific definition of race is impossible," for "physical characteristics are not so inherited as to make it possible to divide the world into races."[10] But race asserts its existential veracity through appeal to the eyes, through assertion of a natural and visible difference, marked in skin color, that helps to seduce equally Du Bois and Outlaw into compliance with racial thinking. It is this seductive visibility of race, this "common sense" evidence from "everyday life," as Outlaw puts it, that we must first come to terms with in understanding the compelling attachment to race maintained by African Americans like Outlaw and Du Bois.[11]

Though race is a discursive construct, one that I argue is inspired by psychic urgencies, race remains compelling to the eyes because racial differences emerge from a grafting of the meanings of the Symbolic onto biology. It is this propensity of race to conflate the Symbolic's discourses with biology that Du Bois and Outlaw promote in clustering race as both sociohistorical and biological. Emerging from the intersection of biology and the Symbolic, race does not manufacture difference but instead structures a prescribed mode of interpretation that grants forms of existent biological difference more critical Symbolic value. The biological fact of phenotypic variations functions in racial discourse as race's alibi, masking the inherent arbitrariness of racial distinction by internalizing and eternalizing difference as an embodied permanency. Because phenotypic differences in pigmentation and morphological variations in bone and hair are often traceable through ancestral lines, these visible differences provide an ostensive basis for a biological notion of race as defined by inheritable characteristics. However, as the history of racial passing in this country attests, such characteristics do not always correlate in predictable ways with racial identity. Though, by grounding itself in the biology of phenotype, race comes to imply deeper dissimilarities in such things as morality, intellect, degrees of licentiousness, violent proclivities, and so on, it is the system of the Symbolic itself that grants race and these implied dissimilarities their value, establishing a differential status that has meaning only within a chain where black adopts its Symbolic significance through its interrelation with and distinction from white. Precisely by grafting itself onto biology, however, race presents itself as pre-dating the system of the Symbolic, masquerading as an inherent component of nature indicative of visible, natural variations in groups of humans.

This ability to grant permanency to difference through biology is both what enables race to function as the accomplice of psychic fantasies aimed at *jouissance* and what Outlaw attempts to reinforce by defining race as a cluster concept. Though Outlaw contends that racism today is caused by "invidious conceptualizations of raciality and ethnicity" and that therefore today "we desperately need . . . settled and widely shared knowledge" of "empirically and socially appropriate identification of persons and groups," Outlaw does not embrace the cluster concept for its empirical or social appropriateness.[12] Recognizing that race's lack of scientific grounding makes it a concept that will always be "subject to challenge and change," Outlaw admittedly embraces the "cluster concept" definition of race for its fluidity and its ability to account for "variation across time and space"; he embraces this definition because it allows him to maintain race and racial distinctions.[13] We note most visibly the contradiction in Outlaw's argument when he asserts that the "continued existence of discernible racial/ethnic communities of meaning is highly desirable, *even if, in the very next instance, racism and invidious ethnocentrism in every form and manifestation were to disappear forever.*"[14] If race, though failing to define its referent, is yet needed to achieve "social peace and harmony" in the face of invidious racism, why this compulsion to maintain race once racism disappears forever?[15] It would seem that what Outlaw seeks is not to establish communities of meaning but to maintain racial communities forged by the memory of this very history of race and racism Outlaw seeks to overcome.

What is revealed in this break in Outlaw's logic, I suggest, is his unconditional attachment to a traumatic history. Outlaw's insistence on conserving the concept of race is determined by his resistance to relinquishing the traumatic past that established this concept. Because America, "from the onset," was "structured, with the assistance of complex doctrines of white racial supremacy, into a racialized, hierarchic nation-state," says Outlaw, reference to the racial past is always necessary for "understanding the historical and social being" that this past has created.[16] But Outlaw's emphasis here is not on understanding the multiplicity of each subject's identity in the present or on recognizing each subject's situatedness along numerous points of cultural intersection; it is, instead, primarily on an effort to perpetuate the process of racializing subjects as African American through linking them to the past.

There is in Outlaw's thinking an imbrication of the historical past with contemporary personal identity such that this past becomes the dominating core of the self. Such an imbrication, I suggest, threatens to ground the psyche primarily in a subjective sense of self built on a relation to the trauma of the past. This process of collapsing one's self with the past of slavery allows for a bond with slavery's trauma that must be conceptualized in the light of what Lacan identifies as the "hauling of the subject, who always drags his thing into a certain path that he cannot get out of."[17] Where for Outlaw reference to this traumatic past remains necessary even in a hypothetical future when this past's influence not only is nonexistent but has disappeared "forever," it is clear that moving past racism should never entail giving up race or the memory of a racial history that once forced certain identities upon African Americans. But most significantly, what Outlaw finally resists giving up, I think, is an attachment to what, at "the onset," initiated America into the racial history that Outlaw will not forget: not just slavery but also the trauma it produces.

Lacan describes trauma as a "form" of the Real that, though excluded from the Symbolic, structures both consciousness and Symbolic activity.[18] Slavery, I argue, is an intrusive traumatic Real with which African Americans like Outlaw maintain a psychological link through adherence to the concept of race. Outlaw's insistence on race breaks free of the logic of his argument about its political utility so as to become, I propose, an "act of homage to the missed reality," a tribute to the inaccessible and unsymbolized trauma emanating from the past of slavery.[19] Where trauma defies Symbolic representation, such insistences on race perform "a rite, an endless repeated act" as a means to "commemorate" the "not very memorable encounter" that I call the trauma of slavery.[20] The insistence simultaneously fends against and facilitates the repetition of this traumatic Real through what Lacan refers to as the *automaton*, "the return, the coming back, the insistence of the signs, by which we see ourselves governed by the pleasure principle" and its "function of fantasy."[21] I thus point to the "sign" of race as unifying for African Americans a returning automaton, a "network of signifiers" entrenched in the fantasy construction of their racial identity.[22]

African Americans maintain an attachment to the fantasy of this racial identity because what lies beyond race's return as the insistent sign, as the sign that African Americans like Outlaw would "drag" and "haul" into the present and future, is the repetition of the Real that cannot be confronted but yet must not be forgotten. The insistent automaton produces race as what Lacan speaks of as the "obligatory card," the card dealt by the Symbolic that must be drawn by the subject, the returning sign that the subject comes to seek after actively because its return masks the repeated Real "beyond the *automaton*."[23] This obligatory card, race, is drawn, dragged, hauled, and insistently conserved by many African Americans as a means of maintaining but not confronting the very trauma of slavery that conditions and accompanies race's compulsory return.

Lack and the Racial Past

We can better understand how the automaton of the racial signifiers impacts efforts to conserve the trauma of slavery if we turn more directly to an analysis of Du Bois himself and of Du Bois' ambivalent attachment to the concept of race. It is clear that Du Bois employs race for its political value. We see his efforts to tie race to politics when he, for example, urges his contemporaries in the Harlem Renaissance to be strategic in their artistic depictions of Negroes, asserting quite famously that "all Art is propaganda and ever must be."[24] But beyond his political reliance upon race, it is the trauma of slavery that I suggest inspires Du Bois' allegiance to this concept. Where I define the trauma of slavery as an attack upon psychic fantasies of being, at issue in Du Bois' work is the effort to establish stable, irrefutable ground for his own sense of being, a process that entails for Du Bois a redefining of the race itself. Yet, I argue, it is as Du Bois comes most fully to embrace his racial identity that he is most directly pinned to the trauma of slavery. Recognizing in America a society that "only lets" an African American "see himself through the revelation of the other world," Du Bois reluctantly embraces the racial identity granted him by the Other.[25] Where this identity links Du Bois to a traumatic past, both the external insistence upon race and, more significantly, Du Bois' own embrace of this concept prevent his easy dissociation from the trauma of the past. To the extent that Du Bois comes to resist understanding his identity as other than racial, Du Bois confronts the automaton of the racial signifiers both as that which binds him to this trauma and as his sole protection against it. Du Bois' most pronounced traumatic confrontation with lack emerges when race produces for him an identity so fully entrenched in the past that there is no room to imagine other avenues of access to being than the one directly contested by this same racial past. Urged to accept an identity so exclusively grounded by his membership in a race already uniquely pinned to notions of inferiority, what Du Bois seeks is to maintain his fantasies of being by fending against the unveiling of a lack presented as the exclusive possession of his race.

This lack, however, is constitutive of each subject, emerging with the onset of subjectivity, which is defined by a splitting of the psyche into its component registers of the Imaginary, Symbolic, and Real. Lack articulates itself around such fantasies as race and racial inferiority to establish the subject's position in relation to being, the illusory sense of psychic unity and autonomy that may be established through domination of one's external environment and others who occupy it. These fantasies mask the fact of each subject's mutual submission to the forced choice that Lacan calls the "vel of alienation."[26] This vel is defined as a compulsory, "lethal" choice between meaning and being, a choice that produces the "*aphanisis*," or "*fading* of the subject," who is ever forced to attain subjectivity via the dominating signifiers of the Other.[27] Subjectivity emerges with entrance into the Symbolic, the world of language and meaning that organizes thought for the subject but alienates the subject from the *jouissance* of being he or she desires. It is this alienation that fantasies of race both mask in those who are able to position themselves in a hierarchal place of dominance and highlight in those who are dominated by the signifiers of the other.

Rethinking Hegel, Lacan illustrates the "essence of the alienating vel, the fatal factor" that defines it, through reference to the choice offered the slave: *"your freedom or your life."*[28] This fatal choice, he explains, is between two elements such that one element "has as its consequence a *neither one, nor the other*": if the slave "chooses life [or meaning], he has life deprived of freedom [or being]," but "if he chooses freedom, he loses both" his life and his freedom immediately.[29] Lacan calls this vel "the primary alienation, that by which man enters into the way of slavery."[30] Expanding on Lacan, I define slavery as not that which alienates the slave, but that which reveals the fact of the slave's deeper subjective alienation in language. Where the typical subject of the Symbolic finds support in the signifier for the fantasies of being that underpin his or her psyche, the slave's confrontation with and lack of control over the signifiers of the Other prevent the easy construction of such fantasies.

Lacan describes these fantasies through his critique of the Cartesian *"I* of the cogito," which he designates the "homunculus," the illusory "presence, inside man" who "governs him, who is the driver, the point of synthesis" for man's subjectivity.[31] This is the self that Lacan says "has not failed to occur in the history of what is called thought" as disguise for the fact of the subject's alienation.[32] The *I* is presented as the subject's true self, as the self that accesses the external world through a manipulation of language and its signifiers. It is the integrity and very humanity of this self that Du Bois seeks to defend in coming to embrace propaganda as a means of manipulating the racist signifiers confronting African Americans in the Symbolic field of the Other. Elaborating on his position on art, Du Bois explains, "The point today is that until the art of the black folk compels recognition they will not be rated as human."[33] In this effort to prove his humanity and secure his fantasy access to being, Du Bois invokes race as a political and psychical tool in battle against a culture that, he notes, deems Negroes "inferior to the dirtiest white dog."[34] Through a continual rethinking of and then final reassertion of the validity of race at the end of his career, Du Bois reveals his domination by the returning automaton of the signifiers of racial identity that both links him to and defends him against the traumatic past that challenges his fantasies of being.

This automaton, the continual return of race as the concept that African Americans like Du Bois both conserve and actively refute, is conditioned by race's ability to operate through a relation to each of the three registers of the psyche. Where race is a social and discursive construct, I argue, one's entrance into the social Symbolic, with the very onset of subjectivity, initiates one into the formations of racial identity. What we will see through Du Bois' example is that, though racial difference is truly grounded not in biology but in discourse, the racial identity one obtains from the Symbolic of the Other has extra-Symbolic and extradiscursive effects on the subject; the images and discursive definitions of the racial self granted the subject are alternately embraced and resisted at levels both conscious and unconscious, registering themselves to varied degrees at the psychic level of the Imaginary so as to found an internal portraiture of the body that is central to the formation of the ego. The politics of race at the level of the Symbolic holds dire stakes particularly for African Americans because race enables the constitution of an Imaginary ego image that simultaneously challenges and asserts the unity of these racialized subjects. Binding this ego's self-image to racial identity through the illusion of race as biological fact, the Symbolic actively constitutes this identity through discourses of race that rhetorically link the racialized self to the history of slavery. In the process, race both masks and reveals personal lack by conflating personal lack with the slave's suffering and trauma. Through this displacement, race binds African Americans to the Real of a traumatic past they both own and disown as they negotiate through a relation to this past a fantasy of race articulated around the promise of being.

Du Bois' own negotiation of this past is emblematic of the ambivalent attachment most African Americans hold to race. This negotiation involves for Du Bois both what he calls his "recoil from the assumptions of the whites" and his development of "racial feeling[s]" as a "later learning and reaction" to racism.[35] These feelings become especially significant as Du Bois looks back at his career and contemplates in his autobiography, *Dusk of Dawn*, what it is within himself that constitutes a "connection, psychical and spiritual, with Africa and the Negro race."[36] Contrary to the focus on logical reasoning one would expect from someone with Du Bois' distinguished academic training, Du Bois describes his racial "tie" to Negroes and Africa as something he "can feel better than [he] can explain," rooting these feelings in race as not a logically defined "concept [but] rather . . . a group of contradictory forces, facts and tendencies" that have guided his actions throughout his career.[37] In this battle between emotion and logic, Du Bois' sense of his "psychical and spiritual" tie to Africa and the Negro race comes to overbalance both Du Bois' conscious awareness of his mixed heritage—"my paternal great-grandfather . . . was white"—and the deeper "culture patterns" he "absorbed" in childhood, which he explains "were not African so much as Dutch and New England."[38] While describing an allegiance to the Negro race that defies the full logic of his own reasoning, Du Bois reaffirms his racial identity most directly through consideration of his biological and historical link to a racial group that extends to Africa:

> On this vast [African] continent were born and lived a large portion of my direct ancestors going back a thousand years or more. The mark of their heritage is upon me in color and hair. These are obvious things, but of little meaning in themselves; only important as they stand for real and more subtle differences from other men. Whether they do or not, I do not know nor does science know today.
>
> But one thing is sure and that is the fact that since the fifteenth century these ancestors of mine and their descendants have had a common history; have suffered a common disaster and have one long memory. The actual ties of heritage between the individuals of these groups vary with the ancestors that they have in common with many others: Europeans and Semites, perhaps Mongolians, certainly American Indians. But the physical bond is least and the badge of color relatively unimportant save as a badge; the real essence of this kinship is its heritage of slavery; the discrimination and insult; and this heritage binds together not simply the children of Africa, but extends through yellow Asia and into the south Seas. It is this unity that draws me to Africa.[39]

Du Bois attempts to establish for himself and African Americans a racial identity that is not simply biological. Like most contemporary African Americans, Du Bois remains at least consciously skeptical of the notion of biological differences among races and grounds difference, instead, in ancestry and history. Thus, what unifies Du Bois, African Americans, and Africans into a single racial group is not primarily biology but their one long memory of the historical disaster and insult that was slavery. As Appiah reveals, however, Du Bois' conception of his racial identity as historically grounded leads him to the affirmation of an illogical non sequitur. Du Bois maintains that the insult and discrimination of slavery "binds together not simply the children of Africa" but also the peoples of "yellow Asia and the south Seas," who do not share the history of slavery. Appiah argues that "what Du Bois shares with the rest of the non-white world" and what binds him to it "is not the insult but the *badge* of insult," the biological skin color that identifies Du Bois as black.[40] Appiah shows that throughout Du Bois' intellectual career the development of his socio-historical argument is restricted by this illogical attachment to a "buried" biological conception of race.[41]

Appiah rightly suggests that a notion of phenotypic difference grounds both Du Bois' sense of his historical lineage and Du Bois' understanding of his relation to other groups. Because of his own insistence upon logic, however, Appiah cannot fully appreciate the function of this buried, illogical attachment to race in Du Bois' narrative, an attachment that, I argue, must first be understood in relation not only to biology but also to the Symbolic and the Real. Appiah undervalues his own recognition that Du Bois' bond "is based upon a hyperbolic reading of the facts" and rejects the obvious rhetorical (thus Symbolic) role slavery plays in defining identity for Du Bois.[42] Du Bois' willful selection of certain groups to which he claims "kinship" and common "heritage," just like his dismissal of Dutch and other ancestors with whom he holds an acknowledged biological and cultural relation, displays a selection process in racial identity that is often both unreasoned and motivated. Defying logical reasoning, race often functions at the emotional and psychic levels. What structure these emotions and give shape to our "racial feelings" are the signifiers of language that themselves remain motivated in their articulation of subjective meaning and identity by a fundamental relation to lack. With the non sequitur, Du Bois establishes through the signifier not an empirical and logical understanding of race but a rhetorical and autobiographical one that both historicizes his identity and pins it to a lack positioned in the traumatic past and remanifested in the present through the continual "insults" of racism. Most broadly, it is this imposition of lack onto personal identity, a process to which other peoples of color are also subjected in varying degrees by racism, that urges Du Bois' identification with these discriminated-against groups. But, most directly, this imposed lack is also what constitutes for Du Bois a link to African Americans as a racial group through his conscious embrace of the past of slavery.

Focusing on this past, Du Bois presents us a narrative of the African American racial self that we may say, with Lacan, "condense[s] in relation" to "a nucleus," to an organizing, hollow center that structures the signifiers of both Du Bois' discourse and his identity.[43] Lacan explains that "when the subject tells his story, something acts, in a latent way, that governs [his] syntax and makes it more and more condensed."[44] What governs Du Bois' narrative is not a movement toward race as the core of the self but rather an identification of race as the signifying mark of a deeper injury and insult suffered by this self. Du Bois' sense of the injuries to which the racialized African American subject is exposed because of race causes him to struggle against the concept of race, but Du Bois fails to discard this concept that both he and science question because he simultaneously finds political value in the deployment of racial identity and, more significantly, substitutes race for another signifier with which race holds a metonymical relation: slavery. These two signifiers, I suggest, are linked within a signifying chain that thus ensures Du Bois' return to race. But the signifier slavery that Du Bois chooses to emphasize does not only recuperate his racial identity; more importantly, it links this identity to slavery's signifieds—insult, discrimination, disaster. As this source of insult and injury, slavery is the nucleus around which Du Bois' narrative and identity condense. I say with Lacan that this "nucleus refers to something traumatic," something beyond slavery itself that "must be designated as belonging to the real" of subjective lack; and I argue that Du Bois confronts this lack, as may contemporary African Americans, precisely because he begins by embracing a hyperbolic, historical relation to the signifiers of race and their injurious signifieds.[45]

The Rhetorical Self, Dominated by the Signifier

In his rhetorical construction of the self as racial, Du Bois subjects himself to a domination by the signifiers of race in ways that can be understood in relation to Lacan's reading of the mechanisms of metaphor and metonymy as central to subjective activity. Lacan's work "links metaphor to the question of being and metonymy to its lack."[46] Metonymy expresses what Lacan identifies as the "properly signifying function" of language, the root effort of language to compensate for lack by routing the subject's desire along a signifying chain in which desire is "eternally extending toward the *desire for something else*."[47] This something else is the plenitude of being that the subject seeks continually to find through the metonymical movement of language, through both the "transfer of signification" from one word to another within a signifying chain and the transfer of desire from one object to another as value and meaning are cast upon them by the signifier.[48] It is this metonymical revaluing of race so as to retain it as a means of compensating for lack that we see in Du Bois. Born in what he defines as "the century when the walls of race were clear and straight" and "there was no question of exact definition and understanding of the word," Du Bois eventually comes to question "the concept of race" because it "has so changed and presented so much contradiction."[49] Insofar as Du Bois reaches toward race as that which promises to fill lack, he struggles with these contradictions, shifting metonymically from the biological to the sociohistorical and eventually coming full circle through the signifier slavery to ground his identity in this very contradiction.

However, the nature of this contradiction is such that it allows Du Bois a restrictive understanding of both his historical and his psychic self. In pinning his identity to slavery, Du Bois moves from the operations of metonymy to a metaphorical process whereby slavery is substituted as the dominating signifier for his (racial) identity. Where metaphor involves the substitution of the signifier for that which it names, the function of metaphor is to remanifest being, to give presence, through language, to absence. Most notable through the subject's self-representation in the signifier of his or her proper name, metaphor allows for the emergence of the lost being in the only form through which it may manifest itself, as what Lacan refers to as "the being of signifierness."[50] This lost being is thus the signified implied in the signifier of the subject's proper name. But what we see in Du Bois is how the signifier of slavery restructures his subjective relation to being.

In Du Bois' narrative, slavery functions as a dominating master signifier that delineates the meaning of Du Bois' racial identity. Not only does it substitute itself for Du Bois' proper name as the signifier that will structure Symbolic representation of his (racial) being, but it also conflates this being with the injury, insult, and discrimination both he and the nonwhite world suffer today and have suffered in the past, thus bonding them in a common identity. This substitution of identity and conflation of feelings is explained by a Lacanian understanding of metaphor as that which brings to a halt the metonymical sliding of desire and meaning through manifestation of a more lasting substitution, a "conjunction of two signifiers" for which there is "the greatest disparity of the images signified."[51] Such

disparity of the signified is what we see in Du Bois when slavery, the new
master signifier of his identity, structures Du Bois' personal feelings and
sense of being, in what he calls a "later reaction" to racism, around racial
feelings that belong to all nonwhites. Slavery is able to produce this disparity that organizes his sliding feelings because metaphor does not involve
juxtaposition of two equally actualized signifiers but is instead a process
in which one signifier has "replaced the other" in "the signifying chain."[52]
In such juxtaposition, the substituting signifier of slavery suppresses other
signifiers of identity, so that they remain present only "by virtue of [their]
(metonymic) connection to the rest of the chain," while it simultaneously
delimits and occludes the signifieds that emerge as an expression of this
identity's psychic and emotional reality.[53] In Du Bois' discussion of his
feelings toward Negroes and Africa, these personal feelings are themselves
the signifieds that will express and further elide his being, articulating this
being around the substitute signifier slavery that displaces the multiple signifiers of Du Bois' personal identity with its dominating historical context.

As signifieds Du Bois' personal feelings begin as what Lacan calls
after Saussure an "amorphous" and "sentimental mass of the current of
discourse," but they become increasingly structured into "racial feelings"
through the agency of the signifier slavery.[54] It is this sentimental mass
of the signified that Du Bois experiences as "contradictory forces, facts
and tendencies" that shuttle him through the changing currents of the
discourse on race. These currents lead Du Bois to question skeptically
"what is Africa to me," while they simultaneously ensure his affections
for Africa, despite his rational rejection of biologically inflected notions
of Africa as the "motherland."[55] The flow of this discourse is so determinative of Du Bois' objects of desire that, though aware of the mixture of
his own racial heritage and cultural background, Du Bois is driven at one
point by what he terms an "ultra 'race' loyalty" to give "up courtship with
one 'colored' girl because she looked quite white" and because, guided by
racial allegiance, he "resented" the potential "inference on the street that
[he] had married outside [his] race."[56] Du Bois' self-admitted subjection to
surrounding discourses on race exemplifies the sentimental mass of the signified as a "continuum," as what Lacan terms a "confused mass" ever open,
through domination by the signifier, to the "immeasurable power of ideological warfare."[57] Du Bois' subjective feelings, in their amorphous metonymic shifting from skepticism and love to allegiance and resentment,

along with his individual identity itself, become the grounds upon which this warfare is waged.

In such warfare, it is the dominating substitute signifier that coheres and grants structure to the sentimental mass of the signified. Slavery as signifier comes to organize both desire and identity for Du Bois because slavery "crystallizes" his feelings and sense of self in what Lacan calls a "dialectic that has as its centre a bad encounter."[58] In psychoanalysis, the bad encounter is a "traumatizing" confrontation in the life of the subject that assumes an "organizing function for development" because it produces an awareness of lack.[59] In Du Bois' case, however, the bad encounter of slavery that organizes his personal biography is external to his biographical experiences. Slavery allows for the historicizing and, thus, depersonalizing of both being and lack for Du Bois. This historicizing becomes possible because the racism of slavery that attempted to elide the being of slaves by pinning subjective lack exclusively to them also produced slavery as a central historical representative of subjective lack for later generations of African Americans. Racial identity itself, whether imposed by racism or willfully embraced by contemporary African Americans as the historical context for self-understanding and being, not only crystallizes for African Americans the indisputable link between slavery and the racism they continue to suffer but also may collapse their personal sense of being with the historical lack emerging from slavery. Racism is key to this conflation. In repeating a process whereby the African American subject's relation to being is again questioned, as it was in slavery, racism grounds the African American subject's psychic sense of lack not in the split self but in the racial past. This crystallization of identity through the bad encounter of slavery is therefore what redefines Du Bois' own desires by obfuscating lack.

Du Bois models the process by which slavery and racial identity may displace African Americans' relation to both lack and being. Lacan ties the subject's loss of being to the exclusion from the Symbolic of those aspects of the subject that defy linguistic circumscription, the drives and desires of the subject that evade representation even in the very process of the subject's articulation of his or her demands. The root of these core drives and desires is the libido as "an internal" tension, a "constant force" that registers what the "sexed being loses in sexuality" upon entrance into the Symbolic.[60] Initially "polymorphous, aberrant," the emerging subject is able to attain pleasure through multiple sources, but sexuality and the signifier both step in to define the regions of the body and the objects of the Symbolic through which the sexed subject may attain pleasure.[61] As a result, the constant force of the libido achieves Symbolic expression only as "partial drives," emerging with only "that part of sexuality that passes into the networks of the constitution of the subject, into the networks of the signifier."[62] As "the most profound lost object," the libido, manifested as an aphanisis of being, fuels desire and sexuality such that it is through pursuit of a mate that the subject attempts typically to compensate for lack, seeking out in love the person who possesses the illusory lost object that will fulfill him or her and make him or her, fantastically, whole again.[63]

However, African Americans like Du Bois, who ground their identity primarily in race, relate to this fantasy of wholeness on a grander scale. As we see above, when he reaches the point of "ultra 'race' loyalty," what compensates for lack in Du Bois is not a connection with a mate but membership in a larger race. In this moment, desire is most directly grounded in the substitute signifier slavery that organizes the sentimental continuum away from personal lack and toward an external bad encounter that presents itself as a fixing manifestation of loss for all members of the race. Because slavery has so bound loss to race, race itself becomes the illusory object upon "which the drive closes" in its pursuit of wholeness.[64] Beyond love of a mate, love of the race becomes the primary means of curing whatever ails the subject and fulfilling all of Du Bois' desires as he begins to define all lack and all suffering as racial.

Here we see how the amorphous continuum of an African American's subjective feelings and desires may be reshaped by existent discourses of race and a privileging of one's relation to the history of slavery. Lacan explains that the continuum of the signified is part of the "double flow of discourse," in which the chain of the signified can be envisioned as positioned below the chain of the signifier so as to form "two planes" that are each "indefinitely subdivided within themselves."[65] This amorphous mass of feelings slides continually "under the signifier," oscillating metonymically across the plane of the signified until through metaphor a "quilting point" is achieved, a knitting together of the tangential planes such that the signifier, in purporting to embody the signified, "stops the otherwise indefinite sliding of signification."[66] For Du Bois, slavery becomes the displacing metaphorical signifier of personal identity, centering a reticulated network of signifiers in which what are substitutionally displaced are those signifiers that mark the self as nonracial, multiracial, or more than racial. On the second plane of discourse, slavery's signifieds—insult, discrimination, disaster—grant linguistic and cognitive structure to the amorphous feelings of desire and lack Du Bois experiences, forming the "lines of force" that organize this plane of the signified in its convergence with the signifier slavery.[67] The end result is a knitting together of the planes so that self-identity is pinned to the master signifier slavery as a linguistic quilting point that names Du Bois' feelings as racial, defines the proper (i.e., racial) objects of his desire, and, finally, binds his being and his lack to the suffering of all nonwhites.

Suture and the Imaginary Ego

This rhetorical foregrounding of suffering is what I find to be the core of Du Bois' ambivalent relation to race. Lacan explains that the quilting point is a "metaphoric creation" manifested in a moment when, ostensibly, "the signifier sticks perfectly to the signified"; in jumping the gap of disparity so as to produce a quilted representation of something it is not, the metaphorical signifier becomes "situated at the precise point at which meaning is produced in nonmeaning," the point at which the signifier emerges in a masquerade representation of the meaningless being that ever defies linguistic and Symbolic representation.[68] In Du Bois, however, the designated feelings of insult and discrimination do not mask but instead unveil the empty place of being that here emerges as an overwhelming experience of lack from which Du Bois can distance himself only by projecting it onto all nonwhites. This failure of the signifier to represent being is what leads Du Bois ambivalently to embrace and reject race.

As Lacan shows, for most subjects quilted by the dominating signifier, "when the upholsterer's needle . . . reappears, it's all over," and the subject, in effect, "joins the faithful troops," donning the uniform granted him or her by the Other of the Symbolic.[69] It is this joining of the racial troops that Du Bois describes as the end result of an African American's "group imprisonment within a group," a confinement that causes the individual to "think of himself not as an individual but as a group man, a 'race' man" with "almost unending" loyalty to this group.[70] Lacan elaborates that from the moment this knitting together of the planes of the signifier and the signified is achieved, "everything radiates out from and is organized around the signifier."[71] The signifier becomes the "point of convergence that enables everything that happens in this discourse to be situated retroactively and prospectively."[72] It is this retroactive situating of his amorphous feelings that Du Bois conducts as he questions his relation to Africa;

but Du Bois' need to do so at the end of his career also displays the limits of race's ability to quilt his identity, exhibiting that any earlier quilting was never fully sufficient in its prospective and futural orientation.

In looking most specifically at his youth, we shall see that though dominated by the racial signifier throughout his career, Du Bois does not consistently and completely embrace this concept. Instead, Du Bois actively contests and negotiates race, ambivalently resisting and accepting the concept because beyond race is a trauma of slavery that extends across time as one long memory that continues to "insult" his very humanity. Not only do these continuing insults remain functional in the quilting of identity for both Du Bois and contemporary African Americans, but, I argue, they also threaten to impair for African Americans what Lacan calls the suturing of the subject. Where the process of quilting describes a joining of the signifier and signified, suture defines a stitching together at the level of the registers that comprise the psyche, a splicing of the Imaginary and the Symbolic across the opening of the Real. This suturing is fundamental to subjectivity because the "meaning" that emerges within consciousness through the metaphorical and metonymical functions of the signifier is finally "the result of an intersection between the imaginary and the symbolic," a linking of the signifiers of the Symbolic with the Imaginary ego constructs of the subject that, as I have argued, are contested for African Americans by a racist Symbolic.[73]

What occurs in the process of suturing is that the fantasies of wholeness that determine the subject of the Imaginary are articulated through and find their support in the Symbolic's signifiers. These signifiers enable a process of "mimicry" as the means of constituting the ego through which the subject "accommodates itself" to its own splitting: by identifying with and emulating the desire and form of the other, the subject establishes this ego as "something that is like a mask, a double, an envelope, a thrown-off skin, thrown off [by the Other] in order to cover the frame of a shield."[74] This skin as an ego granted by the Symbolic is what is fixed to the shield of the subject's Imaginary fantasies of wholeness, serving as "the paper tiger" that sits bonded like a crest upon the impregnable, unified *I* figured by the Imaginary. The crested shield, the illusory unified ego produced in this suturing of the Symbolic and Imaginary, functions as a "screen" before the Real, protecting the subject from an "iridescence" that threatens to "overflow" him or her, a scalding *jouissance* and traumatic lack that may consume the subject.[75] This crest or emulating skin positioned on the shield of fantasy is thus the means through which the subject begins "making a picture of himself," developing from the fantasy of this unified ego a portraiture of the self that may be sutured into the broader tapestry of the Symbolic through the needlework of the signifier.[76]

Lacan explains that, as a result of this suturing, "in most people, the symbolic, the imaginary and the real are entangled to the point where they are continuous, one to another" and linked in the form of what he calls a "Borromean knot."[77] It is this very continuity that may be compromised by racism. Lacan identifies the Imaginary as the "support of [the] consistency" and continuity found in the registers; "this imaginary," Lacan elaborates, is "namely the body" and is "what holds things together," providing the "surface" as "merely skin" that serves to grant the subject his or her only "mental" consistency.[78] The "idea of the self" as "body" "is what is termed the ego," states Lacan, and the "root of the imaginary" ego is "self-love": "I make a bandage of [the body], thus I clean it."[79] What is challenged by racism is the idea of the cleanliness or core value of the racialized subject's body. It is this process of devaluing or dirtying the African American subject's body that impedes the ability of this body to serve as the core of an Imaginary that bandages over the Real and sutures the subject to the racist social Symbolic. If Du Bois only ambivalently dons the uniform and joins the racial troops, it is because he recognizes in race what Lacan calls the "impersonalization" of the signifiers through which the Other seeks to define him.[80] This is the impersonal relation to the concept of race that Du Bois highlights in such statements as "The pictures of my race which were current were not authentic nor fair portraits."[81]

It is an effort at self-portraiture that I find dominating Du Bois' relation to race, such that what he negotiates through the signifier is the Imaginary of his own body. At a most personal level, Du Bois is driven by a competitiveness that weighs his self-worth against that of his white peers. We see this competitive striving emerging in Du Bois at the very moment he comes to recognize both his racial identity and its inherent association with inferiority. In one of the most well-known scenes in *The Souls of Black Folk*, Du Bois describes a day during his childhood when a little white girl's rejection of his gift of a visiting card leads to his recognition that he is not only "different from the others" but also "shut out from their world by a vast veil."[82] Du Bois does not depict his confrontation with this veil and racial identity as particularly traumatic. Indeed, he had "no desire to tear down that veil" because his realization that he "could beat [his] mates at examination-time, or beat them at a foot-race, or even beat their stringy heads" grants him a sense of being, a sense of self-worth that allows him to soar "above" the veil while also holding all "beyond it in common contempt."[83]

What Du Bois competes against, however, is truly an image of self reflected back to him through the racist vision of an other whose views are sanctioned by the larger social Symbolic. The rejection of his visiting card outlines for Du Bois the limited sphere allocated to him within the social Symbolic and the conjunction with lack that this Symbolic seeks to impose upon him. This imposition of lack leads Du Bois to resist a rewriting of the Imaginary identity granted him by the natural processes of subjective inscription Lacan details in his theory of the mirror stage and rearticulates most lucidly in his *Seminar XI*. Lacan defines the mirror stage as designating "the transformation that takes place in the subject when he assumes an image" of self that Lacan calls the "ideal-I" or ideal ego.[84] The child of this stage, still limited in its motor control but nascent in its acquisition of speech, constructs this idealized image as a gestalt, as a conflation of the self, the external world, and the mother who serves the "orthopedic" function of propping up the child (and its identity) in front of the mirror.[85] The gestalt thus orients the developing subject in a "fictional direction," initiating a "discordance with his own reality" that will be from here on in grounded by the notion of "the *I*'s mental permanence" and inviolate unity.[86] These fictions that ground subjective fantasy are precisely what I suggest are challenged when Du Bois encounters through the little girl an altered vision of his identity.

Lacan shows that the subject is inextricably bound to the other. The gaze of the other, he explains, is that through which "I enter light" and "am *photo-graphed*."[87] The other determines one's relation to the Symbolic, embodying that exterior iridescence through which the subject graphs and maps his or her own relation to a tenebrous being. The subject enters the Symbolic by entering the picture of the external world granted him or her by the Other. The prepainted image of the external world, Lacan explains, "is painted" in "the depths of my eye," emerging as that vision of externality inscribed onto the psyche through the Other's portraitures of Symbolic reality.[88] Through the ideal ego and its continual articulation around a vision cast upon the subject, the psyche introjects an "exteriority" that contains within it the "contour" of "the statue onto which man projects himself," the conflated image of the other through whom the subject both takes on an alienating "desire of the other" as its own desire and outlines in the psyche the "form of his [own] body."[89] Where both Du Bois' views of the contours of his own body and his understanding of its dissymmetry from the Symbolic's vision of the statue that contours true (or white) humanity are unsettled by his rejection from the white Symbolic, what Du Bois resists is a grafting onto his psyche of a revised image of both himself and the space he occupies in the external world.

Du Bois strives against this revision by seeking to display his competitive superiority over his white peers. Finding that all "the worlds" and "dazzling opportunities" he "longed for" belong to his white rivals, Du Bois becomes determined that "they should not keep these prizes" and concludes that "some, all," he "would wrest from them."[90] Lacan defines the formation of one's ego around the statue or "imago of one's semblable" as occasion for a "primordial jealousy" existent in man.[91] This conflation of the self with the semblable of the other causes a mirroring of desire, such that the subject sees his or her satisfaction as guaranteed by the objects around which the other's desires gravitate: Lacan explains, the subject "constitutes its objects in an abstract equivalence due to competition from other people."[92] It is this drive to possess the objects that signal satisfaction and psychic coherence in the other that defines Du Bois' relation to his white rivals.

Indeed, it is Du Bois' inability to win these objects that determines his later reorientation toward a fuller desire for the fantasy object of race. As Du Bois encounters more obstacles to his success, the "contempt" he holds for his rivals begins to fade. In confronting and seeking to negotiate the veil, what Du Bois concludes is that "the race problem" was not a "matter of clear, fair competition," and so what had been for him in his "boyhood" the "vision of a glorious crusade" where he matched his "mettle against white folk" becomes for Du Bois as he grows older a "more serious matter."[93] In describing one morning he "can never forget," for example, Du Bois articulates his feelings of helplessness while studying in Berlin with "a big aggressive" professor who walked in and "thundered," mulattoes "are inferior."[94] Du Bois laments, "What contradiction could there be to that authoritative dictum?"[95] I would argue, however, that Du Bois' entire scholarly production is an attempt to refute this increasingly traumatic confrontation with race that, in this instance, left him feeling both that his professor's "eyes [were] boring into" him and that his professor "had not noticed" him at all.[96] Du Bois notes that it is "difficult to let others see the full psychological meaning of caste segregation" but that it became clear to him that his "struggles" and "resentment" had begun "to have serious repercussions upon [his] inner life."[97] Du Bois battles race while also contending against the psychological implications of an assertion of his own lack of being. What makes competition unfair and race increasingly traumatic for Du Bois is that "the basis of race distinction [is] changed [continuously] without explanation, without apology," and what Du Bois seeks is to establish a stable and revivifying notion of racial identity.[98]

In the end, however, so overwhelmed is Du Bois by the shadow of race that by 1940, when he publishes his autobiographical *Dusk of Dawn*, the images Du Bois uses to represent the segregation of African Americans are not simply their separation by a veil but also their "entomb[ment]" in an "impeding mountain."[99] Du Bois comes to assert that "racial identity present[s] itself" as "tightening bonds about [his] feet."[100] Yet Du Bois is drawn to that which binds him; acknowledging that "the process" of forming his "theories of race" was "probably largely unconscious," Du Bois observes that "it is hard" to be "philosophical and calm" when one's "essential and common humanity" is so virulently contested.[101] Bound to a traumatizing racial identity, Du Bois embraces as defense this very traumatogenic identity itself.

Du Bois finally claims this racial identity as a "badge" that both singles one out for injury and protects one from harm. He unveils the paradox of race as automaton, as the signifier that keeps coming back both because it is externally imposed by a racist Symbolic and because it is clung to as a means of self-protection that is simultaneously political and psychic. Notably puncturing the ego in the very process of suturing this ego to the Symbolic, the signifiers of race produce in Du Bois a racial identity that functions mutually to mark the place of a laceration associated with slavery and to scab over this open wound with the screen of the Imaginary's identity structures. The badge of race, like a donned family crest, is what the Symbolic grants Du Bois as the outlines of the portraiture that is to be traced upon the protective shield of the ego. However, because this badge marks an identity not easily integrated into the Symbolic, what it highlights is precisely the site of this troubled Symbolic integration. This visible badge designates the screen of the ego as what Lacan calls the "stain" in the tapestry, the tender "spot" of the psyche indicative of the injured site at which subjective identity scabs itself across the opening of the Real.[102]

Fueled by his awareness of the impropriety of the signifier to define his identity, Du Bois cannot seamlessly suture over the wounds of the past with the identity granted him by the Symbolic. The scar remains visible, marking with the scab of racial identity an injury bound to the signifiers of race that both manifests the "insult" and "discrimination" that assails the ego and simultaneously fortifies this ego through racial identity as defense against these subjectively fragmenting effects of the signifier.

Racial Interpellation, Trauma, and Fantasy

Du Bois' experience with these fragmenting effects of the signifier allows us to articulate more fully a notion of trauma and its relation to African Americans. A fragmenting of the psyche through the signifier is precisely what constitutes the trauma that assails equally Du Bois and contemporary African Americans whose identity remains bound to the dominating signifier of slavery. Through his hyperbolic embrace of the historical past and its signifiers, Du Bois comes to experience the trauma of slavery as the Real, as "that which always comes back to the same place."[103] This ever-present, centering wound, this traumatic Real of slavery, continually torments the African American subject through the capacity of the automaton to initiate with its signifiers a process of "repetition," a re-emergence of a founding event that "can no longer produce itself except by repeating itself endlessly."[104] The traumatic event of slavery remanifests itself through its repetition in the forms of both racism and the "hauling" of racial identity. However, whereas this hauling of race allows African Americans to maintain a relation with the traumatic past and yet not directly confront the Real beyond the automaton of the racial signifiers, racism involves what Lacan refers to as the "function of the *tuché*," the "encounter with the real" that may shatter the subjective self.[105]

I link this *tuché* to the repetition of racist acts produced in the Symbolic as the lineage of slavery, acts through which the confrontation with subjective lack once experienced by the slave repeats itself in the lives of African Americans. This repetition establishes racism as one of those unique moments in which "the real reappears, in effect, frequently unveiled."[106] It is this unveiling of the Real that exposes and links African Americans like Du Bois to the trauma of slavery, urging them to employ race protectively in the constitution of their identity. Racism, I argue, manifests the subjective trauma that interpellates African Americans into racial identity, linking this trauma to that of the slave and this identity to that of the group. Lacan defines trauma as that "which is *unassimilable*" to subjectivity, arguing that trauma marks "a point that the subject can approach only by dividing himself into a certain number of agencies."[107] We may say most precisely that trauma is that which portends the very unsuturing of the psychic registers of subjectivity. In the face of a racism that may produce this unsuturing or fragmenting of the psyche through an unveiling of the Real, African American racial identity often finds its most compelling utility as that which facilitates a resuturing of the shattered subject.

Because racism is often experienced in subtle ways by African Americans, however, and because racial identity also involves the sense of pride we saw especially present in Du Bois during his competitive youth, trauma for African Americans more often entails continual assaults to fantasies of being, not a full-on shattering and unsuturing of the self. As trauma theorist Kai Erikson observes, "Trauma can issue . . . from a continuing pattern of abuse as well as from a single searing assault."[108] But an analysis of how this single searing assault may unsuture subjectivity can help us to specify the mechanisms of racism that conflict African Americans in less apparent ways. Here I would like to more directly present a definition of trauma that will contextualize my reading of Du Bois' impact on an African American scholarship on race that continues his legacy of binding racial identity to slavery. To do so, I will turn momentarily away from Du Bois and toward a central moment of traumatic confrontation with racism depicted by Frantz Fanon in *Black Skin, White Masks*. Clearly Fanon is not African American; however, in depicting the powerful scene of his encounter with racism while disembarking from the train that brings him to France for the first time, Fanon dramatizes the more gradual process by which individuals become interpellated into a racialized identity. As a one-time student of Lacan's, Louis Althusser and his notion of "ideological hailing" or "interpellation" will also be helpful here, for just as "all ideology has the function . . . of 'constituting' concrete individuals as subjects," especially for African Americans, racism has the function of constituting concrete subjects as racialized subjects, granting them a racial identity through an encounter with the remanifested trauma of slavery as the Real.[109]

Fanon's encounter with the repetition of the Real past occurs when he first meets "the white man's eyes."[110] Stepping off the train that ends his journey from the Antilles to France, Fanon is hailed by the other in an Althusserian sense: "Look, a Nigger!"[111] In Fanon's words, "It was an external stimulus that flickered over me as I passed by."[112] This flickering is our first indication of the *tuché*: as Lacan explains, "What is repeated . . . is always something that occurs . . . *as if by chance*."[113] It is a gentle touch, if you will, whose power is not fully registered at first. However, the hail creates a recognition, a responsibility, in Fanon, an ownership of something that demands he pay it homage: Fanon tells us, "An unfamiliar weight burdened me."[114]

This weight marks the initiation of the automaton, "the return, the coming-back, the insistence of the signs" that impose upon Fanon a racial identity grounded in the traumatic history of slavery.[115] Fanon explains that while living among his "own" in the Antilles he had maintained an "intellectual understanding" of race, in which he conceptualized racial identity as something that was not "dramatic" or of excessive importance to his self-identification; but Fanon's confrontation with the signifier nigger forces him to accept a position in a pre-established signifying chain that unfolds through the historical lineage of this word.[116] Fixed in the gaze of "the white man, who had woven [him] out of a thousand details, anecdotes, stories," Fanon is "battered down by tom-toms, cannibalism, intellectual deficiency, fetishism, racial defects," and all of the signifiers he is sure run through the white man's mind.[117] The automaton initiated externally by the other of the Symbolic comes to dominate Fanon's psyche, producing through the repetition of its signifiers the *tuché* as an encounter with personal lack that becomes the very means of establishing Fanon's identity as fundamentally racial.

Fanon's trauma arises in this moment, emerging from the ability of the racist signifier to unsuture him from the Symbolic and Imaginary structures of identity he had maintained, shattering the Imaginary ego and bodily image he had been able to construct free from a portraiture dominated by what he calls an imposed "racial epidermal schema."[118] As Lacan specifies, however, the *tuché* as traumatic encounter with the Real "is essentially the missed encounter" with an event that consciousness cannot assimilate.[119] Instead of conscious meaning, the traumatic encounter produces a void, a Real gap in the universe of meaning, a lack around which subjectivity must resuture itself. Thus, what enters consciousness for Fanon is not the trauma of this unsuturing but the racial identity that now gains prominence in Fanon's self-identification. Fanon misses the Real of his own lack only to the extent that the personal trauma that issues from its unveiling is replaced for Fanon by the automaton that now racially defines him, both protecting him from this lack and binding him to a racial identity grounded in a grander historical unveiling of subjective lack. Fanon says, "My body was given back to me sprawled out, distorted, recolored."[120] Unsutured from a more than racial self, Fanon can only reconstitute his identity and maintain his subjectivity through a resuturing that lacerates the bodily ego with puncture wounds from which issue the black blood of his racial heritage: "What else could it be for me but an amputation," asks Fanon, "an excision, a hemorrhage that splattered my whole body with black blood?"[121]

We can say with Althusser that by Fanon's "mere one-hundred-and-eighty-degree physical conversion," as he turns in recognition that the hail issued through the other's racial signifier is addressed to him, Fanon "becomes a [racialized] subject."[122] Fanon's recognition brings to "consciousness" the "incessant (eternal) practice of ideological recognition" that Fanon has always taken part in on a less "dramatic" level.[123] In this moment, the "racial epidermal schema" confines Fanon, as his blackness overflows into his consciousness: "Some identified me with ancestors of mine who had been enslaved or lynched: I decided to accept this. It was on the universal level of the intellect that I understood this inner kinship—I was the grandson of slaves."[124] Through racism as repetition, Fanon experiences the necessarily missed encounter with personal trauma by means of which he attains a racial identity: black, descendant of slaves.

With this identity, Fanon removes himself from the immediate scene of his own traumatic encounter with personal lack, articulating around the introduced void a new fantasy self that finds its solace in a racial past. In the moment when Fanon's identity is shattered by the gaze of the other and its introduction of the automaton, Fanon first reconstitutes his sense of being by articulating it around the epidermal schema and racial signifiers granted him by the other. "Since the other hesitated to recognize me," says Fanon, "there remained only one solution: to make myself known," to "assert myself as a BLACK MAN."[125] But where Fanon's identity as a black man marks him with a projected sense of inferiority too close to the condition of lack against which he contends, Fanon reinforces his sense of being through a glorification of Africa that revalues the racial signifiers and identity to which he is now pinned by designating African culture as the source of a racial pride: "From the opposite end of the white world a magical Negro culture was hailing me. Negro sculpture! I began to flush with pride. Was this our salvation?"[126] Fanon's salvation is a reinforced link with Africa that allows him to articulate the racial "epidermal schema" as the very core of a new identity capable of sustaining his illusions of being. Now hailed by the discourse of a "magical" past that produces in him not trauma but pride, Fanon displays the ambivalent relation to race, also present in many African Americans, that here leads him to embellishment of the past as counterbalance to the assaults upon being that are staged by the concept of race.

Functioning in conjunction with trauma to ensure the successful interpellation of the African American racial subject, this sense of pride, I argue, often fends against the traumatic Real by helping to rearticulate the past as a new center of identity, as what I would call a new Real wrapped up in the fantasies of the Imaginary. Fanon's response to racism with the construction of his racial identity allows us to specify more fully the temporal function of the Real in its relation both to the trauma of slavery and to a personal trauma unveiled by racism and subsequently tied to slavery. As a result of a personal trauma like Fanon's or Du Bois', the Real is retroactively articulated in such a way that we may speak of it as manifesting two versions of itself. Borrowing the terminology of Lacanian scholar Charles Shepherdson, we shall call these versions the postsymbolic Real and the presymbolic Real.[127]

The postsymbolic Real is always directly tied to traumatic encounters and is constituted through what we have already termed the splitting of the psyche into "a number of agencies" through the function of the signifier.[128] Initially manifested with the subject's entrance into the Symbolic world of language, this Real emerges as a component register of the psyche. What fundamentally institutes trauma is this very splitting of the psyche, which introduces the postsymbolic Real as a void, a gap, at the core of the subjective self. Where the developed subject sutures his or her Imaginary and Symbolic across this gap, what later traumatic encounters in the Symbolic entail is an unsuturing of subjectivity that confronts the fragmented self with the Real lack that subjectivity has up to this point masked from conscious recognition. Here we may define traumatic encounters in the Symbolic as themselves repetitions or remanifestations of the "very split that occurs in the subject" with the traumatic onset of subjectivity.[129] It is this splitting that is repeated in racism and made so appallingly visible in slavery, as confrontation with the Other's signifiers afflicts the subject with an essential void situated in the place where the subject must fantasize his or her being.

Whereas Fanon confronts the repetition of this postsymbolic trauma through a reauthoring of his identity produced by the signifier nigger, Du Bois experiences this trauma as a constant struggle to shore up fantasies of being, a struggle yet punctuated by seminal moments such as the rejection of his visiting card and his encounter in Berlin with the professor who defines him as inferior. We can say through the examples of Du Bois and Fanon that what trauma thus involves is the stroke of the Other's signifier, its barring of a meaning whose failure to arise institutes within the subject a void, an essential gap, in the place where meaning should reside. It is this void that we saw most notably with Fanon in the form of the missed encounter that, through the signifier nigger, supplants identity and being with a lack around which racial identity must be established. At issue in the encounters of both Fanon and Du Bois is a breaking down of these figures' established sense of self and an unveiling of personal lack through their mutual exposure to the racist signifiers of the Other. This personal lack is conflated with the mirrored lack of the slave in an unsuturing that fragments these subjects across time to bind personal lack to the historical past. Trauma here reveals itself as that which forces upon the subject not only a confrontation with the void of the Real but also a resuturing of subjectivity through a rewriting of identity. It is in this rewriting that the presymbolic Real establishes itself, emerging to protect the subject from the postsymbolic trauma that splits subjectivity.

A retroactive product of the subject's fantasies, the presymbolic Real is an illusory version of the past reconstituted by the signifiers of the Symbolic and inflected with the fantasies of the Imaginary so as to produce through the creation of a new identity structure a "sliding-away" from the unbearable trauma of the postsymbolic Real.[130] After the splitting of the subject in the Symbolic, this constitution of the presymbolic Real allows for a "variation" and "alienation of . . . meaning" that, quite simply, goes "some way to satisfying the pleasure principle" and masking lack.[131] The constitutive function of the Imaginary, as it first appears in the initial splitting of the subject, is precisely this masking of lack, a function that produces the Imaginary itself as a fantasy realm of subjective bliss in the presence of the mother; accordingly, as the presymbolic Real arises in defense of the subject traumatized by a confrontation with his lack of being, this illusory Real roots the subject in a new identity formation by binding itself to the pleasure-inducing fantasies of the Imaginary. It comes to figure in the psyche of the traumatized subject as a lost state of pure *jouissance*, a past in which, like the Imaginary bliss of the child's oneness with the mother, lack never existed. It is this past that fuels so many of the racial fantasies that underpin African American identity.

The presymbolic Real often figures in African American identity as the root of notions of both a glorious lost past in Africa and a future bliss that may be refound through racial identity as a source of psychic completion. Especially influential in the decades surrounding Du Bois' own intellectual career, extending through Marcus Garvey's "back to Africa" movement in the 1920s and the Black Power movement of the 1960s, we see hints of this lost African past not only in Fanon's hailing from the mystical world of Negro art but also in Du Bois' own allusion to Africa as the "motherland," the maternal source of his African American identity. In this allusion, we may note the Imaginary function granted "Mother Africa" by African Americans, as Africa becomes not only the source of their racial identity but also the mother of their whole race. Coming to stand as the illusory presymbolic Real, "Mother Africa" emerges as a surrogate or substitute for the Lacanian mother of the Imaginary. In the popular discourse that views African Americans as "brothers" and "sisters," "Mother Africa" figures as the place of a primordial unity that is severed by the institution of slavery, shattering the familial gestalt to cast Africa's children across the diaspora. Thus, what is figured as lost is not the absent being of African Americans that is unveiled by slavery and racism but their Imaginary mother, "Mother Africa." Inspiring both arguments for a return to Africa and desires to unite as a racial family, this Imaginary lost past lends slavery the function that the Lacanian child's fantasies grant to the Symbolic, becoming the illusory destroyer of an Imaginary unity. Thus, both the trauma of the postsymbolic Real of slavery and the postsymbolic personal trauma of racism are excluded in this racial politics through a process where the illusory, presymbolic *jouissance* of Africa is mourned.

Though we see that Du Bois himself remains hesitant strictly to define Africa as the mother of his identity, this notion of a broken unity is precisely what inspires his politics of Pan-Africanism. At a more personal level, it is also this fantasy of loss that Du Bois engages in his contemplation of his ties to Africa, a contemplation that ends in Du Bois' retirement in Ghana, where he lives out the end of his life. Du Bois returns to the arms of a "Mother Africa" he rhetorically constructs through a discourse that engages the Imaginary to define race as a "vast family of human beings, generally of common blood, always of common history, traditions, and

impulses."[132] This definition displays Du Bois' discomfort with the biological conception of race while also gesturing toward similarities of a more
ineffable nature that unify the racial group: Du Bois asserts that although
"race differences have followed mainly physical race lines," no "mere physical distinctions would really define or explain the deeper differences—
the cohesiveness and continuity of these groups. The deeper differences
are spiritual, psychical, differences."[133] Du Bois points to the psychical as
reinforcing and cohering an already racially distinct group, failing to recognize that it is the trauma itself that constitutes the group and its identity, both identifying through racism the designated members of the group
and urging through racial pride an embrace of the interpellation through
which race becomes the compensatory object for lack. As Lacan notes in
discussing the psychic bonds that link individuals to each other, "it is in
their courage in bearing the intolerable relationship" to lack, it is in the
very manner through which the subject reacquires access to an impossible *jouissance*, that "friends recognize and choose each other."[134] African
Americans, I argue, establish and maintain their group identity through
a structured relationship to *jouissance*, through manners of compensating
for lack that are not only expressed in cultural productions like music and
religious practice, but also grounded in fantasies like race.

Though the fantasy figuration of Africa as the site of a lost *jouissance* is
less popular today, this ability it maintains to compensate for lack ensures
the figuration's continued presence in contemporary racial discourse. We
see the maternal metaphor assumed in the very appellation which has come
to be the politically correct designation, "African American," a term that
grounds the racial identity through allusion to Africa as the site of a prior
familial unity. But today, foregoing the need for a return to Africa, contemporary racial politics more often evokes this fantasy of a lost maternal
unity through use of an illusory object *a* that can remanifest the state of
jouissance in America itself. Specifically through the notion of racial unity,
race functions as an object *a* to present itself as the remnant of the lost
past. Insofar as it is linked to the presymbolic Real, the object *a* disguises
itself as the remainder of a forgone infantile *jouissance* and unity with the
mother, standing as the returned manifestation of the presymbolic Real.
As this manifestation of a lost Imaginary bliss, the concept of race functions as object *a* to unify African Americans along the lines of their racial
identity.

What often operates as object *a* in calls for political unity is the racial essence critiqued by Appiah, the assumed guarantor of each African American's place within the race. This impossible fantasy object in each African American grounds the notion of him or her as a complement, a part of the Imaginary gestalt that can be re-established as the race is made whole again through the unification of all of "Mother Africa's" children displaced in America. This focus upon complementarity, as I have already suggested, echoes on a grander scale the central fantasy of the Lacanian subject: the fantasy that fuels desire for a mate through the promise of a re-established unity. However, it is not always the case that this essence is required for racial unity to make its promise of re-creating through complementarity the lost presymbolic *jouissance*.

As we have seen, because the concept of an essence is now often contested, African Americans like Lucius Outlaw turn to less restrictive definitions of race that can articulate a need for racial unity without asserting a racial essence. Though arguing that it is "utterly crucial that the use of 'race' . . . be uncoupled from any presumptions of . . . an unchanging, heritable, race-defining biological essence," Outlaw is yet able to maintain race as a cluster concept that promises "stable, lasting social peace and harmony" through racial unity.[135] Significantly, Outlaw does this by evading an exact definition of the sameness or similarity across the group that justifies its eternal unification even in the absence of racism. Lacan speaks of the illusory object *a* as an "object, which is in fact simply the presence of a hollow, a void."[136] The Lacanian object *a* can maintain its function as a fantasy object only insofar as it is able to remain unfinalizable and unidentified. In moving race from the domain of a biological essence to the sociohistorical realm of a cluster concept capable of accounting for "variation across time and space," Outlaw frees this concept from reliance upon finalizable meaning.[137] This hollowing of race, this separation of race from any identifiable object, actuates race as a metonymic object of fantasy able to propel desire forward through the abstraction of an undefinable, dispersed similarity, an ahistorical sameness, that inspires members of the group to work together and help each other create the future *jouissance* of a time when racism is eradicated and African Americans can coexist in unity.

The Legacy of Du Bois

This politics of racial unity as a pursuit of a future *jouissance* is a direct legacy of Du Bois' thinking. In order to resignify the racial identity pinned to him by the Other, Du Bois begins to assert that not only are African Americans "born with a veil," but their tragic experiences have also "gifted [them] with second sight," with unique understandings that African Americans have formulated into a special "message" for that "other world which does not know and does not want to know [African Americans'] power."[138] Suggesting a future in which the parts will unite into a whole, Du Bois presents each racial group as "striving, each in its own way, to develop for civilization its particular message, its particular ideal, which shall help to guide the world nearer and nearer that perfection of human life for which we all long, that 'one far off Divine event.' "[139] More than mere rhetoric, Du Bois' conception of a special message founds his reading of African American identity itself, his famous notion of double consciousness as the second sight with which African Americans are gifted by the traumas of their history. Registering the sense of fragmentation that issues from trauma, Du Bois defines double consciousness as a "peculiar sensation" of "always looking at one's self through the eyes of others," a sense of "two-ness" that produces the central "strife" of the "American Negro": a "longing to attain self-conscious manhood, to merge his double self into a better and truer self."[140] While Imaginarily presenting the fragmenting effects of trauma and subjectivity as curable through a future when "two world-races may give each to each those characteristics both so sadly lack," Du Bois diagnoses the fragmentation of African Americans as created by the duality of their social identity: "an American, a Negro," two "souls," two "warring ideals in one dark body, whose dogged strength alone keeps it from being torn asunder."[141] In Du Bois' view, the cure, then, for both the African American subject and American culture at large, is the sociopolitical endeavor of African Americans "as a race" to "strive by race organization, by race solidarity, by race unity to the realization of that broader humanity."[142]

What Du Bois points to through double consciousness is a heightened awareness of the other's effects upon one's psyche and social sense of self. His reading of how social reality traumatically impacts the psyches of African Americans is lent support by the observations of trauma theorists like Cathy Caruth, who demonstrates that while "psychic trauma involves intense personal suffering . . . it also involves the recognition of realities that most of us have not begun to face."[143] But, as I have noted, confronting these realities has often meant for African Americans an Imaginary reconstruction of the self. Because the personal and social losses suffered by African Americans in the social reality of the Symbolic are registered as attacks on being, these losses become conflated with psychic lack, and what comes to drive political action in the social sphere is as much an Imaginary effort to mask psychic lack as it is a political effort to protect the self against further social losses. Indeed, once African Americans are interpellated into this identity by race, it is the Imaginary self as racial bodily ego that is assailed through a conflation of loss with psychic lack. Thus, efforts to produce social progress in the Symbolic become directed by a desire to protect and conserve the racial image forced upon the subject by the other, structuring political activity in the social around an attempt to clean, as Lacan says, the restrictive, racial ego image maintained as the fantasy core of the self.

The goal becomes to resignify race, to transvalue it in a positive reading. What is ignored in this process is the option of disputing the very possibility of assigning value through race and the illusory identities it produces. Where in his reading of African American identity Du Bois goes so far as to assert that the duality of double consciousness "yields [the Negro] no true self-conscious," the model of trauma clearly complicates this second sight of African Americans.[144] As Kai Erikson explains, trauma may narrowly refocus one's vision, causing the traumatized to "evaluate the data of everyday life differently, read signs differently, see omens that the rest of us are for the most part spared."[145] What I would like to suggest finally is that the double vision of African Americans often involves not just a heightened awareness of racial realities ignored by an American culture driven by its own scotomization of the past but also an Imaginary rewriting, conducted even by African American scholars, of the narratives that articulate African Americans' relation to this past and its suffering.

Du Bois' own articulation of this past and the special message it has allowed African Americans resounds in the work of contemporary African American critics. Where Du Bois links this message to cultural productions such as music, calling the "wild sweet melodies of the Negro slave" the only "true American music," most scholars correctly read jazz and the blues as among the greatest cultural achievements of African Americans.[146] Significantly, what these thinkers often find in the music is a message about suffering. The blues, in particular, is compellingly read as involving an artistry whereby pain and suffering, the trauma of the past itself, come to found the experience of transcendence and overcoming that is the very aesthetics of the musical form; as Ralph Ellison famously defines it, "The blues is an impulse to keep the painful details and episodes of a brutal experience alive in one's aching consciousness, to finger its jagged grain, and to transcend it, not by the consolation of philosophy but by squeezing from it a near-tragic, near-comic lyricism."[147] Thus, for many African American thinkers, the message presented by African American culture and music is finally an instructive on how to overcome the trauma and suffering of the past.

What I have suggested, however, is the danger of the blues-like approach of keeping "alive," as Ellison says, a past of suffering: the danger that one becomes lost, or even comes to revel, in an experience of suffering, forgoing the effort to transcend the pain that has been transformed into the sustaining music of life, into the very source of self-identity. In much of the scholarship and artistry that follows Du Bois' work, African American identity is sustained in its aspiration toward a unique and transvalued status through a glorification of suffering. The individual blues artist's ability to work through and transcend pain is often presented as the distinct possession of the race itself. By the tail end of Du Bois' life, James Baldwin's essays and fiction come, in particular, to ground a notion that, similar to the blues artist, African Americans achieve through suffering a level of personal growth and development that surpasses the less mature and petty concerns of white Americans.[148] Baldwin writes,

> I do not mean to be sentimental about suffering—enough is certainly as good as a feast—but people who cannot suffer never grow up, can never discover who they are. That man, who is forced each day to snatch his manhood, his identity out of the fire of human cruelty that rages to destroy it, knows if he survives his effort, and even if he does not survive it, something about himself and human life that no school on earth—and indeed, no church—can teach.[149]

Baldwin's resignification of suffering signals the past as a badge of honor, as the source of a maturity and developed manhood that starkly contrasts the lack unveiled in slavery.[150] Though we cannot doubt the potential for personal growth through suffering, it is also true that Baldwin sets the stage for a newly inverted hierarchal relation, whereby contemporary scholars like Cornel West may rightly criticize America's blindness to the racial past while also dichotomously highlighting the inhuman bestiality of the rest of American and world culture. Echoing both Baldwin's focus on maturity and Du Bois' politics of complementarity in calling the blues "a great democratic contribution of black people to world history," West asserts,

> The blues is relevant today because when we look down the corridors of time, the black American interpretation of tragicomic hope in face of dehumanizing hate and oppression will be seen as the only kind of hope that has any kind of maturity in a world of overwhelming barbarity and bestiality.[151]

West transforms suffering into hope. This hope revalues the trauma of the past and hails African Americans toward interpellation by a racial identity solidly grounded in the suffering of this past. Thus, the racial identity that masks personal suffering reintroduces suffering on another level through this identification with the collective. The collective and its cultural productions become the source of a racial pride that enables African Americans to massage the scars left by the traumatic past. But, as it aids in the healing of these wounds, it also awakens the potential for African Americans to revel in the *jouissance* of suffering that their massaging of such wounds reawakens.

Caruth shows that "treatment of trauma continue[s]" to present "a crucial problem" because "relieving suffering" seems to entail "diluting" or "eliminating the force and truth of the reality" that the traumatized face and "quite often try to transmit to us."[152] However, in trying to transmit to the broader American culture not just the often ignored social realities of their lives but also a message so frequently grounded in racial fantasy, African Americans bind themselves to an Imaginary truth driven as much by a recognition of social loss as by a desire to mask the personal lack these losses recall. This conflation of lack and social loss restricts the models through which agency for African Americans is imagined. As Appiah argues, the political efficacy of race is dependent upon one's ability to use race strategically, one's ability to discard race and "to celebrate and endorse those identities [based upon nationality, gender, class, and so on] that seem at the moment to offer the best hope of advancing [one's] goal."[153] However, the concept of race as a complementarity bound to family yet dominates African American politics. So prevalent is it as to influence even thinkers outside of the supposed racial group, like "Jewish" philosopher Anna Stubblefield, who presents as a "prescriptive claim about how people should think of their racial identity" the argument that we ought to

"treat members of [our] racial groups as family," suggesting that "identifying with each other on the basis of race is morally acceptable and does
not require justification."[154] While this racial unity does allow for political
action, it also impairs it, grounding agency upon only one aspect of subjective identity. Political activity, I argue, must differentiate between the need
to recuperate from social losses and the impossible desire to fill psychic
lack that grounds the politics of racial unity.

This desire to escape lack runs counter to the blues artist's desire to
transcend that has come to stand for an African American culture of overcoming. As African American scholar of the blues Leroi Jones notes, "To
a very large extent, [blues] songs are about love affairs which do not, did
not, come off."[155] Where the song of the blues artist dwells upon loss in
order to transform it through aesthetics, the song is also a deep engagement with personal lack: not an effort to mask loss in a vision of complementarity but an embrace of personal fragmentation as a condition of
existence. Emphasizing that the love affair can never come off, that "there
is no such thing as a sexual relation" between man and woman because
what man relates to in his complementary other is the fantasy object he
positions in this other, Lacan speaks of the fantasy of complementarity
as "the fundamental phantasy," arguing that a "subject who has traversed
[this] radical fantasy" to move "beyond the function of the *a*" may "experience the drive."[156] It is this experience of the drive, this recognition of lack
as a propelling condition of existence, that is opened up to the musician,
facilitating through lack the artistic production of something new, something revivifying. While the trauma of African Americans is maintained
through their adherence to an identity dominated by the signifiers of the
Real past, accepting this lack means for African Americans grounding
themselves not singularly in the past but multiply in the fragmentation
that is proper to each subject.

Such grounding first requires an interrogation of one's racial desires,
an unveiling of the traumatic Real that inspires political and individual
action and a distancing from the illusory identity of race that constitutes
for African Americans a central manifestation of the fundamental fantasy. Lacanian theory asserts the subject's capacity to make the Real "itself
speak."[157] I propose that this be the task for African Americans: to become
the agency that makes the traumatic Real of slavery speak, to displace
the trauma from its location within the register of the Real through an
investigation and articulation of this trauma's determinative relation to

personal subjectivity. We have seen how the Real speaks through African Americans like Outlaw, how it urges Outlaw to utter an illogical insistence upon race after race serves the political purpose he is sure it must serve. Political arguments like Outlaw's sustain the trauma by denying its true agency as the source of this insistence upon race. Such arguments collude with fantasies that serve the function of excluding this Real, fantasies about racial essence, lost unity, and future unification—a return of what was lost. As Lacan says, "It is in relation to the real that the level of phantasy functions. The real supports the phantasy, the phantasy protects" and maintains the Real.[158] I wish to position African Americans, therefore, beyond the limit of these fantasies, at the point where the fantasies begin to dissolve as the trauma of slavery and racism is dislodged from the Real through the trauma's entrance into symbolization. To reach this point, the African American subject who is attached to race, who is in effect a subject dominated by a trauma that dictates both speech and identity, must begin to possess the trauma, becoming, like the blues artist, a more conscious agent of its utterances and expressions. Through confronting this trauma at the representational level of the Symbolic, African Americans may thus engage the essential process of contextualizing the traumatic past within the multiplicity of an ever-changing subjective self grounded in lack.

3

APPROACHING THE *THING* OF SLAVERY
Toni Morrison's Beloved

In the previous chapters, I suggested the need for African Americans to transcend the fantasy of race and distance themselves from the trauma of slavery. As a means of displaying how this may be done, I now turn to the literary representation of trauma and race in Toni Morrison's *Beloved*. Morrison's novel, I argue, offers not only unique insight into the relation of African Americans to trauma but also a means through literature of safely encountering and contending against the repetition of this trauma in one's own psyche. Significantly, *Beloved* has emerged as a foundational text in a body of African American literature that is already often defined through a nonpsychoanalytic reference to the concepts of repetition and revision. African American scholar Henry Louis Gates Jr. argues that it is precisely because "black authors read and revise one another, address similar themes and repeat the cultural and linguistic codes of a common symbolic geography" that "we can think of them as forming literary traditions."[1] It is in the context of this literary process of repetition and revision that we may first view Toni Morrison's *Beloved*. At its most basic level, *Beloved* is an imaginative repeating and revising of the history of a slave woman named Margaret Garner, the historical figure upon whom the character Sethe is based. However, what is most compelling about *Beloved* is its articulation of a psychoanalytic conception of the role that repetition plays in the lives of both its African American characters and many of the members of its contemporary African American reading audience.

If the function of repetition is important to psychoanalysis, it is important to the extent that, as Jacques Lacan asserts, "psychoanalytic thought defines itself" in "terms of traumas and their persistence."[2] What Morrison's *Beloved* points to is precisely the persistence of a traumatic past that haunts the present through a subjective, psychic experience of trauma that defies the limits of time and space. Morrison's novel presents us with a literary understanding of a past that functions as what Lacan calls the Real, the Real as "that which is always in the same place," as the "excluded" Thing that is "at the heart of me" as "something strange to me," the "prehistoric Other that it is impossible to forget" or to remember.[3] It is this Real that Morrison's protagonist Sethe attempts to circumscribe in her description of Sweet Home as a place from her past that is "still there," not just in her "rememory," but "out there outside [her] head."[4] Speaking of her traumatic enslavement at Sweet Home, Sethe asserts, "even though it's all over—over and done with—it's going to always be there waiting," because "that place is real."[5]

Beloved's understanding that "some things just stay" founds its articulation of a historical trauma that equally haunts the residents of "124" and contemporary African Americans.[6] The text presents to us a trauma that re-emerges in the moment of our identification with its past location. Speaking of the Real place, Sethe proclaims, "It's never going away . . . , and what's more, if you go there—you who never was there—if you go there and stand in the place where it was, it will happen again."[7] Through Sethe's description of a traumatic past that is always there waiting, Morrison suggests the notion of an African American population continually imperiled, not so much physically as psychically, by the history of slavery. Baby Suggs, Sethe's mother-in-law, declares that "not a house in the country ain't packed to its rafters with some dead Negro's grief."[8] This past grief is depicted in *Beloved* as a repetition that haunts and claims African Americans because they claim the racial past.

I read Morrison's *Beloved* as a textual presentation of race and the racial past of slavery as sublimated representatives of the Lacanian Real. Where race in particular is claimed by many African Americans as a socially accepted object of attachment, *Beloved* is a literary attempt to free African Americans from a self-destructive investment in the traumatic, racial past that frequently grounds their identity as "raced subjects." Lacan defines sublimation as a process that "raises an object . . . to the dignity of the Thing," to the level of the Real.[9] His most telling example of a sublimated figure is perhaps "the image of the crucifixion" that "Christianity has erected in the place of all other gods."[10] Lacan finds in this sublimated image the function of an *Atè*, the "divinization" of a "limit" that simultaneously draws us toward and keeps us a safe distance from that which "represents the disqualification of all concepts," that which represents the void of the "empty" Real.[11] The sublimated image, as *Atè*, as barrier, protects us from a desubjectifying confrontation with the traumatic Real by attracting "to itself all the threads of our desire."[12] But it also effectively traps us at the entranceway unto the beyond of this limit, unto the place where Christianity positions its one "true" God. Like the crucifixion, I argue, race functions as a sublimated object of attachment, leaving many African Americans trapped at the entranceway unto an empty, Real place of trauma that has been taken up by the horror of American slavery.

Morrison states that "there is a necessity for remembering [slavery's] horror" in "a manner in which it can be digested, in a manner in which the memory is not destructive."[13] For Morrison, "writing the book" provides "a way of confronting [the past] and making it possible to remember."[14] This book functions, in my view, for both Morrison herself and her reader, as a new *object cause of desire* that potentially unhinges our attachment both to race as a sublimated *Atè* and to the Real of slavery. *Beloved* adopts the role that Lacan ascribes to the analyst, through whom the subject reorients her or his desire and reaches that point at which she or he "renounces [her or his] object."[15] Where it is race that attracts "to itself all the threads" of many African Americans' desire, leaving them tethered at the limit in a recursive path around the Real past, *Beloved* seeks to enable what Lacan calls a "beneficial crossing of the limit," a crossing that brings the subject back to a place "where the possibility of metamorphosis is located."[16] Aimed most urgently at African Americans, *Beloved* facilitates for each reader a *tuché*, or an encounter with the Real. Taking us through a journey that reveals to us the deadly path toward this destructive Real that one travels in pursuit of race and the traumatic past, *Beloved* enables in readers the capacity for a catharsis, or a "purification of desire."[17] And what the reader's desire is potentially purified of is an attachment to the concept of race that so grounds this traumatic history in our American Symbolic.

The Pursuit of *Jouissance*

I identify in *Beloved* a warning issued to African Americans about the dangers of centering their identity upon the racial past. This warning can be understood in the context of Lacan's description of the subject's pursuit of the sublimated object through which she or he comes to desire and embrace a *jouissance* of suffering. Lacanian theory shows that, in its proper functioning, desire maintains a trajectory around the Real in search of a lost *jouissance*, a lost experience of bliss, of pure lust/unlust, both pleasure and pain, that the subject associates with the Real. Subjectivity arises out of a traumatic split that through the function of language constitutes, on the one hand, the Symbolic world of meaning and the consciousness that perceives it and, on the other, all that refuses symbolization through language, most properly the unconscious and the Real. This traumatic, constitutive splitting of the subject institutes at the heart of subjectivity a sense of loss, a central lack. The very inaccessibility of what is lacking, particularly of what Lacan calls the Real, enables the subject's retroactive articulation of this Real as itself a now absent *jouissance* that can be refound in the Symbolic. Lacanian scholar Slavoj Žižek defines *jouissance* most aptly as an "objectless ecstasy" that is imagined to be lost by the subject and "subsequently" is "attached to some historically determined representation."[18] I read *Beloved* as presenting through its characters a process wherein the traumatic past of slavery comes to represent this lost *jouissance* of lust/unlust for African Americans, embodied as a historical representative of subjectivity's originary trauma.

My contention has been that slavery comes to represent the Real because it visibly repeats and makes manifest, in the Symbolic, the subject's true psychic condition of lack, each subject's enslavement to a Symbolic universe in which she or he is ever deprived of a full sense of being, of a full psychic sense of completion and wholeness. By defining both the slave and his or her descendant as subhuman, slavery and the racism that emerges with it confront these racialized subjects with an identity that threatens to shatter that which is absolutely essential to each subject's psychic life: the fantasies of self that mask the traumatic fact of lack. Because this threat to subjective fantasies of being appears so visibly in slavery, slavery itself becomes for many African Americans a "historically determined representative" of the Real, a manifested lack, marking a specified moment in time from which issue those stereotyped, racist notions of personal identity that seek traumatically to overlay and stifle these subjects' productive and enabling fantasies of wholeness and self.

The psychic need for such fantasies has led African Americans to embrace and themselves redeploy the concept of race, but the history of slavery yet predetermines the contours and function of this concept. I suggest that by pinning lack to racial identity slavery not only has arisen as a representative of the constitutive trauma of subjectivity, but also has conflated social losses with psychic lack for many African Americans, making it possible for them to experience losses suffered at both the personal and the historical/racial levels as attacks upon their being. Through race, slavery contextualizes and makes intelligible both their identity and their experiences in the racist Symbolic, emerging for many African Americans as the Real void into which all losses fall and the "excluded" center around which all subjective meaning gathers.[19] With personal access to being thus imbricated with racial identity, race has concomitantly emerged for many African Americans as Lacan's object *a*, the fantasy object that promises to guarantee the fullness of an identity that is both individual and communal, a group identity that can return African Americans to the *jouissance* of that illusory wholeness which is figured as having been shattered by slavery in a primal, historical confrontation with lack. However, an obsessive attachment to the sublimated object *a* of race poses significant dangers to African Americans. Where desire is fundamentally that through which the subject is propelled forward in his or her search for the objects that promise to compensate for psychic lack, not only can race stall the metonymic functioning of desire, through its sublimation and masquerade as the only source of selfhood and being that is worthy of the subject's attention, but it can also lock the subject into an all-consuming relationship with the Real.

The character Beloved enables our understanding of the dangerous function of this sublimated object *a* of race. Lacan describes the object *a* "as an empty body, a ghost," an "enfeebled *jouissance*" of the Real.[20] Beloved, as Sethe's object *a*, embodies for Sethe both the *jouissance* of the Real past and the horrific specter of Sethe's psychic death. She emulates the role of race, as the illusory, intangible object that grants African Americans a sense of being and identity, the impossible, fantasy possession of all African Americans that not only links them through time as an exclusionary group, making of them African Americans, but also lures them psychically to the trauma of the past.

As a haunting manifestation of this racial past, Beloved displays a ten-
uous, often willed relation of African Americans to the "sixty million and
more" dead slaves of Morrison's epigraph, a racial relation that is based
both on notions of ancestry and on the psychic compulsions of fantasy.
Just as African Americans remain temporally removed from these dead
"ancestors," electing to, as Morrison's excerpt from Romans 9:25 states,
"call them my people, which were not my people," Sethe claims in Beloved
a daughter who is not strictly of her engendering; Beloved's own claim to
Sethe is her ability to conflate Sethe's face with that of an African mother
who picks "yellow flowers in the place before the crouching" of the slave
ship and then jumps into the sea to escape the "men without skin."[21] As a
child of slavery's Real past, Beloved reaches out across time not for Sethe
specifically but for someone willing to stand in as "the underwater face she
need[s]," for anyone content to embrace the identity substitutions through
which race, as object *a*, binds one to the Real of slavery.[22] Through Sethe's
hasty proclamation of Beloved as her child, with the single word "mine,"
Sethe embraces the *jouissance* of a Real saturated with both her own personal suffering and the trauma of a people grievously slighted, coming to
echo with her utterance of the word "mine" what Stamp Paid calls the
"mumbling of the black and angry dead."[23] She displays not the possibility of one's recovery of what is lost but that dangerous obsession with the
fantasy object that draws African Americans to the devastating trauma of
slavery that threatens to consume Sethe's subjective self.

Morrison's *Beloved* and Lacan's seminars both make salient this possibility of a subject's consumption by the representatives of the Real she or
he embraces. Though Morrison herself speaks of *Beloved* as a "paying-out
of homage still due,"[24] she maintains that "we need to rethink the subtle
yet persuasive attachments we may have to the architecture of race" and
the past that designed it.[25] This identification of a persuasive, and even
dangerous, attachment to the objects to which we pay homage is what
centers Lacan's reading of Christianity. Lacan argues that in its imitation
and representation of that which is positioned in the beyond, the "central image" of the crucifixion poses a threat to desire, which for Lacan is
integral to subjectivity.[26] This "exemplary image," says Lacan, "absorbs all
other images of desire in man with significant consequences."[27] Not only
is the crucifixion an "image of the limit in which a being remains in a state
of suffering," but it also engenders in its worshippers a fixated desire, an
irresistible allegiance to that image through which "Christianity has been

crucifying man in holiness for centuries."[28] It is this type of crucifixion, this sacrificing of one's self to a sublimated image, that I find operating in Morrison's text as a strict allegiance to the traumatic past.

Morrison reveals that the idea of writing *Beloved* came to her as she was "considering certain aspects of self-sabotage, the way in which the best things we do so often carry seeds of one's own destruction."[29] In stepping out of the beyond to claim Sethe as her mother, Beloved comes precisely to embody for Sethe a sublimated representative of the Real, a destructive Thing that Sethe claims as her own "best thing."[30] Emerging first as the object *a* that promises to fulfill Sethe's longing for an impossible return to a fantasy state of completion and oneness with her lost child, Beloved is soon transformed into what Lacan calls after Freud *das Ding*, or the Thing, the embodiment of the Real, in the presence of which one can experience only ceaseless, unchanging suffering.[31] Before Beloved's arrival, "all that mattered" to Sethe was "keeping the past at bay," avoiding the Real of her trauma by choosing never to "go inside."[32] But, convinced that Beloved's appearance indicates her slain child "ain't even mad" with her, Sethe begins to speak for "the first time" of events from her past that justify the murder.[33] Beloved, as object *a*, as the fantasy of a ghostly *jouissance* around which Sethe's life already traces a centrifugal path, entices Sethe to claim the Thing of the Real as her own. Though Beloved makes present the traumatic past of slavery, repeating it in Sethe's life, Sethe confuses Beloved with the internal "parts" of her that are "precious and fine and beautiful."[34] Beloved becomes a cherished internal pain that Sethe refuses to give up, Sethe's own precious, best Thing.

Lacan argues that when the subject is assured she or he has found that which allows access to the lost *jouissance* of the Real, as "if under some monstrous spell," the subject at times cannot "resist succumbing" to the offering up of "an object of sacrifice" to what is positioned for the subject in the beyond.[35] Sethe's sacrificial offering is both her own sanity and her very existence as a desiring subject. Finding in Beloved what she thought she had lost forever, Sethe is "wrapped" in the "timeless present," desireless with "no plans at all" for the future.[36] Lacan shows that it is in a "state of wishing for" the Real and "waiting for it" that "the optimum tension will be sought," and "below that there is neither perception nor effort."[37] In embracing Beloved as the object *a* that fills her lack, in aiding Beloved's return from "the timeless place," Sethe becomes a *full*, desireless subject with nothing to inspire in her the effort to carry on into the future.[38] She reaches what Beloved calls "the join," and what Lacan calls the *joiner*.[39] In this *joiner*, Lacan tells us, "the subject can achieve nothing but some form of psychosis or perversion," where this psychosis is marked precisely by a fullness, in the presences of the Real, that eliminates the dimension of desire and all subjective aspirations.[40] It is this self-destructive, desubjectifying fullness that Morrison's *Beloved* suggests African Americans move toward when embracing completely the racial past of slavery; and it is the novel itself that enables a possible separation of the subject from the trauma of this past.

Atè and the Illusory Self

In *The Ethics of Psychoanalysis*, Lacan presents a reading of Sophocles' *Antigone* that makes plain the possibility of an audience's safe encounter with and separation from the Thing of the Real through the mediation of a literary text such as *Beloved*. For Lacan, the text of *Antigone* becomes the means through which, to the audience, a sublimated *Atè* is made manifest in all its alluring and deadly beauty. *Antigone* designates the place of this *Atè*, both revealing the very limit beyond which lies the desolate Real and displaying to the reader the consequences of trekking past this limit. Beyond *Atè* lies only death, the dissolution of subjectivity in the presence of the Real, but Lacan's assertion is that "it is always through some beneficial crossing of the limit that man experiences his desire."[41] For Lacan, "the function of desire must remain in a fundamental relationship to death"; and, through the text, we journey into the beyond and experience something of our own relation to death.[42] In such journeyed returns, Lacan shows, the subject comes to learn "a little more about the deepest level of himself" and "the pole of [his] desire."[43] Lacanian theory recognizes desire as "nothing other than that which supports an unconscious theme," that which, when properly oriented away from the false gods of our sublimations and when maintained at a safe distance from the Real, "roots us in a particular destiny" and protects us "from all kinds of inner catastrophes," including "neurosis and its consequences."[44] By granting the subject this knowledge of desire and death, the text of *Antigone* enables a "tempering of desire," allowing for "the disruption" of the subject's unconditional attachment to his or her destructive, sublimated objects.[45]

Lacan reads the character Antigone as herself constituting for the reader an alluring *Atè*, a "violent illumination" that both "attracts us and startles us" with its relation to death.[46] This function as *Atè* is precisely what Morrison's Sethe also serves for *Beloved*'s reader. Lacan explains that the Greek word *Atè* is linked to and "found in" the word "atrocious."[47] *Atè* identifies "the limit that human life can only briefly cross."[48] What we see in both Antigone and Sethe is a desire that breaches the limit of the atrocious, a desire that brings them to the "level of the monstrous," beyond "the limit of the human."[49] Antigone is fueled by her unbending intent to bury her brother, pushing "to the limit the realization" of a "pure and simple desire of death" by accepting Creon's decree that she be buried alive in her brother's tomb.[50] In going past the limit of the atrocious, Antigone unveils for us the abysmal emptiness of the Real place beyond *Atè*. Through this unveiling, she comes to stand for us at the threshold of the beyond as barrier, as the "fascinating image" that "dazzles us and separates us" from a direct confrontation with the Real.[51] Antigone embodies *Atè*, revealing to us, "only in a blinding flash," that which Sethe also makes manifest to *Beloved*'s reader: the absolute condition of "man's relationship to his own death," the desire for the atrocity of the Real that continually draws us to the beyond.[52]

Lacan ties the lure of the Real to humanity's propensity to "mistake evil for good."[53] In Sethe we see what it means to embrace the ultimate evil of the Real itself as the good, the evil of a traumatic *jouissance* that Sethe pursues through Beloved. Initially, while plotting and executing her escape from Sweet Home, Sethe is guided by her insistent desire to get her milk to her children and live on in freedom; but, when tracked down by schoolteacher, Sethe discards all laws of morality, grounding her notion of the good only on what Lacan describes as an "order of law" that "is not developed in any signifying chain," an ethics that is founded upon the Real beyond the law.[54] Sethe becomes irreconcilable, unbending to the end, intent upon her desire for death. Like Antigone, Sethe believes that her life can only be lived from what Lacan calls "the place of that limit where her life is already lost, where she is already on the other side."[55] Traumatized by both the experience of slavery and her later act of infanticide, Sethe ends her own life with Beloved's death. Her death in life is marked by the disappearance of the whites of her eyes on the day of the murder, their replacement by "two open wells" that do "not reflect firelight."[56] She is "blind" to this world, possessing an unflinching gaze that is fiercely directed at death itself.[57] Denver tells us that her mother is "the one who never looked away," not "when a man got stomped to death by a mare" nor when a "sow began eating her own litter."[58] This fierce willingness in Sethe to face death head on is what most disturbs and fascinates the reader.

For the reader, Sethe's unflinching gaze, like that of Antigone, is "the line of sight that defines desire" in its relation to death.[59] Lacan argues that man can have access to his own horrifying "death instinct, to his own relationship to death," only insofar as he "articulates a signifying chain" that enables him to come "up against the fact that he may disappear from the chain of what he is."[60] *Beloved* as text and Sethe as protagonist allow the articulation of such a chain. The text encourages us to experience Sethe's pain, to insert ourselves into its narrative as subjects who are ourselves faced with an evanescent disappearance, of our psychic sense of being, from the Symbolic chain of who we are. Freed of Symbolic impediments founded upon moral definitions of the good, not only does Sethe show desire to be in its essence grafted upon the Real, but she also becomes for us the *Atè*, the "lure" that "keeps us awake" and "helps us adjust" to this most essential desire for death.[61] We can say in Lacan's words that Sethe "crosses" the "invisible line" of "outrage" and is "insensitive" to this crossing; but, in the process, she reveals to the reader what is at stake in such a crossing.[62] Through her desire for death and the slow movement toward a psychosis-inducing self-conflation with the Real, she unveils for us what Lacan calls "the important risk" of "aphanisis," quite simply "the loss of desire" and the dissolution of one's status as a desiring subject that may result from pursuit of the Real past.[63]

Sethe burns with a desire for this Real, radiating an effulgent passion that *Beloved* intends the reader to feel and experience but not emulate. Bringing us to the precipice of that abysmal conflagration that is Sethe's infernal *jouissance*, the text encourages all of its readers, whether African American or not, to rally against the racial past and its haunting psychic legacy. Most notably through the character Ella, the text models for its readers a hermeneutics by which they are to safely confront the Real past and bring its trauma to an end. Through Ella, *Beloved* encourages readers to engage the past not only by becoming a part of the telling of this very fragmented American tale but also by supplementing Sethe's experience with an understanding of their own varied relation to race and the traumatic Real of slavery.

Ella's distinct understanding of the past is conditioned by the fact that her "puberty was spent in a house where she was shared by father and son, whom she called 'the lowest yet.' "[64] Unlike Sethe, however, Ella asserts that "the future [is] sunset" and "the past something to leave behind."[65] Ella resists her past "taking possession of the present" by embracing the pain of others.[66] Aiding Stamp Paid in rescuing runaway slaves, Ella stops to listen "for the holes—the things the fugitives [do] not say."[67] Able subjectively to insert herself into their stories, Ella fills these gaps in the slaves' narratives with her own understanding of suffering. Ella measures "all atrocities" against her own torment at the hands of "the lowest yet."[68] When seeing Beloved for the first time, Ella also sees the "hairy white thing, fathered by 'the lowest yet,'" that she had "delivered, but would not nurse"; and it is "the idea of that pup coming back to whip her" the way Beloved whipped Sethe that "set her jaw working": from Ella's determination to "stomp out" the past emerges the "holler," the cry, the primal scream that begins the exorcism of Beloved.[69]

This effort to stomp out and exorcise the past preoccupies the text, and Morrison repeatedly presents it as a process dependent upon a subject's embrace of others' stories of trauma. The final page of the novel asserts, "This is not a story to pass on."[70] Playing on a dual meaning in the words "pass on," the narrative affirms that it is precisely by not passing by this story casually but actively embracing its narrative of trauma that we prevent its suffering from being passed on into the future. By repeatedly conveying this affirmation, first in Ella's actions, then in Denver's ability to imagine how "it must have felt for her mother" as she tells Sethe's stories, and again in Paul D's desire to "put his story next to" Sethe's, *Beloved* encourages its readers to use the text to begin articulating the narrative of their own varied and individualized relation to the traumatic past.[71] While implying an especial symmetry between the experiences of many African Americans and Sethe, *Beloved* seeks to battle the past and restructure the racial Symbolic by involving all of its readers in a process of engaging and mediating the Real through the signifier.

Lacan says that "the magic circle that separates us" from the painful *jouissance* of the Real "is imposed by our relation to the signifier."[72] Through the signifier, the subject articulates the fantasies that allow safe access to *jouissance*. What we find in *Beloved* is the assertion that the traumatic past of slavery leaves African Americans more deprived than are most other subjects of control of the Symbolic's signifiers, and thus more open to the painful *jouissance* of the past. Especially through the character schoolteacher, *Beloved* highlights as traumatic a persistent and almost casual ability to name the other that, in an American Symbolic grounded in notions of race, is often claimed as the unspoken privilege of racial whiteness. This continual onslaught within the Symbolic of the signifiers that seek to redefine them is the source of the psychic trauma suffered not only by the slave but also by contemporary African Americans.

As is characteristic of those who have lived through a traumatic experience, Sethe cannot directly identify the source of her trauma; she is aware, however, that it is connected to the fact that, as she says, "schoolteacher was teaching us things we couldn't learn."[73] Schoolteacher asserted to his slaves that "definitions belonged to the definers—not the defined," and what he attempted to teach the slaves of Sweet Home was a new self-definition.[74] Sethe and the other slaves initially "laughed about" schoolteacher's brand of what we may call scientific racism.[75] Sethe relates to Beloved, "I didn't care. . . . schoolteacher'd wrap that string all over my head, 'cross my nose, around my behind. . . . Number my teeth. . . . I thought he was a fool."[76] But Sethe soon begins to learn the traumatic power of definitions when she overhears schoolteacher's use of the word "characteristics": "That's not the way. . . . I told you to put her human characteristics on the left; her animal ones on the right."[77] This word, "characteristics," is what conveys to Sethe the traumatic knowledge she "couldn't learn."[78]

I showed in chapter 2 that encounters with trauma involve a breakdown in the structure of identity maintained by the subject. This breakdown begins to occur, in Sethe's case, the moment she confronts the signifier that challenges her self-definitions. Through schoolteacher, Sethe begins to encounter the truth about her place in the social Symbolic of slavery, the truth that she continues to resist; as the scene between schoolteacher and his pupils plays out in front of her, Sethe "commence[s] to walk backward."[79] "Lifting [her] feet and pushing back," Sethe "bump[s] up against a tree" and begins to sense the irresistible but still faint presence of something that will *repetitiously* present itself to her in the form of a "prickling" in her scalp.[80] Sethe says that after bumping into the tree her "head itched like the devil. . . . Like somebody was sticking fine needles in [her] scalp."[81] This prickling marks the presence of an insistent, traumatic signifier that Sethe's conscious mind cannot assimilate.

Lacanian scholar Charles Shepherdson usefully describes the breakdown of identity that occurs in trauma as an experience "in which two chains of signifiers, previously kept apart, are suddenly made to intersect."[82] This intersection creates not meaning, as I have argued, but a void, a collapsing of identity upon the confrontation with something that is unassimilable, something that Shepherdson describes as "an obscure 'knowledge' . . . a 'forbidden knowledge' that remains excluded the moment it appears."[83] Initially "soft" and "trusting," Sethe and her view of the world are radically altered by what she overhears.[84] She confronts through schoolteacher the signifier that promises to grant her the only knowledge that is truly forbidden within a subject's fantasy of self, the knowledge of her inescapable dependence as a desiring subject upon the signifiers of the Other. In actuality, what psychically traumatizes Sethe is not her powerlessness against the slave master, but her powerlessness against words. Sethe's ultimate aim is not simply to escape schoolteacher. What Sethe strives for, both for herself and for her children, is precisely what the subject can never fully have in life: freedom from the signifier.[85]

Sethe achieves only a small sense of this freedom when she escapes Sweet Home. Her pursuit of this freedom is what inspires her murderous act, but Sethe cannot fully explain the relation between the murder and freedom. When asked by Paul D why she committed the murder, Sethe speaks instead of how it felt to have her children with her after escaping Sweet Home:

> It was a kind of selfishness I never knew nothing about before. It felt good. Good and right. I was big, Paul D, and deep and wide and when I stretched out my arms all my children could get in between. I was *that* wide. Look like I loved em more after I got here. Or maybe I couldn't love em proper in Kentucky because they wasn't mine to love.[86]

What Sethe herself calls a "circular" and indirect answer to Paul D's question about the murder touches on the knowledge Sethe cannot articulate about being subjected to the Other's signifiers.[87] Sethe's discussion of her freedom in terms of a newfound selfishness and possessiveness alludes to her ability in the North to construct more freely a fantasy of being, a fantasy self that is thus felt to be more "deep and wide" than any she has ever known.[88] Finding in her freedom a new "selfish pleasure," Sethe establishes over the unbearable *jouissance* of lack that slavery attempts to force upon her what Lacan calls a "dominance of the signifier."[89] Strictly speaking, this dominance is the pleasure principle itself, that which circulates within the Symbolic the semblance of *jouissance* that keeps the subject a safe distance from the Real. Because Sethe now is not forced to submit consciously to the Other's signifiers, she encounters, in the Symbolic, an experience that for her is both "good and right."[90] It is the transitive nature of this experience that ultimately pushes Sethe to kill.

In spite of Sethe's inability to explain fully what motivates the killing, Paul D yet isolates in her words a truth that transcends his own complete understanding: "to get to a place where you could love anything you chose—not to need permission for desire—well now, *that* was freedom."[91] The full implication of this truth is masked from Paul D because, having "never stayed uncaught" for "seven years" after his escape from Sweet Home, Paul D longs for a freedom he associates with a yet distant fantasy "place."[92] What Sethe appreciates better than Paul D is that reaching such a place of complete freedom of desire and autonomy from the Other means also making an absolute choice to accept one's own Symbolic death. As Lacan states, there is "an emergence of the subject at the level of meaning only," and meaning can only be granted by the Symbolic of the Other; thus the subject must make an absolute choice between freedom outside of the Symbolic and life in the Symbolic, wherein "if he chooses freedom, he loses both immediately," and "if he chooses life, he has life deprived of freedom."[93] This insight into the nature of desire and freedom, I have argued, is at the heart of Lacan's assertion that existence in the Symbolic is inextricably linked to "alienation, [to] that by which man enters into the way of slavery."[94] It is toward this Symbolic slavery that Sethe ultimately directs her murderous act of resistance.[95]

Where Sethe cannot sustain her illusory freedom of being in life, in the Symbolic, she seeks it in death. Sethe says of Beloved, "If I hadn't killed her she would have died."[96] Through the murder, Sethe tries to maintain for herself and her child the fantasy of a complete and autonomous self that schoolteacher threatens. Speaking of the murder, the narrator reveals:

> The truth was simple, not a long-drawn-out record of flowered shifts, tree cages, selfishness, ankle ropes and wells. Simple: she was squatting in the garden and when she saw them coming and recognized schoolteacher's hat, she heard wings. Little hummingbirds stuck their needle beaks right through her headcloth into her hair and beat their wings. And if she thought anything, it was No. No. Nono. Nonono. Simple. She just flew. Collected every bit of life she had made, all the parts of her that were precious and fine and beautiful, and carried, pushed, dragged them through the veil, out, away, over there where no one could hurt them.[97]

Without thinking "anything," Sethe makes an impulsive, unconscious choice to drag her children through the veil. Significantly, her choice is made in response both to schoolteacher's presence and to the piercing beaks of the hummingbirds that flock Sethe's mind as schoolteacher steps into her yard. Replicating the prickling in Sethe's scalp that she felt upon hearing the word "characteristics," this image of needled beaks piercing her head marks the repetition of the psychosomatic symptoms that take the place of Sethe's conscious confrontation with the Other's signifier. Lacan argues that in the psychosomatic a "signifying induction at the level of the subject [occurs] in a way that does not bring into play the *aphanisis* of the subject."[98] Sethe here stands at the threshold of a limit that she cannot pass, spared a confrontation with her subjective aphanisis only by an induction that already half marks the presence of the truth she cannot confront. Finding that the only defense available to her in the Symbolic is an impotent litany of no's, Sethe chooses instead to breach the limit and step across the veil.

This self-destructive act of liberation is what most directly positions Sethe as *Atè* for us. In seeking a physical death that is to spare her from a Symbolic death, Sethe shows us exactly what is at stake in the pursuit of absolute freedom. As Lacan explains, "In the conditions in which someone says to you, *freedom or death!*, the only proof of freedom that you can have . . . is precisely to choose death, for there, you show that you have freedom of choice."[99] But Sethe fails to execute the suicide that would establish her full freedom of choice, and her success in killing only her child brings the reader with her to the place where both Sethe and the reader must confront and grapple with the traumatic past that comes to permeate Sethe's existence. We stand with Sethe at this place of *Atè*, watching as precipitously she approaches the absolute desirelessness that she will encounter in the full presence of the Real.

Beloved's return brings Sethe to this Real, producing in her the belief that she can safely engage and remember the Thing her conscious mind has defensively forgotten. Sethe says, "Now I can look at things again because she's here to see them too."[100] As Beloved "joins" with Sethe, Beloved becomes the suffering that Sethe will not allow to disappear, the interior self that Sethe will protect from aphanisis at all cost. It is this Thing of hers, more important than Sethe herself, that Sethe attempts to preserve in attacking Mr. Bodwin. Unable to break free of the signifier's repetition, Sethe is convinced not only that Bodwin is schoolteacher "coming into her yard" again, but also that "he is coming for her best thing."[101] Once again Sethe "hears wings," as "little hummingbirds stick needle beaks right through her headcloth into her hair"; and once again Sethe utters her impotent no's, as she lashes out impulsively, attacking Bodwin with an ice pick.[102] Caught in the repetition of the past and its signifiers, Sethe is saved only by the ability of her daughter, Denver, to use the signifier to create for herself and Sethe a return path from the Real.

Separation from the Thing

In a strictly Lacanian application of the word, the true "hero" of *Beloved* is Denver. The hero, Lacan tells us, is someone who does not give "ground relative to [his or her] desire."[103] To the extent that both Sethe and Antigone unswervingly follow their desire for death into the zone of the Real, this definition is clearly applicable to each of them. But, for Lacan, what justifies the hero's journey into this zone is the fact that through this journey "something is defined and liberated."[104] In discussing the hero, Lacan seeks to establish an ethics that is focused on "nothing less than the impossibility in which we recognize the topology of our desire."[105] Where the subject who remains in this zone can achieve nothing but a desireless state of psychosis, in a truly clinical sense, not "giving ground" on one's desire means above all achieving a "return" from the Real that "involves some gain," a return that involves the subject's placement on the "track of something that is specifically [his or her] business."[106] It is only when the subject returns to a safe distance from the Real that agitates and orients his or her desire that the subject can live out his or her destiny in the Symbolic.[107] Of all of *Beloved*'s characters, it is Denver alone who is able independently to make this return journey and, in the Symbolic, establish herself on the tracks of her desire.

Denver may be conceived of as positioned initially within the Lacanian mirror stage.[108] Like the child of this stage, Denver develops from the maternal figure of Sethe the sense of a bodily self that remains dependent for its coherence on the watchful mother whose presence it confuses with its own. While learning from Baby Suggs to "always listen to" and "love" her own body, Denver simultaneously believes that it is only "as long as her mother [does] not look away" from her that her body can be spared from devolving into something that is "more than vision" itself can "bear."[109] But Denver also seeks out the absent father, Halle, as paternal metaphor, as the signifier of lack that breaks the bond between mother and child and precipitates entrance into the Symbolic. Denver thus exists in a liminal state where she depends on Sethe but longs for her father.

While Denver exists in this condition of stasis and liminality, she displays to the reader an uncomfortable but necessary alternative to Sethe's relation to trauma. Denver simultaneously fears and seeks both the Symbolic and the Real. In pursuit of the Real, Denver searches for "the thing" in her mother "that makes it all right [for Sethe] to kill her children"; she explains, "I need to know what that thing might be, but I don't want to."[110] Denver expresses a cautionary fear of the Thing, adopting the necessary distance so lacking in Sethe from the sought-after Real. But while remaining sufficiently distant from the Real, Denver also possesses a paralyzing fear of the racist Symbolic, a fear that the novel suggests both Denver and the reader must conquer. Denver is convinced that the "thing" in her mother came "from outside the yard," and her fear is that it can "come right on in the yard [again] if it wants to."[111]

It is Baby Suggs who presents Denver with the means through which Denver moves forward from her place of stasis. Baby Suggs counterbalances Denver's fear of Sethe's Thing with stories about "all [of Denver's] daddy's things."[112] Introducing Denver to the beliefs that guided Halle's most noble actions and made it possible for him to buy his mother's freedom, Baby Suggs informs Denver that her daddy always said, "if you can't count they can cheat you," and "if you can't read they can beat you."[113] This image of an "angelic," unreachable, father who himself navigates the Symbolic and manipulates its signifiers is what continually draws Denver's imagination toward the "little *i*" and the "sentences [that rolled] out like pie dough" from her lips at Lady Jones's school.[114] Denver hungers to complete the narcissistic mirror stage so that this *i* can become the point of articulation of a self that develops through identification with the paternal metaphor and separation from the mother.

Denver is key to our understanding of the agency the signifier holds over the Real. She is the mirror image of her mother, possessing the same indomitable will and uncompromising drive, but aiming heroically at the Symbolic itself. Lacan maintains that the "difference between an ordinary man and a hero" is that "for the ordinary man the betrayal that almost always occurs" at the hands of those he trusts makes him able "never again [to] find that factor which restores a sense of direction" to him.[115] Betrayed and abandoned both by a grandmother who no longer wants to face the "bitterness of life" and two brothers who would rather "fight [in] the War" than live with the "killing woman" that is their mother, Denver does not "know where to go or what to do."[116] Caught in the middle of a love-hate relationship between her mother and the manifested Thing-of-a-sister that threatens to consume all in its path, Denver finds a sense of direction only in her hopeless hope that Halle is "coming" for her.[117] But it is Denver's persistence in the tracks of her hopeless desire for the absent father that makes of her a hero. Lacan states that "the path of the hero is traced" in "each of us," and "it is precisely as an ordinary man that one follows it to the end."[118] As an ordinary and very helpless girl, Denver makes a path for herself toward the paternal metaphor and the signifier, relying only upon the power of her own determination not to give ground on her desire.

In Denver we find modeled what we may call a "desirousness" that steers us clear of Sethe's path. As Lacan shows, "It is in seeing a whole chain come into play at the level of the desire of the Other that the subject's desire is constituted."[119] Like the analyst, Denver serves, in *Beloved*, the function of "the subject who is supposed to know" desire, who presents one with an experienced desire that "intervenes" to make possible the process by which desire "renounces its object."[120] Honed in the experience of her mother's trauma, Denver's desire emulates the analyst's "desire to obtain absolute difference" from the Real Thing and the mother; and as we see Sethe consumed by the Real of the racial past, Denver's desire models most aptly the process of our own separation from this past.[121] In analysis, Lacan says, the subject "counts the vote relative to his own law," to a law that is "in the first place always the acceptance of something" that "strictly speaking [is] *Atè*."[122] Similarly, through Denver, the reader comes to calculate his or her own distance from that law of *Atè* that can protect him or her from the trauma of the racial past.

The reader's appreciation of this need to escape the past and its repetitious signifiers is meant to coincide in *Beloved* with his or her appreciation for, or even identification with, Sethe's pain. Denver's own link to her mother is what enables her escape from Sethe's presence and her retreat from the overwhelming *jouissance* of Beloved and the Real. Like Denver, we remain ambivalently linked to Sethe as the murderer whom we pity, and it is this link that is meant to aid our own separation from the Real of the racial past. Lacan states that when approaching the Real, if "the subject turns back on his tracks," she or he does so to prevent "from assaulting the image of the other," from assaulting that on "which we were formed as an ego."[123] Where Denver's only sense of self is mirrored in the image of her mother, Denver makes the decision to "leave the yard" and "step off the edge of the world" to save Sethe's body, and her own, from Beloved.[124]

As it becomes obvious to her that "her mother could die and leave" her, Denver begins to steer clear of the path both she and the reader take while identifying with Sethe.[125]

Denver tries to preserve the image of the other on which she depends. When she sees Sethe "carrying out Beloved's night bucket, Denver race[s] to relieve her of it."[126] "Frightened" as Denver is of "the thing in Sethe," it "shame[s] her to see her mother serving a girl not much older than herself."[127] Denver witnesses firsthand her mother's degradation, and she is personally embarrassed and threatened by it. She sees Sethe's willful starvation, as Sethe goes without, "pick-eating around the edge of the table and stove," so that Beloved's "basket-fat stomach" can stay full.[128] The job Denver had embraced, of protecting Beloved from the woman whose body mirrors Denver's own, finally changes to "protecting her mother from Beloved" when Denver recognizes the full extent of the damage done to her mother's body: it "rocked Denver like gunshot" to see "Sethe spit up something she had not eaten."[129] Denver comes to realize that her own well-being is tied to the preservation of this woman in whose tracks she follows. And through Denver's eyes, we see the danger to ourselves of the route Sethe takes. Denver makes possible our perception of Sethe as having crossed that limit of *Atè*, beyond which the reader should not trek. While the text initially urges us to insert ourselves into its narrative and form an identification with both Sethe and the racial past she embraces through Beloved, Denver's spectatorial presence aids our recognition of the perils inherent in this path toward the past.

As *Beloved* brings the reader to the point of desiring a separation from Sethe's path, the text seeks to redirect both the reader and Denver toward the Symbolic and its signifiers. *Beloved* identifies the act of storytelling as crucial to such separation. It is not, however, the paternal figure of her father that finally allows Denver to construct a subjective identity in the Symbolic, but the maternal keeper of her father's stories. In Lacan's work, the paternal metaphor is *only* a metaphor for the process of separation itself, and Denver reaches the Symbolic through the agency of Baby Suggs, the maternal figure that initiated her into the act of storytelling.[130] It is Baby Suggs whose voice comes to Denver "clear as anything" as Denver stands on the porch unable to leave her yard.[131] Denver finds herself unsure of what to do when Baby Suggs herself has said that "there is no defense" from what is out there.[132] Baby Suggs suggests, however, that it is the stories of the past that will themselves protect Denver, asking Denver, "You mean I never told you nothing about Carolina," or "your daddy," or "how come I walk the way I do?"[133] Indicating that she has already prepared Denver for the outside world, Baby Suggs encourages Denver to "know" that there is "no defense" and "go out the yard" anyway.[134] Urging both Denver and the reader toward the terrifying Symbolic that produced the traumatic past, *Beloved* asserts through Baby Suggs that it is after we have already engaged the trauma of the past and the Symbolic in which it circulates that we can begin to free ourselves of the past. This engagement is what enables what Lacan describes simply as "distance," the gap between the way the subject once expressed her or his "instinctual drives" and the way she or he expresses it after the process of "arranging and organizing them" is made available to the subject.[135]

Denver uses the stories of the past to reorganize her desire and resist the drive for death that she is exposed to through Sethe. Enabling her finally to leave the yard, these stories not only separate her from the maternal other, but also give birth to Denver as a subject fully positioned within the Symbolic. Here, in this terrifying place of the Other, Denver reacquaints herself with Lady Jones, the woman who, in addressing her as "baby," inaugurates "her life in the world as a woman."[136] Spoken "softly and with such kindness," this word, "baby," presents Denver with a maternal affection that both stems from a Symbolic Other and, unlike Sethe's affection, does not consume her.[137] Lady Jones' affection and help come with a price that must be paid in the Symbolic itself. What Denver is forced to realize is that "nobody was going to help her unless she told it—told all of it."[138] And Denver begins to elicit the help she needs precisely by coming to embrace and utilize the signifiers that she had sought since her childhood.

It is Denver's telling of her mother's tale to the community, and the ability of its members to find in this tale the unspeakable traumatic truth beyond what even Denver can articulate, that cause the gathering at Sethe's doorsteps of the thirty women who exorcise Beloved. Seeing "themselves" in Denver, the women join Ella in uttering a purgative, primal scream that rocks both Beloved and Sethe.[139] The narrator tells us that they take "a step back to the beginning": "in the beginning there were no words," only "the sound, and they knew what that sound sounded like."[140] This sound, as primal scream, is what Lacan refers to as the *cry*, as that which "fulfills the function of discharge" and first marks the psychic presence of the yet unarticulated Thing.[141] It is the "bridge" to the Thing, which would "remain obscure and unconscious if the cry did not lend it" the "sign that gives it its own weight, presence, structure."[142] Yet unable to utter the words that are to name Sethe's and their own trauma, the women "search for the right combination, the key, the code, the sound that broke the back of words"; it is by finding this sound that they produce the wave that cleanses Sethe "like the baptized in its wash."[143]

This baptism is as much for the reader as it is for the thirty women and Sethe. It involves what Lacan calls "catharsis" or "abreaction," the "discharge of an emotion," where "an emotion or a traumatic experience may" have left "something unresolved."[144] With the reader having moved through an ambivalent emotional identification with Sethe to a recognition, through Denver, of the urgent need to separate from both Sethe and the racial past, this *cry* lends voice, in the stead of the reader's own utterance, to the unnamed and individualized emotions that accompany each reader's full recognition of her or his own subjugation to the racial past and the signifiers of race. Lacan shows that in the play *Antigone* the chorus takes care of our emotions for us, responding as readers should to all that occurs in the text so that readers do not have to themselves.[145] By gauging their individual responses against that of the chorus, readers partake of a journey in which as "spectator[s]" they are not left "in ignorance as to where the pole of [their own] desire is" or as to their relation to its "pathological interests."[146] In a similar way, the community of thirty produces in place of the reader the cry that is the final vehicle through which the subject is brought to some consciousness of that level of unconscious pleasure and pain she or he experiences through relation to the *jouissance* of the past.

But this cry that resounds within the place of trauma in which the women stand yet demands a response from the reader. It beckons from the reader not only his or her recognition but, more imperatively, his or her utterance of the word that saves, the "me" that is the subject's only salvation. For the reader, the cry is voiced by the women in their capacity as Symbolic Other, as the Other through whom the reader gathers his or her own defenses against the Real Thing. It finds its parallel in what Lacan describes as the familiar cry of "You!" that "may appear" on another subject's lips in a "moment of utter helplessness, distress, or surprise," the call to action that emanates from the Symbolic Other most fundamentally and originally as a call to embrace actively that subjective positionality within the Symbolic that makes action itself possible.[147] This "You!" always functions, according to Lacan, as a "pronoun of interpellation," a replay of the constitutive call to subjective status in the Symbolic.[148] It is a cry that reaches the subject as though it were an accusatory "You!"—an interpellation to which the subject simply responds, in "refusal" and in "apology," with the word "Me?"[149]

In answering "Me?" the subject is "made responsible or accountable for something" that is simply the "I" of subjectivity, the defense granted him or her by the Symbolic against that "unforgettable Other" of the Real, which must necessarily cast the subject down from the "height" of its presence.[150] Where *Beloved* itself is the cry that announces to the reader the terrible pain and trauma of a past that not only still haunts African Americans in the present but also yet besieges the Symbolic with its evil *jouissance*, what the text ultimately requires of the reader is a rearticulation of the subjective "I." In aiding the reader's recognition of race as that which shackles African Americans to the *jouissance* of slavery, *Beloved* presents the potential for a traversal of race as that "fundamental phantasy" through which the subject seeks to access being.[151] It is in the beyond of this fantasy, at that point where the subject confronts his or her own lack, that the subject must come to "recognize" him- or herself.[152] Confronting then rejecting *jouissance*, *Beloved* opens up the possibility for an identity grounded in the metonymy proper to desire, so that the subject may become liberated to find him- or herself within a multiplicity of ever-shifting identity formations. But Lacanian theory shows that even in analysis the fantasy maintains a binding presence and must be confronted multiple times. Called by the Symbolic to voice that response that will eject him or her from the Real place of his or her *jouissance*, the subject most naturally resists. On its own, the cry, when emanating only from the Other, is insufficiently capable of producing a separation from *jouissance*.

It is only after Sethe herself repeats the cry first uttered by the women, thus making herself responsible for the traumatic truth it announces, that Sethe finally speaks what will be her last words in the text: "Me? Me?"[153] As Sethe begins to weep, giving voice to the unarticulated pain that emerges with her conviction that her "best thing" has "left" her, it is Paul D who positions himself as the Symbolic Other from whom emanates the accusatory "you": "You your best thing, Sethe. . . . You are."[154] Sethe's journey begins to end, as will the reader's own journey, only when she starts to accept and articulate a notion of self that stands distantly apart from the racial past that traumatizes her. In uttering, with her tentative uncertainty, the word that promises to save her—"Me? Me?"—Sethe herein marks the beginnings of a reconstructed fantasy of self through which she may resist the insistence of those signifiers presented to her by schoolteacher and the racial past. Through Paul D, Sethe finally starts to accept for herself the task upon which is rooted the very praxis of psychoanalysis: the effort to establish that illusory " 'I' which is supposed to come to be where 'it' was."[155]

This task is what *Beloved* leaves also to its readers, most especially to its African American readers, whose racialized identities open them up so perilously to the trauma of the Real past. Like Sethe, African Americans must establish in the place of the "it" granted them by the racial signifiers of the American Symbolic an "I" that does not seek to find itself in a crossing of that limit beyond which lies the traumatic Real of the racial past. *Beloved*, as *Atè*, defines this limit, bringing its readers back to a safe distance from the Real while also revealing to them the point beyond which that essential illusion of self is shattered. In having returned from the beyond of this point, Sethe seems to have found in Paul D someone who, in his words, can "gather" the "pieces" of who she "is" and "give them back" to her in "all the right order."[156] Through *Beloved*, we too gather the pieces of our selves. But, while *Beloved* introduces us to the process of mapping our own relation to the Real as defense against the racial past, the task remains ours to carry out this process to some hoped-for conclusion in our own Symbolic universe beyond the text.

4

THE OEDIPAL COMPLEX AND THE MYTHIC STRUCTURE OF RACE
Ellison's Juneteenth *and* Invisible Man

My argument thus far has been that slavery has produced an upsurge in *jouissance* that continues to shape the psychic and social interactions between white Americans and African Americans. This argument correlates with Lacan's observation that "in the course of man's history things have happened to him that have changed the subject's relation to being."[1] In discussing the altered relation to being that emerges through slavery, I have focused primarily upon African Americans, showing throughout that fantasy is essential to Symbolic and psychic representations of being. I would now like to turn more directly to a mythic, oedipal fantasy structure that tends to underpin the narratives of racial identity and the Symbolic representations through which not just African Americans but also white Americans seek to access being. This turn brings us not to a focus on the traditional Freudian narrative based on the figure of Oedipus Rex but instead to a rearticulation of this myth expressed in the narrative of Hamlet, an individual whom Lacan reads as an image of "the modern hero," a "second Oedipus Rex."[2] What is particularly modern about Hamlet is his defiance of a Symbolic universe dominated by the will of the Other, a will embodied by the figure of the usurping king. Lacan presents *Hamlet* as focused on the "decline" of the Oedipus complex, situated in the moment when the "subject feels the threat of castration."[3] It is this struggle against an alienating and castrating Symbolic that, I suggest, aligns especially African Americans with the experience of Hamlet.

Indeed, my particular interest in this chapter is in using Hamlet's narrative as a bridge allowing us access to an understanding of more contemporary articulations of the oedipal fantasies of whites and blacks as they are represented in two works by Ralph Ellison. Specifically in the prologue and first two chapters of *Invisible Man* and in his posthumous publication *Juneteenth*, Ellison conveys how racial fantasies express a mythic structure that mirrors the decline of the Oedipus complex and the struggle against the Symbolic found in *Hamlet*. Significantly, Hamlet's narrative diverges from the focus on slaying the father presented in the story of Oedipus, depicting instead the desire to murder and avenge one's self against the *usurping father*, the one who has taken the place of the biological father. This is a narrative that correlates well with the history of slavery, in which the white master was granted the prerogative to, like King Claudius, slay the father and both take on his patriarchal position and possess his wife as the master's woman. Through Ellison's own presentation of his characters' relation to black and white paternal figures, what we see is that this history of slavery offers structure for the formation of a myth through which antagonism toward alienation in the Symbolic is refocused into antagonism toward the slave master and his white descendants as privileged occupants of a Symbolic in which alienation for African Americans is heightened by racial oppression.

We may say that, through a racializing of the oedipal myth as crucial grounds for African Americans' battles against a white patriarchal Symbolic, "an essential relationship of the [African American] subject to his being is localized and fixed."[4] In this myth, being is viewed as the purloined possession of the usurping white Symbolic and its patriarchal figures, against whom the African American subject is pitted. Still, in truth, being designates a loss suffered by all subjects through entrance into the Symbolic. And whites, too, resist this fundamental alienation through use of oedipal racial fantasies, thus revealing a central dependence on the racial other in the attempts of both African Americans and white Americans to establish a mythic relation to being. Myth, Lacan stipulates, is "a chronicle expressing in an imaginary way the fundamental relationships characteristic of a certain mode of being human at a specific period."[5] It is what structures a sense of self contextualized within the dominant discourse of the times. The specific period Ellison focuses on is the 1950s. Set in a historical moment before the establishment of the restraints placed upon racism by the civil rights movement, Ellison's works display core dynamics of racial hatred that still linger today in more veiled manifestations. They allow analysis of race as an embraced identity that, I will show, urges African Americans toward a neurotic rejection of the Symbolic and white Americans toward a perverse embrace of its supplied transgressive fantasies as a route toward recuperation of the being it alienates. What I will convey through Ellison's work is the way that the oedipal structure combines with the narratives that emerge in the wake of slavery to found racial relations between whites and blacks that aim precisely at being. In this emergence, racial conceptions of the self and the other become both expressive and determinative of oedipal impulses, making mythic and stagnant conceptions of both the individuals who occupy the oedipal structure that race establishes and the proclivities that drive these individuals.

The Oedipal Complex and Subjective Relation to the Symbolic

The Oedipus complex for Lacan is not about a transgressive desire to kill the father but rather about the subject's submission to the law, for which the father is merely a metaphor. Involving "the quintessential charting of the relationship of the subject" to "the locus of the inscription of the law" that Lacan refers to as the Symbolic, oedipal dramas articulate the subject's entrance into the Symbolic world of meaning, into the sphere of the law of desire, through language.[6] This entrance alienates the subject because it occasions a "splitting" of the subject's enunciated demands from his or her biological and psychic needs.[7] When need is necessarily "put into [the] signifying form" of an articulated demand, what is produced is a "deviation of man's needs."[8] In this deviation, that which is "alienated in needs" by their "pass through the defiles of the signifier" constitutes a "primal repression," a loss that cannot "be articulated in demand."[9] Through language, the subject's needs only "come back to him in an alienated form," such that a given "demand in itself bears on something other than the satisfaction it calls for."[10] Lacan states that it is a "demand for a presence or an absence," for that loss that will seal the split instituted in the subject by language.[11] This split produces the "radical form" in which love between parent and child presents itself as a demand for "the gift of what the Other does not have," namely, the means to make the subject whole.[12] The child's demand for proofs of love resonates with a desire for something beyond what the Symbolic may offer, a "desire [that] begins to take shape in the margin in which demand rips away from need," as the subject comes to be "nourished by the imaginative dimension" that ever falls short of delivering the fantastical pleasures of a reconstituted wholeness.[13] It is from this insatiable desire for what is lost in the split, this fundamental rejection of alienation within language and the Symbolic, that the contentions marking the oedipal complex with its signature patricidal inclination emerge.

The oedipal drama pits the child against the father as the paternal representative tasked with enforcing the child's acceptance of loss. In the face of this splitting of desire from need and demand, the "true function of the Father," or of any living other who takes up the place of paternal metaphor, "is fundamentally to unite (and not oppose) a desire to the Law"; it is to bound desire within the constrictive ambit of the Symbolic.[14] This binding occurs when, in the law of the Symbolic, the subject comes to recognize a form of "power" and "potency" that may compensate for his or her loss.[15] Through successful identification with the metaphorical representation of the law, the subject comes to accept his or her "self-sacrifice," his or her loss of "that pound of flesh which is mortgaged in" the subject's "relationship to the signifier" through the alienation of the subject's needs.[16] What the subject finally identifies with is the Symbolic itself, which grants him or her access to the signifiers that may designate for the subject the place of the object *a*, the object that "satisfies no need" but that through the function of fantasy takes "the place" of "what the subject is—symbolically—deprived of."[17] This loss is what is meant by the term "castration," as that which "regulates desire" and instates the decline of the oedipal complex.[18] Castration "means that jouissance" and wholeness have "been refused in order to be attained on the inverse scale of the Law of desire."[19] At the "final outcome of his Oedipal demands, the subject, seeing him or herself castrated in any case, deprived of the thing [that will satisfy him or her], prefers, as it were, to abandon a part" of the self for entrance into the Symbolic, the place in which the subject "must find again in the very discourse of the Other what was lost" by the subject the "moment" he or she "entered into this discourse."[20]

But what we see in race is a resistance to accepting the loss of castration, a resistance that is more readily facilitated for whites by the signifiers of the Symbolic than it is for African Americans. Lacan argues that in castration it is the phallus that represents the pound of flesh, the unalloyed *jouissance*, lost to the subject. The phallus, Lacan emphasizes, is not "the organ" but is instead a signifier, a "signifier that has no signified."[21] It is the master signifier, the signifier I have already defined as whiteness in the American racial Symbolic. Within the confines of our white heterosexist Symbolic, whiteness as phallus emerges as "the privileged signifier" of alienation, the signifier that purports to signify what cannot be signified.[22] Lacan stresses that, aimed at an Imaginary state of wholeness and supremacy, the phallic "signifier of power, of potency," only "symbolize[s] the place of jouissance" through fantasies about "exclusion[s] from the specular image," fantasies of what may "fall[] off" from the Imaginary self, making of the phallus a representation of a "part that is missing in the desired image" of completion.[23] In this vein, whiteness presents itself as the castrated phallus that can grant wholeness and psychic completion to the Imaginary form. Both symbolizing the ideal and creating an unachievable desire to attain this ideal, whiteness as phallus is always positioned one step away from the subject's grasp.

Still, because the phallus at which white subjects grasp grounds the Symbolic in an ideal of whiteness, this phallus also facilitates an identification with the Symbolic that is less frustrated for white Americans than for African Americans. The impossibility of white Americans grasping or achieving whiteness is finally determined by whiteness' own successful self-presentation, at a purely discursive level, as the phallus that, once attained, will negate the castration produced by the Symbolic. This discursive supremacy of whiteness as phallic signifier of the impossible ideal, in actuality, splits whiteness away from any embodied individual who may call him- or herself white. But though unable to incarnate the ideal beyond its own discursive representations, racial whiteness devolves into an Imaginary self-presentation as the object *a* that promises this fantasy wholeness, a presentation that in the racist Symbolic is often more compelling than the promises made by racial blackness as object *a*. Involved in a struggle for supremacy germane to all forms of the object *a* associated with racial identity, whiteness feigns exceeding its status as object *a* by cyclically establishing itself as the glorified phallus that can be only desired and not incarnated. As the object *a* that discursively achieves the status of phallus, whiteness thus pins the white subject to the Symbolic by persuasively promising an impossible manifestation of the ideal he or she desires.

In contrast, it is because racial blackness as object *a* is so manifestly distant from the ideal of whiteness that has achieved phallic dominance that the position of African Americans within the Symbolic that whiteness structures is so contentious. Whiteness' masquerade as the phallus hampers African Americans' fantasy connection to a viable object *a*. Lacan explains that "it is from the phallus that the object [*a*] gets its function in the fantasy."[24] Desire for the object is constituted through the object's presentation as "reference" for the phallus, allowing the "imaginary object" to "condense in itself the virtues or the dimension of being."[25] The problem confronting African Americans is that blackness as object *a* is not valorized as a referent of being by the broader Symbolic that the phallic signifier of whiteness centers. And, at the same time, the racialized identities of African Americans prevent their easy identification with the figures designated as embodiments of the paternal metaphor and possessors of the phallus. It is only when the subject forms an identification with this paternal metaphor positioned as having the phallus that the oedipal complex goes into its decline. Through such identification, the subject is brought into the Symbolic and his or her desire is curtailed to the prevailing images of the object *a* the Symbolic supplies. What we see in both *Hamlet* and Ellison's works, however, are oedipal conflicts and transgressive desires that continue within the Symbolic because of characters' inability to identify with the paternal metaphor that is meant to bind their desires to the law of the Symbolic; and in Ellison's portrayal, it is race itself that leads both blacks and whites beyond the Symbolic toward an illicit pursuit of the Real that promises *jouissance* but only stifles desire.

Hamlet, *Invisible Man*, and the Ancestor

Hamlet famously gives voice to his own antagonistic relationship to the Symbolic with the assertion that "the time is out of joint" and he was "born to set it right."[26] Marking his distance from the Symbolic through a focus on the times, Hamlet draws our attention to temporality as a factor that proves significant in both his own relation to the Symbolic and that of African Americans. Lacan reads Hamlet as a subject who finds "his sense of time in his object," a subject who "repeats the initial germ of his trauma" by clinging to the dead ancestor as the object that defines his relation to the Symbolic.[27] Similar to my earlier descriptions of African Americans' link to an unsignified trauma from the past that is hauled into the present through race and racism, Lacan describes in Hamlet a subject plagued by an injury suffered upon a paternal ancestor who cannot facilitate entrance into the Symbolic because he cannot be adequately mourned in the Symbolic's current structure. Unlike in Oedipus' narrative, the crime centering both Hamlet's narrative and the narrative of self that grounds African American identity "has already taken place at the level of [a] preceding generation."[28] The intergenerational trauma that haunts the subject as a result of this crime occurs because "the rites" that would discursively integrate into the Symbolic the loss suffered in the past "have been cut short and performed in secret."[29] Where this secret performance often occurs at the unconscious level for African Americans, through a process whereby race is hauled into the present, it occurs in *Hamlet* through acts of homage to the father in which the father's surrogates, like Polonius, are murdered by the grieving son. At root here is an effort to supplant the paternal figures of the Symbolic with an image of the dead ancestor or his descendant as phallic authority. This process, however, threatens to leave uncovered the place of loss, because the Symbolic itself resists the ancestor as an Imaginary compensation that can ground a self-image of potency and completion.

The absence of an adequate phallic figure with which to identify helps leave exposed the traumatic Real of slavery with which African Americans continue to contend. Arguing that "the one unbearable dimension of possible human experience is not the experience of one's own death, which no one has, but the experience of the death of another," Lacan specifies that "the hole that results from this loss" constitutes "a hole in the real," such that "what is rejected in the symbolic register reappears in the real."[30] This reappearance, however, comes to structure the Symbolic around its very exclusion. It is this repetition in the Symbolic of a traumatic loss positioned in the Real that I have shown through my discussion of the signifiers of race as the automaton agitated by the Real. As Lacan elaborates, "The hole in the real that results from loss, sets the signifier in motion."[31] Since "there is nothing of significance that can fill that hole in the real, except the totality of the signifier," this "hole provides the place for the projection of the missing signifier"; and, with the rejection of the phallic signifier as that which will seal this gap, what arises is an "appearance of ghosts and specters in the gap left by the omission of the significant rite."[32] It is to these ghosts of the past, thus conjured by the signifiers of race, that African Americans pay homage through racial identity.

However, this attachment to the ghostly ancestor is precisely what is problematized in Ellison's works. Particularly in the prologue of *Invisible*

Man, Ellison ties the social exclusion of African Americans from the Symbolic both to racism and to a vision of the self and the Symbolic grounded in a reductive, mythic narrative of the slave's—the ancestor's—perpetual rivalry with the slave master and the Symbolic. As context for its presentation of this myth, the prologue begins by introducing us to the novel's nameless narrator, who emphasizes his identity's lack of full integration into the Symbolic by defining himself as invisible, as an almost ghostly "spook" whom people "refuse to see."[33] In terms that echo Lacan's view that man "hallucinates his world," the narrator presents his invisibility in the Symbolic as the result of "a peculiar disposition of the eyes of those with whom I come in contact . . . the construction of their *inner* eyes, those eyes with which they look through their physical eyes upon reality."[34] This invisibility and this distance from the Symbolic lead to an antagonism in the narrator. Driven by his sense of invisibility, the narrator springs upon and head-butts a "tall blond man" one night, demanding that the man apologize for not seeing him after *the narrator* "accidently bump[s] into [the] man."[35] Though the fact that it is the narrator who fails to see the man leads us to recognize that through race he too hallucinates his world, the narrator suggests that his distance from the Symbolic grants him clearer sight. His clarity is marked by a particular awareness, "a slightly different sense of time," an ability to perceive "its nodes, those points where time stands still or from which it leaps ahead."[36] By stepping into these nodes, by choosing to "slip into the breaks and look around," what the narrator comes to confront is the past of slavery as the root of an oedipal metaphor that centers the meanings he finds in the Symbolic.[37]

Entering these nodes of time through a drug-induced vision, the narrator finds in the past a complex narrative of love and paternal relation that he wishes to dismiss and transform into the more established structure of a racial oedipal rivalry. Paralleling the structure presented in Hamlet's tale of the usurping king's claim to all he surveys, the narrator's vision stresses the licentious, free rein of the phallic authority. Confronted in his vision by the complexity of a slavery in which "slaveowners . . . bid for [the] naked body" of a "beautiful girl the color of ivory," the narrator seeks clarity by maintaining racial categorizations that ascribe specific roles to individuals based upon race.[38] His vision can imagine coexistence with the phallic authority only as based upon hatred. When this vision conjures the image of a slave mother who, after killing the master who fathered her children, willingly attests, "I dearly loved my master," the narrator dismissively responds, "You should have hated him."[39] The slave mother explains, "Because I loved my sons I learned to love their father though I hated him too."[40] However, bound to his own altered oedipal structure of hatred for the white father, the narrator proposes simply that "maybe freedom lies in hating."[41] The mother struggles to convey the full complexity of a relationship that cannot be reduced to racialized positionings, suggesting that she is guided by love for both her sons and their father, divulging that "I loved him and give him the poison and he withered away like a frost-bit apple."[42] She emphasizes that "them boys woulda tore him to pieces with they homemade knives" if she had not poisoned him, but the narrator can neither fully reject nor embrace this oedipal impulse to slay the usurping white father.[43]

The narrator recognizes that he is having this vision because he has "become acquainted with ambivalence."[44] In avoidance of this ambivalence, he seeks clarity through simplicity, resisting the complicating insight granted by the mother's reading of her sons as bent on revenge. She conveys, "They gits to laughing and wants to kill up the white folks. They's bitter, that's what they is."[45] This bitterness, from which she wishes to protect both her husband and her sons, strikes a chord with the narrator. In hindsight, as he tells his story, the narrator concludes that, in the vision, "I had discovered unrecognized compulsions of my being—even though I could not answer 'yes' to their promptings."[46] But neither can he reject them fully. Viewing "recognition" as "a form" of "responsibility" that he simply "won't buy" and noting how complexity in meaning "inhibits action," the narrator can resist the "incompatible notions that buzzed within [his] brain" only by employing the racial structure as a ready-made means of defining the enemy.[47] While forestalling immediate action, the narrator yet waits in "hibernation," in "covert preparation" for when "the moment for action presents itself."[48]

The narrator seeks to "carry on a fight" against the whites who do not see him—"the sleeping ones"—"without their realizing it."[49] His strategy expands on one articulated, in the first chapter of the novel, by his grandfather on his deathbed when the narrator is still a young boy. Before dying, the grandfather, serving as direct paternal ancestor, reveals to the family, "Our life is a war and I have been a traitor all my born days, a spy in the enemy's country."[50] In a directive addressed most specifically to the narrator's father, who will now become the patriarch of the household, the grandfather presents "meekness as a dangerous activity," as a means toward revenge; he utters words that will haunt the narrator "like a curse," urging his son, "I want you to overcome 'em with yeses, undermine 'em with grins, agree 'em to death and destruction, let 'em swoller you till they vomit or bust wide open."[51] Thus echoing the ancestor's edict uttered by Old Hamlet's ghost to his son, the charge to both "revenge" and "mark"—or remember—him, the grandfather admonishes the narrator's father both to "keep up the good fight" after he is "gone" and to "learn" his path of vengeance "to the younguns."[52]

The narrator's own fight against the sleeping ones shows his final embrace, across the generations, of a path that expresses allegiance to the ancestor through rivalry with the Symbolic. As a young boy, however, the narrator finds himself in a state of disarray, unable to decipher his grandfather's meaning. Torn between his childhood desire to find a place for himself in the very Symbolic that he will come to despise as an adult and the instructions of a paternal figure whose authority the racist Symbolic delegitimizes, the narrator displays the kind of ambivalence at the level of his desire that is elucidated in Lacan's reading of Hamlet. Defining Hamlet as the image of a "man who has lost the way of his desire," Lacan shows that "the dependence" of Hamlet's "desire on the Other subject forms the permanent dimension of Hamlet's drama."[53] In this drama, Hamlet finds himself tasked by the father as subjective other to kill the king with whom Hamlet identifies. Lacan stresses that Hamlet's identification reaches such a degree that in a tournament against Laertes, the other whom Hamlet "admire[s] the most," Hamlet "takes up the side of Claudius," choosing to wear "another man's colors," the colors of the usurper, in a battle that results in Hamlet's death.[54] Also identifying simultaneously with the desire of the mother that remains directed at the phallic king, Hamlet is unable to act on his task of vengeance. Both Hamlet and Ellison's narrator remain incapable of action because the figures with whom they identify are multiple and conflicting. Though the narrator is "told" he "take[s] after" his grandfather, he views the grandfather as an "odd old guy."[55] Unable to identify fully with the grandfather's position or to see the grandfather as the paternal metaphor that can structure his desire and situate him securely within the Symbolic, the young narrator instead "visualize[s]" himself "as a potential Booker T. Washington."[56] What he finds, however, is that the philosophy of this substitute father figure grants him no agency in the racial Symbolic of the story, which is dominated by the desires of racist white men.

The narrator confronts these desires when he is offered an opportunity by the school superintendent to give a speech that echoes Washington's Atlanta Exposition speech in its view that "humility was the secret, indeed, the very essence of progress."[57] This speech, by substituting the grandfather's insurgent meekness with the passivity of Washington's humility, offers the narrator a means of winning the favor of "the town's leading white citizens," men who can help determine the narrator's position in the Symbolic.[58] As a condition for giving his speech, however, the young narrator humbly accepts the superintendent's request that he first fight before these men in a battle royal. Thus "hiring himself out," like Hamlet, to box against fellow black boys for the entertainment of white men, the narrator suffers through the match, enduring its degradation in eager anticipation of his speech, because he is convinced that "only these men could judge truly [his] ability."[59] But while the narrator identifies with these men's phallic authority, finding in them a power and potency that can evaluate and define his Symbolic value, the men stifle the narrator's phallic aspirations, continually emasculating him and reminding him of his Symbolic castration.

Before his degradation in the match, the men emphasize this castration and display to the narrator his limited access to the Symbolic by parading in front of him a "magnificent blond—stark naked" with a "small American flag tattooed upon her belly."[60] Marked with this symbol of America above thighs that "formed a capital V," the blond woman embodies the site of an unattainable pleasure made available only to those whom the American Symbolic defines as having the phallus.[61] Indeed, in Lacanian terms, she represents precisely the phallus itself, emerging for this moment as a manifested signifier of the possession that is desired by all but purportedly available only to the white men. As the signifier that "provides the ratio of desire," the phallus defines desirability itself among the varied objects of the Symbolic.[62] What Ellison's narrative presentation of this blond recognizes is that in our white heterosexist Symbolic, it is often white women who are tasked with "being" the phallus that sets the standard of desirability so that white men, through their illusory possession of these women, can be seen as "having" the phallus.[63] The blond as phallus, as signifier of the "Other's desire," thus personifies the fantasy site of a *jouissance* that is accessible only to those who, unlike the narrator, have access to the object *a*, to the fantasy object of whiteness.[64]

Unable to attain this object *a*, the narrator is excluded from a comfortable place in the Symbolic by a castrating racism that simultaneously delegitimizes available black paternal authorities and supplies justification for his rejection by these white phallic authorities. He maintains an ambivalent desire for the Symbolic's embrace that is signaled by his conflicting responses to the unattainable blond who is flagged as its representative. The narrator states, "I was so strongly attracted" to her that "had the price of looking been blindness, I would have looked."[65] But, still driven by a disdain for this woman and all the desirable elements of the Symbolic she represents, the narrator counters her desirability with a description of her eyes as "smeared a cool blue" the "color of a baboon's butt," adding that he longed to "spit upon her."[66] Because he finds in her an image of what he most desires but cannot have, the young narrator simultaneously wants to "caress her and destroy her, to love her and murder her."[67]

His ambivalent desires for the Symbolic she represents are only further frustrated by his dependence on the desires and instructions of the white men around him. The narrator describes how, both controlling and confusing his desire, "some" of the men "threatened" him if he looked at the blond "and others if [he] did not."[68] Incapable of negotiating the multiple desires that confront him, the young narrator finds that even the speech that was meant to win these men's affections cannot establish for him a palatable place within the Symbolic realm of desire and language. His failure both to please these men and to actualize his grandfather's advice to make them vomit and bust is visible when he finally gives his speech. At this critical juncture, the narrator can only mutter impotently in front of the crowd of white men, who both ignore and mock his words as his "dry mouth, filling up with blood from [a] cut, almost strangle[s]" him.[69] His clear powerlessness in this moment roots both his emerging invisibility and his nascent oedipal hatred of the Symbolic in his inability to identify with a paternal authority that can facilitate his occupation of a less frustrated position in the Symbolic.

Fantasy and Racial Interconnectivity

Even after this experience of rejection, the young narrator continues to identify most completely with the phallic authority of white men. Despite the internal conflict caused for him by the multiple desires of the men during the battle royal, their explicit direction, in the form of the scholarship they grant him after his speech, allows the narrator to imagine the clearest path for himself within the Symbolic. So urgent is his need to identify with the Symbolic through the dictates of white men that, despite his grandfather's appearance in a dream cautioning him to read the scholarship as just another effort by these men to "Keep This Nigger-Boy Running," the young narrator chooses to attend the college for Negroes to which the men direct him.[70]

However, through the narrator's experiences at the college, described in the novel's second chapter, Ellison expands his focus beyond the narrator's efforts to secure a stable place in the Symbolic. Focused most directly on showing that both African Americans and white Americans rely upon fantasies of race to express oedipal desires in defiance of the laws and restraints established by the Symbolic, this chapter emphasizes that the respective roles African Americans and white Americans play in their own and each other's transgressive oedipal fantasies are yet determined by the divergent positions they occupy within the Symbolic. Through a focus on the narrator's interaction with a rich white man named Mr. Norton, with whom the narrator again tells us he "identified," the chapter displays how whites and blacks are interconnected not socially or economically but on the level of the fantasies through which they utilize each other to Imagine and compensate for their mutual condition of lack.[71]

As the narrator drives Mr. Norton across the college campus and beyond its grounds, Mr. Norton expresses his own sense of his dependence on the racial other, conveying to the narrator that even as a young man he had always felt the narrator's "people were somehow connected with [his] destiny."[72] Mr. Norton conceives of this racial interconnectivity in terms of power. Content in the results of his financial patronage of the college, Mr. Norton defines his "real life's work" as his "first-hand organizing of human life."[73] He stresses the prestige granted him by aiding the college's African American students, explaining that through their success he "become[s] three hundred teachers, seven hundred trained mechanics, eight hundred skilled farmers, and so on."[74] But while African Americans are indeed involved "quite intimately" in Mr. Norton's "life," it is not for the reasons Mr. Norton articulates. It is, instead, because they are "bound to a great dream and to a beautiful monument" Mr. Norton has made to the memory of a deceased daughter for whom he still maintains repressed, illicit oedipal desires.[75]

Though African Americans provide a means for Mr. Norton to mask these desires for his daughter in erecting through his patronage of them a "monument to her memory," African Americans also serve as a destabilizing force that helps destroy this fantasy and unmask the repressed truth that guides Mr. Norton's life.[76] Lacan maintains that "only the Other is able to mark [the] position" of the subject's "*jouissance*," and it is through Mr. Norton's encounter with the figure of Jim Trueblood, a black share-cropper who impregnates his own daughter, that Mr. Norton comes to recognize his deceased daughter as a representative of the *jouissance* he has eternally lost.[77] Describing her from the start as a "perfect creation" not "of this world," a "biblical maiden" who was "too pure for life," Mr. Norton divulges, "I could never believe her to be my own flesh and blood."[78] His illicit desire for this object of purity, this ideal phallus that he could never conceive of possessing, becomes clear when he hears from the narrator of Trueblood's actions. Declaring, "I must talk with him," Mr. Norton, we are told, "clambered out" of the car and "almost ran across the road to the yard, as though compelled by some pressing urgency."[79] When confronting Trueblood, he blurts out, with "envy and indignation," "[you] have survived," "[you] have looked upon chaos and are not destroyed!"[80] Registering the oedipal nature of his envy, he asks Trueblood, "You feel no inner turmoil, no need to cast out the offending eye?"[81]

Through Trueblood's survival, Mr. Norton begins to conceive of his own missed opportunity at bliss, at committing the transgression that would signal his unshackling from the ethical restraints that place a limit on achievable pleasure within the Symbolic. This unshackling implies a transgression that Mr. Norton had resisted in himself but readily associates with blacks. His envy reveals how African Americans' struggles in the Symbolic lead to fantasies of their complete freedom from the Symbolic and its restrictions on desire and pleasure, positioning whites as the only ones subjected to the Symbolic's alienating law of desire. Though he cannot understand how Trueblood can "explain his doing" such "a monstrous thing" to his own daughter, Mr. Norton reveals his belief in the connection between blacks and licentious sexual activity when he first hears from the narrator of only the daughter's pregnancy out of wedlock, saying, "But that shouldn't be so strange. I understand that your people—Never mind."[82] Recognizing his own confinement by the ethical regulations curtailing desire to the limits of the Symbolic, Mr. Norton leaves unarticulated his racial fantasy about the lascivious proclivities of African Americans. But grounding Mr. Norton's fantasy relation to African Americans is a supposition of their access, through their salacious activities, to the bliss of what Lacan calls simply an "other satisfaction" than that available within the Symbolic's regulated boundaries.[83] Within these boundaries, what the subject experiences is only "phallic jouissance," produced through the signifier as that which structures a fantasy of being.[84] But because fantasy cannot satisfy need, phallic *jouissance* always "come[s] up short" for the subject, always "prove[s] inadequate, deficient, lacking, failing," and it thus leaves the subject longing for an "other satisfaction," a "pure jouissance," that "could never fail."[85] It is this pure *jouissance* that is masqueraded by the phallic authority and that, paradoxically, is here pinned to Trueblood.

Though, given his racial and economic status, it is Mr. Norton who is positioned in the Symbolic as having the phallus, what Mr. Norton finds in Trueblood is a figure he believes capable of accessing an unrestrained *jouissance* and bliss he himself yet lacks. To Mr. Norton's mind, Trueblood, unimpeded by ethical and moral laws, has the phallus, standing in the position of not just the phallic father but the "primal father" that "can only be an animal," the "father prior to the prohibition of incest, prior to the appearance of the Law."[86] Significantly, it is Trueblood's visible alienation within the Symbolic and his racial incompatibility with the white forms it sanctions as the supposed pinnacle of humanity that positions him as primal father. He stands as the fantasy figure that the phallic authority strives horrifically to embody, the father whose "satisfaction . . . knows no bounds."[87] So powerful is the dream of this boundless satisfaction that Freud himself famously presents this fantasy figure in his myth of the father of the primal horde, who is both idealized and killed by his sons for his unrestrained access to all the women of the tribe.[88] Lacan duly dismisses this myth, recognizing it as a mere fantasy expressing even in Freud a cultural "bias that falsifies the conception of the Oedipus complex right from the outset, making [Freud] consider the predominance of the paternal figure to be natural, rather than normative."[89] He stresses that all subjects, even the phallic father, are barred from being; and as a mere signifier of this fantasy bliss of unrestrained access to *jouissance*, Lacan stresses, the phallus "is bound to nothing" and to no one.[90] However, one of the uses of race is precisely to facilitate the fantasies that establish an illusory bond between the subject and the phallus that signifies *jouissance*, and in Ellison's narrative we see the circulation of the phallus as a signifier that through the fantasy of African American sexual prowess is temporarily bound not to the white father but to the black man.

Through this circulation of the phallus, Ellison depicts a vision of the fantasy lives of white American men, displaying the dependence of white fantasies of being on racial constructions of African American identity. The circulation is driven by the Imaginary, which directs white subjective fantasies in ways that defy Symbolic reality, securing illusory access to *jouissance* for whites by fantastically granting to black men what all subjects lack. The Imaginary bestowal of the phallus onto Trueblood has the immediate effect of producing in the white men of the story a certain "jealouissance," a jealousy over the *jouissance* of the racial other, but it also serves the greater purpose of leaving open the possible existence of an "other satisfaction" to which these men may aspire.[91] While the "envy" ascribed to Mr. Norton as he listens to Trueblood stems from Mr. Norton's attribution of pleasure to this racial other, we also find that Mr. Norton and other white men pay Trueblood for his telling of his story, thus, in a display of power, transforming his story into their own immediate source of phallic pleasure, while simultaneously grounding their fantasies of access to an "other satisfaction" productive of pure bliss. Trueblood therefore becomes a tool, financially manipulated to reaffirm the fantasies of his white patrons, but what is finally traumatizing to Mr. Norton is that for him the opportunity promised by fantasies of wholeness is lost: the daughter who assures him access to illicit *jouissance* is dead.

Mr. Norton had positioned this daughter as a compensating phallus, as the representative of a pure bliss ever lost to him but yet still ever present in the beyond, a goddess-like "maiden" whose ethereal presence would satiate his existence. His own subjective lack was made bearable through her surrogacy as a figuration of a loss he could mourn, assuage, and please through his life activities. Serving to build a monument to her memory, his philanthropic activities were conditioned by the fantasy object *a* of his personal beneficence, a kindness centering an identity that he felt resonated with principles that would please her, ideals that could bring him closer to her blessed purity, granting him some semblance of access to the *jouissance* of this phallus. Thus achieving a phallic *jouissance* marked by both a sense of self-worth and a degree of power over the lives of others, Mr. Norton remained content with his safe distance from the divine unattainability of his daughter. However, what finally overwhelms Mr. Norton after he hears Trueblood's story, what leaves him "lying very still" in a daze and "barely breath[ing]" with his "bluish" lips "parted," is the shock of having lost forever a singular source of *jouissance*, an "other satisfaction" that, in his fantasies, embodied an otherwise unattainable purity of bliss.[92]

Lacan calls the "other satisfaction" not only the *jouissance* that supposedly "never fails" but also the *jouissance* that "shouldn't be."[93] He conveys that our belief in the existence of this pure *jouissance* "contaminates" and impoverishes all the forms of satisfaction we are able to achieve, such that "all of the [other] jouissances are but rivals of the finality" and ideal it represents.[94] What so devastates Mr. Norton is the emergent belief that he has lost the chance to attain this incomparable ideal by rebuking transgression. Upon recognizing in Trueblood the possibility of transgressing without personal destruction, and, upon being confronted with his own desire to do so, not only is Mr. Norton deprived of the fantasy of his pure intentions—once guaranteed by the object *a* of a beneficence through which he formed a resonance with this leavened being—but he is also overwhelmed by the conviction that the pure *jouissance* promised by his daughter is forever lost to him.

To be clear, however, what Mr. Norton loses is not simply his fantasy image of this pure daughter but, more devastatingly, the very fantasy structure through which he compensates for his own subjective lack. Lacan explains that after "the radical loss" of the "phallus occurs" for the subject through his or her initial entrance into the Symbolic of language, he or she "responds then to the necessity of this mourning . . . precisely with the compensation of his [or her] imaginary register and with nothing else."[95] What we see in Mr. Norton is the collapse of this compensatory register as the racial fantasies that support it begin to shift. Racial difference had once guaranteed for Mr. Norton a sense of superiority as a "bearer of the white man's burden."[96] It had convinced him that the purity of his daughter was already marked in her white, "delicate, dreamy features," a delicate purity that made her in death a natural representative of the unattainable "other satisfaction" that, by its mere ethereal existence, made only bearable the diluted phallic *jouissance* Mr. Norton acquired as a fantasy source of being through his philanthropic activities.[97] But, in constructing the racial other as illusory possessor of the phallus that he has lost the chance to obtain, Mr. Norton dismantles the Imaginary structure that until this point has driven his life and compensated for his psychic lack. Where this fantasy structure of Mr. Norton's relied heavily on a static belief in African American inferiority, Mr. Norton is undone by a mutability that Ellison shows is built into this belief itself. Mr. Norton's case makes clear that, driven by an Imaginary that helps define the relation to being that is held by whites and African Americans, the inferiority, or even subhumanity, ascribed to African Americans fantastically constructs them as serviceable representatives of both excess and insufficiency; what produces the psychic disarray confronting Mr. Norton is this shift in fantasy whereby the serviceable African American's insufficiency of being, his very inhumanity, becomes the grounds for a conviction of his excessive, primal access to the very thing Mr. Norton lacks.

While the lacking phallus circulates more freely in the Imaginary depicted by the story, however, making itself open to possession by the hypersexual African American, it remains beyond the reach of African Americans in the Symbolic here portrayed. Trueblood himself is painfully aware that he lacks the power and prestige associated with the paternal wielder of the phallus. In telling his story to Mr. Norton, Trueblood acknowledges that since the incident he has done well because whites want "to hear about the gal lots of times" and they give him "somethin' to eat and drink" in exchange, but he also stresses that "no matter how biggity a nigguh gits, the white folks can always cut him down."[98] Indeed, Trueblood's troubles begin because of his limited access to material in the Symbolic, because "it was cold" and he "didn't have much fire" and was forced to "sleep together" in the bed with his wife and daughter.[99] In a description that, through the concept of manhood, ties sexuality to status in the Symbolic, Trueblood relates that he went to sleep that night thinking " 'bout how to git some grub for the next day and 'bout the gal [his daughter] and the young boy what was startin' to hang 'round her."[100] Where both his inability to provide for his family and his sense of the boy's encroachment upon the daughter who always viewed him as "her favorite over" her mother challenge his manhood, Trueblood seeks not just sustenance that will fulfill a need but also an invigorated sexuality and manhood that will secure a fantasy sense of being.[101]

Trueblood struggles to maintain this sense of manhood in a Symbolic that questions his very humanity. Through his efforts to do so, we see the significance of the sexual to fantasies of being. It is by means of the promise set forth by "the sexual relationship," the illusory oneness secured by the coming together of the subject and the sexual other as object of love, that the subject navigates his or her experience of lack within the "closed field of desire" availed to him or her by the Symbolic.[102] Staying within this field, Trueblood achieves some semblance of *jouissance* by lying in bed recalling the pleasure of his past, replaying memories of "a gal" he "had" in Mobile with whom he lived and slept in a house not far from the waters where musicians played on passing ships.[103] He relates, "Me and the gal, would lay there feelin' like we was rich folk and them boys on the boats would be playing sweet as good brandy wine."[104] But where thoughts of riches and a gal from his youth who called him "daddy" massage his wounded manhood, Trueblood is unsettled in hearing his own daughter say "daddy" in her sleep, as she begins to mumble words "like a woman says when she wants to tease and please a man."[105] As Trueblood grows increasingly "mad wonderin' if it's that boy" she is dreaming of and "worryin' 'bout [his] family, how they was goin' to eat and all," he feels his sense of control and authority over both this family and his larger environment dwindle.[106] Trueblood's fantasies of bliss, the phallic *jouissance* supplied to him within the closed field of the Symbolic by his memories of the past, are undercut in this moment by his inability to affirm in reality his sense of manhood, and he is thus drawn toward the *jouissance* of transgression.

As his dreaming daughter begins "touchin' him" and "movin' close" to him, Trueblood both expresses and masks his transgressive desires by slipping into a dream of his own.[107] What confronts him in the dream, as the dream figures him traveling to a white man's house in search of "fat meat" for his family, entering into the man's front door even though he "knows it's wrong," is the image of a woman he is "scared to touch . . . 'cause she's white."[108] We see here in Trueblood's dream the melding of transgressive desires with race. Existing in a Symbolic that often associated sexual transgression by black men with the rape of white women, Trueblood signals his unconscious desire for his daughter through this displacement facilitated by racial taboos.[109]

But when Trueblood wakes from his dream, he has already penetrated his daughter. His transgression becomes a metaphor through which Ellison conveys the life situations in the Symbolic of many African Americans. Trueblood realizes that he must exit his daughter, but he also cannot move, because he "figgers if [he] moved it would be a sin."[110] Suggesting that this dilemma of "how to git [him]self out of the fix [he's] in without sinnin'," the paradox of how to "move *without* moving," describes "the way things is always been with" him, Trueblood highlights a struggle that characterizes the experiences of African Americans more generally.[111] In a Symbolic that has historically restricted the freedoms of African Americans, from its legalized enslavement of blacks to its later imprisonment of those who seek their rights through civil disobedience, the pursuit of equality for African Americans has often stood in opposition to the law. Thus the very effort to secure a place for one's self in the Symbolic has frequently entailed transgressing against the Symbolic's established legislations.

The core problem confronting African Americans, Trueblood's narrative suggests, is how to maintain one's fantasy sense of being in a Symbolic that seeks to deny one the means of grounding such a fantasy, a Symbolic that structures a route to *jouissance* only through the path of transgression. Caught in such a bind, Trueblood relates that "there was only one way I can figger that I could get out: that was with a knife."[112] But this castration called for by the tight spot he is put into by a Symbolic that deprives him of sustenance and encourages his emasculation is something that Trueblood refuses to accept. Trueblood chooses, instead, to sin, to move, as the "very thought of the fix" he is in "puts the iron back" in him.[113] Where his dream of the white woman already reveals his association of transgression with a crossing of boundaries set by whites, Trueblood breaches the ethical limits of desire, fully embracing the act of fornication with his daughter, by envisioning his pursuit of transgressive *jouissance* as an act of racial insurgence. Recognizing that he is "lost" whether or not he commits to sinning, Trueblood decides to find satisfaction in his situation, identifying with a "fellow . . . down in Birmingham" who "locked hisself in his house and shot at them police until they set fire to the house and burned him up."[114] Trueblood relates, "He mighta died, but I suspects now that he got a heapa satisfaction before he went."[115]

Ellison depicts through the extremity of Trueblood's pursuit of satisfaction not merely an interconnection between transgression of legislated laws and maintenance of a self-sustaining fantasy of being but also an effort to transgress the *ethical* laws that protect us from the evil impulses of our drive for *jouissance*. He displays a succumbing to the seductive *jouissance* of a bliss that may lead not to an impossible freedom from the Symbolic but to self-destruction or to an increasingly stunted relation to the Symbolic and the desire it grounds. Without a place of comfort in the Symbolic, Trueblood is tempted through his visions of insurgent rebellion by a self-destructive drive for the absolute *jouissance* pursued "when a real drinkin' man gits drunk" or when "a real sanctified religious woman gits so worked up she jumps outta her clothes, or when a real gamblin' man keeps on gamblin' when he's losin'."[116] This is a *jouissance* that may take one beyond the limits of the Symbolic and the law. It threatens a collapse with the Real, with an unbearable bliss of pain and pleasure. It extolls a breaching of barriers, sanctifying itself as the great good, as the "other satisfaction" that is immediately accessible and that makes paltry the promises of desire that leave the subject longing only for a future bliss. But, through experiencing this *jouissance*, Trueblood paradoxically regains his manhood, choosing finally to forgo *jouissance* for an effort at making a place for himself in the very Symbolic that obstructs his dreams and desires.

Though attacked by his wife after the incident, with an axe that does not castrate him but cleaves a chunk of flesh from his face, Trueblood is able to suture together for himself a new identity that redeploys the Imaginary fantasies of his past to make possible his stable existence in the Symbolic of the present.[117] Standing his ground despite his wife's insistence that he leave and her assertion to him that "no man'd do what you did," Trueblood maintains, "I'm still a man" and a "man don't leave his family."[118] Trueblood's will to stay and his definition of manhood do not reject the transgressive desires by which the Symbolic pins him to animalism, but they do reframe them within a vivifying fantasy. Embracing these desires as human and simply stating, "I ain't nobody but myself," Trueblood turns to animals to produce a narrative that grounds his Imaginary sense of manhood in an image recalled from his days as a young man in Mobile.[119] Returning to the scene of himself lying in the room with his "gal," Trueblood relates that the music on the boats approaching reminded him of when you go hunting quail and "you can hear the boss bird whistlin' tryin' to get the covey together again" even though he "knows you somewhere around with your gun."[120] Trueblood assigns dignity to the boss bird's acceptance of its fate and its dedication to organizing its covey in spite of its lack of control over this fate, saying, "Them boss quails is like a good man, what he got to do he *do*."[121] Through this construct of manhood that transcends the Symbolic's alignment of his race with animalistic desires, Trueblood thus redefines himself as a man, as the boss of the family. Like the boss quail, he carries on by doing what he has to do to move forward in the Symbolic, finding a way for himself after being placed in the tight spot of transgressing the Symbolic's established edicts and laws. Though he cannot undo this transgression, Trueblood seeks to sin no more, embracing fantasy instead as a means of constituting his manhood and navigating the castrating Symbolic.

The Symbolic and Death, and the Neurotic and Perverse Allures of Race

This focus upon black manhood and transgression of the law remains central to Ellison's work and to its investigation of the African American struggle to establish a fiction of being in the racist Symbolic. In *Juneteenth*, Ellison returns to a vision of being as tied to sexuality and manhood in order to contemplate more fully how fantasy may limit and enable agency. Ellison's novel tells the story of a black preacher named Alonzo Hickman and the child of unclear racial origins whom Hickman would embrace as his own, a boy Hickman names Bliss. Now a reverend, Hickman was once a man engaged in full pursuit of the *jouissance* of the here and now, a gambling man and a drinker, a music man and a con artist. However, Hickman's life changed after he was driven to rage and revenge when the white mother who would birth Bliss accused Hickman's brother, Robert, of a rape that never truly occurred so that she could mask the identity of her real lover. Hickman's journey away from this place of hatred and all that results from this journey form the core of Ellison's contemplation.

The long path toward forgiveness begins for Hickman when the mother confronts him after her actions have already led to the lynching of his brother and the death of his mother. When she audaciously enters Hickman's home seeking sanctuary from those who resent the idea of her fornication with a black man, Hickman is "already feasting on revenge and sacrifice, telling [him]self: Those eyes for Bob's eyes; that skin for Bob's flayed skin; those teeth for Bob's knocked-out teeth; those fingers for his dismembered hands."[122] Driven by a lust for revenge that seems to rival even that of Hamlet, a lust that isn't simply "personal," but that makes Hickman embody "a thousand in [their] ache for vengeance," Hickman binds racial hatred to his need for justice, confessing, "I had prayed for the end of her and all like her."[123] Overwhelmed by not just his personal loss but generations of loss, Hickman seeks an impossible reparation through revenge, wondering hopelessly, "But what can I take that can replace [Robert's] wasted seed and all that's now a barbaric souvenir floating in a fruit jar of alcohol and being shown off in their barbershops and lodge halls and in the judge's chambers down at the courthous?"[124]

As the law itself conspires against his manhood and that of his people, Hickman, like the man from Birmingham idealized by Trueblood, becomes "dedicated to one last act," "dead set to drown" this mother in "deathblood" along with himself.[125] Having already prepared "for seven months to take a few of them along" with him, Hickman embraces death with a rifle, "a shotgun and two pistols" at hand.[126] Psychologically he conflates white people like this mother and death itself as the enemy to which his life will be sacrificed. Indeed, whites come to embody death for Hickman, standing, through the Symbolic's idealization of whiteness, as the representatives of the very Symbolic that oppresses his freedoms and deals subjective death to his being. His conflation of the white heterosexist Symbolic with death justifies Lacan's assertion that "the whole oedipal schema" introduced initially by Freud "needs to be re-examined" for its implication of a "fourth element" beyond the subject and the parental pair, the element of death.[127] Associated most fully with the father but pinned to all who stand as representative of the alienating Symbolic, this element is introduced by "the narcissistic relation" to the paternal metaphor called for by entrance into the Symbolic.[128] The ego that emerges in this narcissism, urged to model itself after the ideal Other defined by the Symbolic as "more advanced, more perfect," and submitted to the external definitions of self established by the signifiers of the Symbolic that make this other the ideal, is experienced by the subject as something "foreign to him but inside him."[129] Thus the struggle against this ideal Other, who has become conflated with the Symbolic as its embodied representative, entails a struggle against the extimate Other—both intimate and external—who is inside the self; and this struggle can lead to self-destruction.

The issue Ellison presents through Hickman is how to free the self from the Symbolic while still occupying it, how to strike at the source of one's alienation without suffering psychic or existential self-destruction. This is precisely the dilemma faced by Hamlet. Lacan observes that Hamlet cannot strike at Claudius, the usurping figure that wields the phallus that grants structural coherence to the Symbolic, "until the moment when he has made a complete sacrifice" of "all narcissistic attachment": not when he has rejected Claudius as an ego ideal he valorizes but when he is "mortally wounded" and is on the doorsteps of death.[130] He escapes alienation from the Symbolic only by sacrificing the life he leads in it. Hamlet thus represents the dangerous path the subject embraces in his or her pursuits of freedom from alienation, displaying the psychic perils that, I suggest, confront especially African Americans in their battles against an alienating and oppressive social structure.

Within this structure, race and racism seek to drive both African American and white Americans toward pathological extremes that breach the limits set in place by the laws of desire. Here Lacan's models of neurosis and perversion shed light on the psychic impact of racialized relations to being. Neurosis and perversion are names for two of the major psychic structures under which all subjects fall. They designate two divergent manners in which subjects may relate to the lack that emerges with language to constitute the barred subject as a subject. Where all subjects compensate for lack through a fantasy that positions them in relation to a fantasy object that promises wholeness—as Lacan indicates in his formula for fantasy, $\$ \Diamond a$, read as the barred subject in relation to the fantasy object—in perversion, as I will discuss below, the "accent is on the object *a*," such that the subject him- or herself seeks to become the object that promises completion to the Other; in neurosis, however, the "accent [is] on the other term of the fantasy, the $\$$."[131] While these accents in the fantasy define psychic structures that are complexly determined by factors both individual and social, racism seeks to drive African Americans toward the position of the neurotic by assaulting their fantasy of being and emphasizing their status as barred subjects, while it urges many white Americans toward perverse submission of their morality and desire to the authority of the white Other with whom they are called to identify. Each racialized subject, whether designated as white or African American, can contend against these urgencies toward neurosis and perversion by embracing alternate fantasies of being, beyond race; but the accent becomes more pathologically intense as the subject comes to adhere more fully to a dominating, racialized fantasy of being.

The particular relation to being that is adopted by both Hickman and Hamlet leads one toward an embrace of neurosis. Lacan, indeed, identifies Hamlet as a neurotic, as someone for whom lack itself, the "impossible" loss, becomes a centering "object of desire."[132] The neurotic, Lacan suggests, desires both what cannot be regained and the perpetual state of lack that is allowed through mourning of this unrecoverable loss. The "obsessional neurotic in particular" is characterized by the fact that "he emphasizes the confrontation with this impossibility," he "sets everything up so that the object of his desire becomes a signifier of this impossibility," thus accentuating his condition of lack through a desire directed at what he cannot have.[133] Focused on the impossibility of regaining what he or she lacks in the very attempt at its recovery, the neurotic "cleaves to [his or her] castration."[134] Though castration urges the neurotic "deep down" to feel he or she "is the most vain thing in existence, a Want-To-Be," a subject utterly devoid of being and completely unrecognized as valuable in the Symbolic, the neurotic "figures that the Other demands" his or her "castration," and so what the neurotic will not do is "sacrifice [this] castration to the Other's jouissance."[135] It is this cleaving to castration, this insistence that his lack will not be the source of the Other's *jouissance*, that drives Hickman to embrace certain death.

Like the neurotic, who refuses to "sacrifice his difference," to give up the lack he is sure is only instated within him by the Other, Hickman clings to racial identity as a means of defining the enemy through whom he and his people have suffered the blow of a historical and subjective loss.[136] Just as "Imaginary castration" becomes so bound to the neurotic's ego that his "proper name bothers him," that "deep down the neurotic [becomes] Nameless," so too does Hickman seek to bind his ego to the self-effacing category of race, thereby deriving for himself the means of avenging loss through insurgent, self-destructive assault upon the racial other.[137] Lacan elaborates that, bound to loss, the "neurotic's fantasy," what "the neurotic wishes for," is "clearly the dead Father . . . who would be the perfect master of his desire."[138] This father perilously emerges as an exultant representative of loss in the fantasy life of the neurotic through a "split" or a doubling of the "father's function" in relation to the Imaginary and the Symbolic.[139] Because the neurotic recognizes the father as visibly failing within the Symbolic to embody the ideal father or ego ideal of the Imaginary, both this failed father and his neurotic progeny come to stand in rivalry with the usurping father of the Symbolic, who presents an Imaginary perfection that pronounces their mutual lack. The neurotic questions his or her self-worth, convinced that he or she has inherited the lack of the "deficient father," and the neurotic thus, like Hamlet, binds his or her own desire to a dedicated effort at redemption of this progenitor of lack.[140] Through this father, the neurotic takes "flight" from his own desire and, instead, "substitutes" it for "the father's demand."[141] This substitution is what makes plain the pitfalls of an African American allegiance to the lost ancestor as the dead progenitor who cries out for vengeance for whole generations of loss. The danger to the African American subject is precisely this kind of neurotic sacrificing of the self for the desires of the dead, for the glorification of loss. And in both Hamlet's case and the case of Hickman, this self-sacrifice is conceivable only through personal death.

In order to avoid such death, however, Hickman chooses another path, one that is germane to the historical experiences of African Americans. He chooses religion, embracing it as an alternate source of being. In Hickman is embodied a religious philosophy that makes suffering in the Symbolic bearable through the promises of bliss in the future. Already a "slave to what a human is supposed to be," Hickman, without quite knowing why he is doing it, takes part in the birth of the child, first reaching for his "Papa's old straight-edged razor" not to kill the racial other but to sever the baby's umbilical cord, and then tying the baby's navel with his recently departed "Mamma's embroidery thread."[142] Not only does Hickman give up the immediacy of the *jouissance* brought on by the debauchery of his past lifestyle and resist the self-destruction of revenge for generations of loss, but he also accepts the mother's son, Bliss, as his own, gifted to him in the mother's attempt to "give" him "back" his brother.[143] Guided by the hope that her son will "share" in Hickman's Negro life and whatever it is that allowed him to help her, "the forgiveness [his] life has taught [him] to squeeze from it," the mother steers Hickman back to a religious path taken also by Hickman's own father but long ignored by Hickman himself.[144]

However, Hickman soon moves from emulating this dead father's desirous relation to religion toward actively substituting his own desires with what he reads as the demands of the Holy Father. While religion saves Hickman, it also stifles his ability to act, leading him to counter the Symbolic's oppressions and its idealization of the white paternal metaphor by granting agency foremost to the biblical Father. Teaching the young Bliss that blacks in slavery were left "without the right to do or not to do, to be or not to be," Hickman contends that his people "were born again in chains of steel" because God "means for [them] to be a new kind of human" or an "element" in this new people.[145] Arguing that "we started out with nothing but the Word—just like the others, but they've forgot it," Hickman asserts that blacks are "handicapped" and suffer "hard times and tribulations" because "the Lord wants [them] strong."[146] Through his focus upon "patience," upon an assertion that "God's time is long," Hickman recalls the suffering of the past while still maintaining a hope for the *jouissance* of the future that stifles his activity in the present.[147]

Despite his own problematic distance from the present, however, Hickman produces a reading of the relation of African Americans to time that is suggestive not only of the dangerous lure of a neurotic fixation upon lack, against which African Americans may contend, but also of the perverse desire to mask lack through self-objectification that may envelop white Americans. For Hickman, the mutual fixation of blacks and whites upon race as an apparatus of being entails a divergent relation to what he calls "continuity," a differential relation to time that, we see, also distinguishes neurosis from perversion.[148] Where in neurosis the focus is on continuity, on the neurotic's perpetual condition as barred subject in the Symbolic, in perversion the fantasy relation to being is grounded "outside of time," in "space," binding the subject to the expediency of immediate acts committed "in a vain detour aimed at catching the jouissance of the Other."[149] Hickman recognizes that, as with neurosis, African American identity grounds itself in continuity, extending to slavery and beyond. He explains that his "great-great-granddaddy was probably a savage, eating human flesh," and "a thousand times in the turmoil" of slavery "bastardy" and "shame" had been mixed for his people, but, he asserts, "out of all that" he became a preacher.[150] By contrast, he argues, when "standing in the doorway of manhood and womanhood," whites reach a point when they can "recognize no continuance of anything . . . not love, not remembrance, not understanding, sacrifice, compassion—nothing."[151]

Hickman associates the movement of whites into adulthood with a "desire to cast out the past and start out new," a process that involves a changed sentiment toward the other.[152] Evoking the history of white child care by black nursemaids in America, Hickman observes that "most of [the] deaconesses" in his congregation "had been nursing white folks' chillun from the time they could first take a job," and turning "over the responsibility of raising a child to another woman" also means turning "over some of the child's love and affection along with it."[153] Yet, he contends, there reaches a point when that first "baby love" must be seen as "wrong" by the white child, a point when continuity is broken and the very "foundation of the world" crumbles for the child entering adulthood.[154] Hickman points to a quelling of emotive attachment to the racial other that racism encourages more broadly as a means of establishing the superiority of white Americans, a rejection of the fundamental interconnectivity of the subject to the racial other.

What Hickman's reading allows us to see is that if race urges for African Americans a resistance to submission to the *jouissance* of the Other, it urges in whites a perverse self-transformation into "the instrument of the Other's jouissance."[155] This perversion is not defined strictly by "aberration in relation to social criteria" or "anomaly contrary to good morals."[156] It is defined, instead, by the white subject's performance for the Other's "entirely hidden gaze," the imagined gaze that "is not necessarily the face of our fellow being" but simply a masked "x," an undefined Other the subject assumes "is lying in wait," observing and evaluating his or her actions.[157] This is the Other that, for instance, we saw earlier in the transcendent figure of the deceased daughter who dictates Mr. Norton's relation to the racial other. What Hickman identifies in white aspirations for being and superiority is a process by which affection is determined by the definitions of self and other enforced by the signifiers of the Symbolic in an effort to buttress the white subject's Imaginary relation to being. Hickman describes the racist Symbolic as centering a disembodied Other that functions as the barometer of personal affections, a "weather man" that whites put "in control" of their emotions, making it so that "laughter cracks down like thunder when tears ought to fall."[158] This Other that must be "consulted" and that causes their "tears to become specialized" makes whites "fall out of rhythm with [their] earliest cries" and lose touch with their most core desires.[159]

It is through this sacrificing of one's desire to the Other that one, as with neurosis, reaches a pathological extremity in perversion. An instructive example of this extremity is the violent excess that can characterize sadomasochism, a subcategory of perversion, which emerges when "the sadist himself occupies the place of object" to "the benefit of another, for whose jouissance he exercises his actions as sadistic pervert."[160] Here we find a "reciprocal relation of annihilation" that characterizes perversion most broadly, whereby not only is one subject "reduced" to being an "instrument" of the other's enjoyment, but the other is "reduced to being only an idol," the "inanimate" embodiment of an "ideal" established in a relationship that "dissolves" this other of "being."[161]

The original Symbolic Other for the pervert is the mOther, who only indirectly links the pervert's desire to the law of the Symbolic while representing an impossible Imaginary ideal that this Symbolic cannot manifest. Perversion is about "how the child, in its relation with its mother," with the Other whose presence founds the Imaginary relation of the gestalt that the child will later produce in his or her fantasies as a lost ideal of bliss and contentment, "identifies with the imaginary object of her desire," with the desired phallus that, paradoxically, "the mother herself symbolizes" in the heterosexist Symbolic: the child attempts to secure the mOther's affections and fulfill her desires by becoming the phallus she lacks, thereby aspiring toward completion of a gestalt that would encapsulate both the mOther and the emergent perverse child.[162] Thus, a "phallocentrism [is] produced" in perversion, a recognition of the paternal authority and its laws. But while the "decline of the Oedipus Complex" should produce within the subject "an identification [with the law] known as the superego," an internal agency that polices desire and limits it to the promises of delayed gratification offered by the Symbolic, in perversion this complex remains unresolved; it is, instead, an insistent pursuit of the immediate *jouissance* personified in the external authority of the mOther that prevails.[163]

This structure whereby the perverse subject aligns him- or herself most fully with the mOther who both is and lacks the phallus, and not with the father who has the phallus and embodies the law, goes some way toward explaining the *aggressivity* and acted-out aggression that can result, in direct defiance of the law, from the pursuit of whiteness. Where whiteness comes to stand in the position of the phallus that the mOther herself occupies, it is whiteness that signifies a recoverable bliss; whiteness itself comes to function as the self-completing Other with whom the subject must bond in the gestalt of racial identity, the disembodied Other whose recognition the racialized white subject seeks through the extremity of her or his actions. What whiteness encourages is a transgression of the law that is aimed at unmediated access to the *jouissance* of the Real this mOther symbolizes. However, the white racist, as pervert, can only position him- or herself at "the limit" of "recognition" by this Other.[164] Unable to embody the object, the *a*, that is meant to serve as "reference" to the phallus, the object that is figured as capable of completing the mOther and satiating the self in the Real bliss of her presence, the white racist "can only be sustained with a precarious status which, at every moment is contested, from within."[165] This self-contestation, emerging from the impossibility of becoming the white object *a* that references the illusory white phallus, produces a "fundamental uncertainty" in the perverse relation to whiteness, such that the subject's personal distance from the ideals promised by whiteness leaves him or her incapable of "becoming grounded in any satisfying action."[166] As this subject "exhausts himself in pursuing the desire of the other," in masquerading him or herself as object referent to the whiteness extolled as phallus by the racist Symbolic, the subject becomes "a pure thing, a maniac," spanning the spectrum of the "human passions," from "shame to prestige, from buffoonery to heroism," in an endless display of his or her allegiance to the disembodied Other through his or her condemnation of the racial other.[167]

The Perverse Desire for Whiteness

This perverse structure is what we see emerging in the figure of the young boy Bliss that Hickman comes to claim as his son. Through Bliss we witness the allure of both whiteness and the perversion it allows. Though Bliss truly loves Hickman, he begins to view Hickman ambivalently as "the true father, but black, black" after learning that his mother is white.[168] With Hickman himself unable to say rightly whether Bliss has black "blood," Bliss is placed in the unique position of not having his racial identity determined by the external Symbolic. Instead, he chooses his race, but is yet able to do so only with recognition of the limitations placed upon black identity. Hickman himself facilitates this choice by teaching Bliss that it is only through their suffering that blacks are redeemed in the eyes of God. Instructing Bliss to embrace meekness, Hickman describes Jesus to him as someone who suffered "not like a God, but like any pale, frail, weak man who dared to be his father's son."[169] Tying both this weak man and black manhood to a state of divine disempowerment, Hickman asserts that in his condition of suffering Jesus was "just a little child calling out to His Father," crying out on a "cross on a hill, His arms spread out like [Hickman's] mammy told [him] it was the custom to stretch a runaway slave when they gave him the water cure," filling up his "bowels" so he "lay swollen and drowning on the dry land."[170] Confronted by this lack of power represented by black manhood and the lack of concern represented by the gaze of the Holy Father who watches on as Christ, "crying from the castrated Roman tree," calls out "WHY HAST THOU FORSAKEN ME," Bliss, instead, seeks after the white mOther who has forsaken him.[171]

While Bliss, as pervert, seeks this mother's recognition out of a need to feel completeness through her love, he also comes to identify phallocentrically with the white Symbolic she occupies out of a recognition of the power it embodies, out of an attempt to himself embody the white phallus it glorifies. Lacan's observation that "the pervert imagines he is the Other" explains this visible slippage here manifested between being the phallus and having the phallus, whereby the white pervert, seeking after the affection and approval of whiteness as mOther, can *have* access to this white ideal, can entice its embrace, only by purporting to him- or herself *be* its incarnation, its referent.[172] Initially following in Hickman's footsteps by seeking to become a preacher, Bliss abruptly diverts from this path when a white woman in a crowd of black followers storms the stage to claim him as her child. Though she is "crazy" and not his true mother, Bliss is drawn to her because he believes he senses fear in the crowd's response to her.[173] This sense of power through whiteness is only reinforced for Bliss when he, "against the law," enters a whites-only movie theater by pretending to be white.[174] Here, in the presence of the enchanting celluloid visions of the ideal represented by the glamorous white faces on the screen, Bliss not only fantasizes a conjoining of his lost mother's face with that of a beautiful white actress but also develops the audacity to imagine the powerlessness of a white man, thinking to himself of a movie usher working the doors he must enter, "You're not a man . . . only a big boy."[175] Able to belittle a white man by himself masquerading whiteness, Bliss comes to seek the immediate bliss of whiteness in rejection of the suffering and delayed glory promised by blackness. His desire for immediate bliss is conveyed initially by his need to be "paid" with ice cream for his preaching and by his ultimate conviction that "every time a preacher turns around he has to give up something else" that brings him pleasure.[176] In embracing whiteness, Bliss thereby rejects the perpetual "added yearning" and eternally unsatisfied desires he associates with both blackness itself and the holy profession of preaching.[177]

In keeping with Hickman's reading of white adulthood, however, this trajectory toward whiteness leads Bliss also to reject his natural affections for blacks, as he perversely transforms blacks into the means through which he, as instrument of the Other, proves his allegiance to the Symbolic to which he believes the mOther directs her desires and affections. When the "crazy" woman who calls him her child disrupts the religious gathering, Bliss is taken away for his own protection by a female member of the congregation named Sister Georgia. As she cares for him in her home and puts him to sleep in her bed, Bliss finds himself "wishing" Sister Georgia were his mother, feeling that "she was what he'd never allowed himself to yearn for."[178] But in the midst of scenes where Sister Georgia oscillates between telling Bliss she is able to care for him because she knows "all about little boys" and teasing him that when he pees he sounds "like a full-grown man," Bliss is caught in a liminal position between childhood and manhood; and he enters manhood finally through a transition that both asserts his identity as white and awakens his sexual desires for Sister Georgia.[179]

Bliss' manhood emerges in a dream that binds him to a perverse desire to become the white ideal by literally splitting his old identity as Bliss from his new white self. The "crazy" woman had hailed him by the name Cudworth when she stormed the gathering, and he comes to accept this identity when in his dreams he sees her "taking hold of him," with her "hands white against his own" white hands.[180] Like the pervert who "even in his dreams" can only "be satisfied in an inexhaustible captation of the desire of the other," Bliss readily embraces his mOther's desire by embracing her fantasy call to whiteness, concluding, "We are the same— Cudworth am I"; and "before he realize[s] it," he finds himself split off from this not yet fully emerged identity, as he dreams himself "looking across a narrow passage into a strange room where another, bolder Bliss was about to perform some frightful deed."[181]

Just as the pervert's dilemma highlights a deeper "division from the self which structures the Imaginary," the fantasies that play out in Bliss' dream lead him to experience the Other as the self.[182] What he sees as he looks at his newly formed white self is his "own hand reaching out like a small white paw" that signals the animal passions awakened by his whiteness, as he lifts "the hem of [Sister Georgia's] night-gown" to peer "into the shadow of a mystery."[183] Bliss' natural need for a mother's love and the oedipal desires that are routinely repressed in the subject gain expression through his use of race to sexualize this woman he once wished to embrace as a mother. Guided by a Symbolic that already pins the animalism awakened in him to black sexuality, Bliss recalls "fragments of stories about digging for buried treasure" as he stares at the "bushy slope where he thought he would find a cave."[184] As he fantasizes about the "iron-bound chest" he "had uncovered," the treasures and pleasures he had accessed through viewing Sister Georgia's black nakedness, what Bliss encounters instead is the animalistic image of a flock of "white geese" emerging from the chest, becoming as he watches a "troop of moldy Confederate cavalry galloping off into the sky with silent rebel yells."[185] The treasure he had sought thus reveals itself to be nothing but the racist construct of a moldy past awakened in its silence by the Imaginary fantasies of an emergent racial identity.

By embracing this identity, Bliss not only comes to reject blacks as the source of what Hickman calls his "first . . . baby love," eventually growing to become a white senator named Adam Sunraider, but also grows to be "considered the most vehement enemy" of blacks "in either house of Congress."[186] As Sunraider splits away from Bliss, becoming a man who is "self-castrated of [blacks'] love" in a land that encourages whites to "deny [this love] by law," he becomes perversely self-conflicted, literally performing an identity for the gaze of the unseen Other on the Senate floor while still being driven by his "baby love" to urge blacks toward uprising in anger over his words.[187] Plagued by the "fundamental uncertainty" that characterizes the pervert in his impossible attempts to incarnate the ideal, Sunraider cannot fully embody the whiteness that would sever his ties to Bliss and African Americans.[188] He thus seeks to "speed up the process" of their freedom, viewing the holiday of Juneteenth, commemorating the day over two and a half years after the Emancipation Proclamation when "words of Emancipation" finally reached slaves in Texas, as emblematic of African Americans' delayed freedom and blind adherence only to the "illusion of emancipation."[189] Through the cruelty of his words, he wishes to "extend their vision until they disgust themselves, until they gag."[190] But Sunraider remains a conflicted soul, coming to live the life Hickman warns him against when he is a child: "You have to watch yourself, Bliss," Hickman cautions, "otherwise you won't know" whether "you're yourself or what somebody else says you are."[191] Bliss becomes, through the figure of Sunraider, a vision of the white phallus, donning this identity in an attempt to please the disembodied white Other of the Symbolic but standing in conflict with the core sentiments of a childhood that continues to bind him to the racial other.

In this state of conflict, what Sunraider cannot figure out is the perennial American challenge of how to embrace the abjected other wno is already incorporated within the psyche of the racialized self, what both he and Hickman identify as "the mystery of the one in the many and the many in the one, the you in them and the them in you."[192] Sunraider's inability to solve this mystery leads not only to his failure to accept Hickman as "the dark daddy of flesh and Word" but also to the patricidal hatred that causes his own abandoned son by a black mother to gun him down on the Senate floor.[193] Hickman, however, recognizes this problem as its own solution, noting that this mystery of the me in the you, the Other in the self, is "a rebuke to the universe of man's terrible pride."[194] Designating the extimate Other as intimate to the self, Hickman asserts that this mystery marks "the shape and substance of all human truth."[195] Indeed, this is the very truth of the human psyche unveiled by Lacanian theory and its reading of the oedipal complex, the core "dependence of [the subject's] desire on the other subject," who not only is offered as the instrument through which the subject structures his or her fantasies of being but also maintains the capacity to model to the subject a more healthy desire.[196]

In a recognition of the other that transcends racial differences, Hickman is able to find one such model in the figure of Abraham Lincoln. Standing at the Lincoln Memorial as he seeks to devise a means to warn Sunraider of the impending attempt on his life, Hickman identifies in Lincoln's somber visage an "air of peace and perception born of suffering."[197] That "look and what put it there," says Hickman, not only make Lincoln "one of us" but also make him "one of the few who have ever earned the right to be called 'Father.' "[198] Here Hickman approaches a truly Lacanian understanding of the father as he who models desire and binds it to the Symbolic. Articulating a route toward freedom that is invested not merely in the social but also in the personal, the psychic, Hickman asserts that "he's one of us, not only because he freed us to the extent that he could, but because he freed himself of that awful inherited pride they deny to us."[199] What Hickman thus finds in Lincoln is the figure of a father who urges freedom through acceptance of castration, acceptance of the lack that is masked in the pride of racial whiteness that Lincoln forsakes. Where Lacan asserts that what all subjects "must be able to get used to [is] the real" of their own castration, Hickman recognizes castration as something that must be embraced equally by blacks and by whites.[200]

However, Hickman's understanding of the function of castration is incomplete. Accepting castration for Hickman also means, as I have suggested, accepting a lack of agency. Hickman begs his God, "teach me, Lord, to move on and yet be still," rearticulating the African American effort to move without moving as a desire to accept the stillness of unchanging social circumstances while moving on from the pain and anger they had brought on in him in the past.[201] Having already divested himself of all personal agency, Hickman comes to see Sunraider instead as "our young hope, as our living guarantee that in our dismal night [God] still spoke to us."[202] Similar to the narrator's grandfather in *Invisible Man*, Hickman hopes that Sunraider will "speak for our condition from inside the only acceptable mask," from within "the councils of our enemies."[203] As Hickman's hopes are shattered by Sunraider's willingness to use Hickman's people as props in his own performance of whiteness, it becomes clear that Hickman's error is that he "had hoped to raise" a man like Lincoln, not to become one himself.[204] From Lincoln he was "forced to learn" that man, "at his best, when he's set in all the muck and confusion of life and continues to struggle for his ideals, is near sublime."[205] But, in the end, Hickman lacks the courage himself to aspire to the sublime.

From Hickman to Obama

Hickman's dependence on the other for change and agency within the alienating Symbolic thus serves as an instructive to raced subjects, especially to African Americans. Set in the 1950s, his story and the narrative of *Juneteenth* articulate the kind of awakening that would lead black preachers of the era to become the fathers of the civil rights movement. It lays bare the psychic and social impediments inherent to struggles against both oppression and alienation, displaying the perverse and neurotic positions that race still encourages us today to adopt. In our own era, African American leaders, including President Barack Obama himself, have urged a similar recognition of the mystery of the me in the them. In his second inaugural speech in 2013, Obama sought to "affirm the promise of our democracy" by encouraging Americans to "recall that what binds this nation together is not the colors of our skins or the tenets of our faith" but our "allegiance to an idea" that "all men are created equal."[206] In what reads like a corrective to Hickman, Obama asserts that "while these truths may be self-evident, they have never been self-executing," and "while freedom is a gift from God, it must be secured by His people here on Earth."[207] But though Obama claims agency for the self, his own rise to power occurs without a concomitant empowerment of the black ancestor as paternal metaphor.

The son of a white mother, Obama, unlike Bliss, embraces his black identity, positioning himself as a potential paternal metaphor for future generations while following in the footsteps of the great black preachers. His most direct link to this tradition is the figure of Reverend Jeremiah Wright, whose tutelage to Obama arguably situates Wright as a surrogate father figure after the deaths of Obama's biological father and white grandfather. Articulating its own variety of the narrative of the pastor and the politician who abandons him, Obama's rise to power is accompanied by his severing of ties to this black father figure who maintained questionable views on the issue of race in America. This split from what we may call, after Bliss, "the dark daddy of flesh and Word," constitutes Obama's rejection of the ancestor's directive to mark and avenge the transgressions of the racial past. It actualizes a disruption of the continuity with the past that secures racial identity for African Americans. But the challenge it leaves unresolved is how to remain free of this past while still grounding the self in a freedom that defies the perverse glorification of the Symbolic's white ideals. Though Obama's recognition of the me in the them resists the psychic urgencies of racial identity, it only continues a long struggle to create a viable replacement for the black ancestor and the white paternal authority as contending mediators of a psychic relation to the Symbolic.

CONCLUSION
Beyond Race, or The Exaltation of Personality

Centering this study is the recognition that race functions not only at the social level but also at the psychic. We can more precisely say that the staying power of race, the inability to discard it despite our awareness of its illusory groundings, is founded in race's capacity to structure a relation to *jouissance* for the subject of race. Beyond its Symbolic value, race grounds the fantasies and transgressions through which both African Americans and white Americans access a semblance of being. With race thus conflated with being by the historical trauma of slavery, with it functioning as the central apparatus through which raced subjects define their own and the racial other's relation to the *jouissance* of being, contending against race means contending against the fundamental fantasy of the desiring subject, the aspiration toward wholeness that founds subjectivity itself. But what I would like to suggest here is that the alienation of especially the African American subject, which has been emphatically displayed in the racist Symbolic that justifies oppression through disregard for African American fantasies of being, has produced in many African Americans a cynicism toward the Symbolic that is an essential defense against psychic alienation.

I have shown that Lacan defines alienation as the effect constituted upon the subject by language. "Man," Lacan says, "is ravaged by the

Word," experiencing through the signifier the "death" that "brings life."[1]
In ascending toward subjectivity through language, the subject sacrifices
an essential part of the self in order to conform to the definitions of self
that are imposed by the Symbolic. The subject is constrained by the limits
of the signifier and thus "designates his being only by barring everything"
of the self that escapes linguistic signification.[2] But, Lacan maintains, the
signifier is also "the cause of jouissance," the means of articulating an illusory recovery of the lost being.[3] I have shown how the master signifier of
whiteness seeks to recover this being for the white subject but more often
denies it to blacks. As Lacan elaborates, "Every dimension of being is produced in the wake of the master's discourse—the discourse of he who,
proffering the signifier, expects therefrom one of its link effects."[4] African Americans struggle against the effects of the master signifier of race
originally proffered by whites through seeking to resignify its value and
reaffirm a fantasy of being. But this struggle at the level of the Symbolic is
both necessary and insufficient.

The necessity involved here is determined by the fact that the exalta-
tion of whiteness as master signifier and the structuring of desire within
the Symbolic around the white phallus impair the ability of African Americans to identify with the Symbolic itself and to establish the fantasies of
being that facilitate a psychic sense of contentment. Thus, it would seem,
what is needed in race relations is access by both African Americans and
white Americans to vivifying fantasies of being. This need is supported
by the fact that the limitations placed upon *jouissance* by the Symbolic
through its shaping of fantasies of being enable a possible mediation of
aggression toward the other. Where the subject "cannot recognize himself" except "by alienating himself" in the desire and image of the Other,
what the subject most naturally aims at in his or her "aggressiveness"
toward the racial other is an effort to "refind" him or herself "by abol-
ishing the ego's *alter ego*."[5] This alter self, experienced in the "extremity
of [an] intimacy that is at the same time excluded" internally, is what the
racial other comes to personify for the raced subject, such that the racial
other stands as "the locus of the decoy in the form of *a*," in the form of
the object that embodies a fantasy manifestation of what is essentially lost
to the subject.[6] It is for this reason that Lacan contends, "A solid hatred is
addressed to being."[7] Thus it is at the level of fantasy, through the operations of the fantasy object *a* that designates a relation to being, that this
aggressivity must be mediated. Through a redefinition of the Symbolic and

its signifiers, language may attain a mediating function in which "it allows two men to transcend the fundamental aggressive relation to the mirage of their semblable."[8]

Making a place for African Americans in the Symbolic therefore means the destruction of old fantasies of race, but, I contend, it does not mean the creation of new ones. This study ultimately refutes the concept of race, designating it as a primary source of subjective alienation. We may say that with race the master signifier structures identity in such a fashion that between the raced subject's "proper name," as the signifier of his or her identity, and the signifiers of race, a "poetic spark is produced" that "metaphorically abolishes" this identity, transforming the subject into his or her race.[9] Race thus perfectly exemplifies the process through which the subject, as Lacan states, is transformed into a signifier and deprived of being. Yet the paradox I have shown is that raced subjects remain bound to race because through it they dangerously recover a fantasy sense of being. Race, emerging from a traumatic past that eruptively manifested *jouissance* through sanctioned acts of transgression, perilously exacerbates illicit desires for *jouissance* by fixing *jouissance* to the racial other. Through positioning the other as a source of *jouissance*, race co-opts the function of the phallus by defining desirability in the Symbolic, and what it defines as desirable is the Real of an exultant bliss to which not only the Symbolic but also the self and other that occupy it are subordinated. Bound through race to the *jouissance* of the traumatic past, the subject of race remains alienated by the desire of the Other, by the racist Symbolic that "proffered" the terms of race that African Americans ascribe to even in their efforts to redefine them.

What is needed, therefore, is a "separation" from the Symbolic and the master signifier of the Other that grounds it in the *jouissance* of race.[10] This separation must be founded, first of all, on a recognition of the interdependence of the subjectivities of the self and the racial other. The fact of the extimacy of this racial other, who is internal to each American's subjective sense of self, is exemplified in the racial fantasies that structure both subjective and national identity for Americans. In the first chapter of this book I showed how the identity of the slave master depended on that of the slave, and I suggested in chapter 2 how slave songs and jazz music became integral to American identity. The implication here is the need to conceive of individuals in terms of broader cultural identities that transcend racial differences and acknowledge interconnectivity across groups. This is the solution I pointed to in my reading of Ellison's *Juneteenth*, which presents the figure of Abraham Lincoln as a paternal authority that transcends race. Present in Ellison's work is an urgency guiding us toward recognizing the vast diversity in American identity and the disparately intermingled racial lineages that root America in cultural hybridity, not racial separation.

This hybridity, what Du Bois conceives of as the problem of the "two warring souls in one dark body" that characterizes African American double consciousness, is the very extimacy that Ellison rightly celebrates in his own life.[11] Usefully modeling for us his own relation to the Symbolic in his essay "The World and the Jug," Ellison speaks of ancestral figures that shape his role as artist. Where Ellison admits that an African American author such as Richard Wright may be seen as a "relative" of his, it is white writers like Hemingway and Faulkner that he counts as his "ancestors."[12] The title of Ellison's essay stems from his rejection of the notion that the traumatic experiences of African Americans have cornered them into a place of "unrelieved suffering," as though they are trapped in an "opaque steel jug."[13] Ellison asserts that "if we are in a jug it is transparent, not opaque, and one is allowed not only to see outside but to read what is going on out there."[14] It is this ability to see outside the limitations imposed by race that enables Ellison to claim Hemingway and Faulkner as ancestors. Ellison explains that "one can do nothing about choosing one's relatives," but "one can, as artist, choose one's 'ancestors.' "[15]

In choosing his ancestors, however, Ellison attempts not to discard his relatives but rather to foreground the urgencies of his own desires and drives. Privileging an understanding of the self in the active choice he makes in his identification with the other, Ellison explains, "Hemingway was more important to me than Wright . . . not because he was white" but "because he appreciated the things of this earth which I love and which Wright" didn't "know," and because "all that he wrote" was "imbued with a spirit beyond the tragic with which I could feel at home."[16] Seeking after that with which the self is most at home, Ellison extends beyond race toward a hybridized cultural identification with Hemingway precisely because the spirit of Hemingway's writing is "very close to the feeling of the blues" that also speaks to Ellison's sense of self.[17] Forestalling an identity grounded singularly in the metaphor of race, Ellison pursues this sense of self through its accumulation in the metonymic movement of self-identifications that are driven by an individualized artistic desire to explore the homely spirit of tragedy.

What Ellison ultimately models is a desire grounded in cynicism toward notions of race and racial lineage. This cynicism, I suggest, establishes a liberating distance mutually from the alienating desire of the Symbolic Other and from the avenging desire of the racial ancestor. Lacan makes clear that "desire is a defense" against alienation, a defense that "reverses the unconditionality" in which "the subject remains subjected to the Other" who, in this case, binds him or her to a psychic relation to race.[18] Lacan argues that "what the subject has to free himself of is the aphanisic [or fading] effect" to which the subject is submitted by the signifiers of the Symbolic, and the way that the subject does this is through "scepticism" as what Lacan calls "a mode of sustaining man in life."[19] Where "man's desire is the Other's desire," granted to the subject and structured for him or her by the Symbolic Other, a "cynic[ism]" by which the subject questions the desire of the Other is the stance that "best leads the subject to the path of his own desire."[20] Along this path, the subject must articulate what Lacan calls the *Chè vuoi?*, the simple question, "What does he want of me?"[21] This question creates distance between the conflated desires of the subject and the Other, allowing for the emergence of something more properly subjective and personal to the subject. As Lacan argues, "if there is a position that one can essentially qualify as subjective," it is "clearly" the position of "doubt."[22]

This position is one uniquely available to the African American subject, as a subject who is continually urged toward an antagonistic relation to the Symbolic Other. In his reading of James Joyce, Lacan shows how this antagonism can lead to an exploration of one's own desires. Like African Americans in their relation to the ancestor, Joyce is a figure who has been confronted with the belief, Lacan states, that "his father was lacking, radically lacking."[23] This confrontation complicates Joyce's relation to the Symbolic. Unable to identify with the Symbolic, Joyce takes to an extreme the sense that the Symbolic and language are imposed upon the subject, the feeling, I argue, that is also experienced by African Americans submitted to the Symbolic's racist signifiers; Joyce comes to sense that "language" is a parasite, a "veneer," a "cancer which afflicts the human being," and he therefore moves to embrace "equivocation" as his "only weapon" against the Symbolic.[24] This equivocation leads to not only a restructuring of Joyce's desires but also their resituation in direct relation to his own Real.

Joyce develops what Lacan calls his own *sinthome*, as a substitute for the function of the father. Where subjectivity is comprised of the three registers of the psyche—the Imaginary, Symbolic, and Real—it is the father that functions metaphorically as sinthome, as the knot that ties together the registers into a unified subjective self.[25] The sinthome is the root of the ego, which is, at the decline of the oedipal complex, modeled after the agency of the paternal metaphor as ego ideal. It is this modeling of the self after the Symbolic Other that leads to alienation in the Symbolic. But as "heir" to a father found lacking, Joyce is able to assume through equivocation the position of the "heir-etic" who questions both the father and the Symbolic.[26] This equivocation occurs at the level of the emergence of the "personal" as the "support of the subject," at the level where "personality" comes to stand as not a link to the Other but a "link between [this] sinthome and the unconscious, and between the imaginary and the real."[27]

Though the unconscious, "structured like a language," incorporates within it the signifiers of the Other that make complete liberation impossible, this linking occurs through Joyce's embrace of the individual lack that centers his personal, unconscious relation to being.[28] It starts with a recognition not only that the ancestor lacks but that so too does the Symbolic itself. It acknowledges a "lack inherent in the [Symbolic] Other's very function as the treasure trove of signifiers," an incapacity in its purported function of defining the subject's identity, desire, and lack.[29] Insofar as "the Other is called upon (*chè vuoi*) to answer for the value of this treasure," insofar as the heir-etic child of the Symbolic puts the Symbolic Other to the impossible task of naming the lack personal to his or her subjectivity, this cynical subject begins the process of making a name for him- or herself.[30] Instead of paying homage to the dead ancestor or bowing to the definitions imposed by the paternal authority of the Other, what is availed the subject is the capacity to valorize his or her own "proper name," designating it as the only signifier to be paid the deference he or she bequeathed to the Other.[31] It is this signifier that must come to stand for the lack, the absence, that is his or her being.

Radically altering one's psychic relation to the Other, the process of self-naming I here advocate both redirects the urge to grieve the ancestor and repudiates the racialized designations through which the Other seeks to confine the subject in the steel jug of the Symbolic. What is ultimately entailed in this self-naming is the subject recognizing his or her "own image" as "a mortal cause, and griev[ing] this object" as a loss, as an emptiness around which the subject's own personality must be built as an incrementally expansive structure to contain this internal absence.[32] In establishing such personality, the goal is not to escape lack but rather to ground the self within it, to, more precisely, build the self around its sustained void. Lacanian theory shows that the only way "to found wisdom [is] on lack," which presents the single viable source of self-recognition afforded the subject.[33] The absent image, as container, as personality, must be cultivated and built up "*ex-nihilo*," from nothingness, as psychic defense against the alluring phallus and objects *a* that act as the decoys for desire within the confining ambit of the Symbolic.[34] By recognizing this absence as the true pathway to desire, and by coming to travel this discovered path, the subject of race may not only attain the means of expressing the multiplicity of an identity and desire unhinged from the fantasy *a* of race, but also potentially direct him- or herself toward a goal that centers the very practice of psychoanalysis: not just a transcendence of race but a transcendence of the fundamental fantasy of recoverable loss that drives subjective and racial desire. What Lacanian theory posits is the possibility that, after the experience of actively mapping one's own relation to the fantasy object is undertaken by the subject, this "experience of the fundamental phantasy" can become "the drive" by which desire is then "agitated"; unveiled by the theory is the potential that, in cynically questioning the fantasy of race, the subject may confront the very lack that fuels all fantasy and all desire, the lack that must be subjectified as the empty core of a newly adumbrated self.[35] Lacan importantly cautions that the "loop" of the subject's fantasy often must be "run through several times" before the subject abandons it. I propose, however, that because of the cynicism already central to their relation to the Symbolic, African Americans are uniquely positioned to embrace this very daunting task of transcending both race and the fundamental fantasy it supports.[36]

NOTES

Introduction

1 Angela Corey, quoted in "What's Next in the Florida Loud Music Killing Case," *Washington Post*, February 18, 2014, http://www.washingtonpost.com/news/post -nation/wp/2014/02/18/whats-next-in-the-florida-loud-music-killing-case/.

2 Throughout, I shall use the term "Other" in its capitalized form to reference Lacan's big Other, which Lacan defines as language itself, designating it simultaneously as the Symbolic order and the order of the law of desire. All lowercase usage of the term "other" references most essentially the fantasy or Imaginary other, the object *a* that is given body by, for example, the racial or sexual other.

3 For useful studies on this kind of speech, see Randall Kennedy, *The Persistence of the Color Line: Racial Politics and the Obama Presidency* (New York: Vintage Books, 2011); Stephanie Li, *Signifying without Specifying: Racial Discourse in the Age of Obama* (New Brunswick, N.J.: Rutgers University Press, 2012); John Hartigan Jr., *What Can You Say? America's National Conversation on Race* (Stanford, Calif.: Stanford University Press, 2010); and Eduardo Bonilla-Silva, *Racism without Racists: Color-Blind Racism and the Persistence of Racial Inequality in the United States*, 3rd ed. (Lanham, Md.: Rowman & Littlefield, 2009).

4 See Michael Dunn, Michael Dunn Trial—Day 5—Part 2 (Dunn Testifies), http://topic.ibnlive.in.com/ajit-pawar/videos/michael-dunn-trial-day-5-part-2 -dunn-testifies-TLdjAJiOqoE-1881933.html; and Web Extra: Letters Written by Michael Dunn from Jail, http://www.firstcoastnews.com/story/news/local/ michael-dunn-trial/2014/01/24/michael-dunn-jail-letters-jordan-davis/4836401/.

5   Dunn, Letters, May 7th.

6   Dunn, Letters, May 7th.

7   Dunn, Letters, July 12th, emphasis in original.

8   Dunn, Letters, May 20th.

9   Dunn, Letters, July 3rd.

10   Dunn, Letters, May 15th.

11   Dunn, Letters, February 24th.

12   Dunn, Letters, July 12th, emphasis in original.

13   Dunn, Letters, February 20th.

14   Jacques Lacan, *The Seminar of Jacques Lacan Book XX: Encore*, trans. Bruce Fink (New York: Norton, 1998), 24.

15   Lacan, *Encore*, 63, 95, 6.

16   Lacan, *Encore*, 44.

17   Lacan, *Encore*, 100.

18   Lacan, *Encore*, 99.

19   Cory Strolla, quoted in "Attorney: Dunn 'Overcharged' due to Trayvon Killing," *USA Today*, February 13, 2014, http://www.usatoday.com/story/news/2014/02/13/attorney-says-michael-dunn-overcharged-due-to--trayvon-martin-death/5457507/.

20   Strolla, quoted in "Attorney."

21   Dunn, Michael Dunn Trial—Day 5.

22   Dunn, Michael Dunn Trial—Day 5.

23   Dunn, Michael Dunn Trial—Day 5.

24   Dunn, Letters, July 12th.

25   Dunn, Letters, July 12th.

26   Dunn, Letters, July 12th.

27   Dunn, Letters, June 14th.

28   Dunn, Letters, July 3rd.

29   Dunn, Letters, January 30th.

30   Barack Obama, quoted in "Obama: 'If I Had a Son, He'd Look Like Trayvon': President Obama Addresses the Trayvon Martin Shooting from a White House Rose Garden Event," *NBC News*, March 23, 2012, http://www.nbcnews.com/video/nbc-news/46834310#46834310.

31   Obama, quoted in "If I Had a Son."

32   Obama, quoted in "If I Had a Son."

33   Barack Obama, "Remarks by the President on Trayvon Martin," WhiteHouse.gov, July 19, 2013, http://www.whitehouse.gov/the-press-office/2013/07/19/remarks-president-trayvon-martin.

34   Obama, "Remarks." Massey and Denton provide compelling evidence of the calculations that went into defining social space for African Americans through biased housing practices that facilitated the formation of ghettoes in America. Douglas S. Massey and Nancy A. Denton, *American Apartheid: Segregation and the Making of the Underclass* (Cambridge, Mass.: Harvard University Press, 1993). For more on disparities in enforcement of the law, see Michelle Alexander, *The New Jim Crow: Mass Incarceration in the Age of Colorblindness* (New York: New Press, 2012).

35   Obama, "Remarks."

36   Dunn, Michael Dunn Trial—Day 5.

37   Eric Holder, "Attorney General Eric Holder's Remarks on Trayvon Martin at NAACP Convention (full text)," *Washington Post*, July 16, 2013, http://www.washingtonpost .com/politics/attorney-general-eric-holders-remarks-on-trayvon-martin-at-naacp -convention-full-text/2013/07/16/dec82f88-ee5a-11e2-a1f9-ea873b7e0424_story .html.

38   Holder, "Remarks."

39   Colin Powell, appearance on *Meet the Press*, January 13, 2013, http://www.nbcnews .com/id/50447941/ns/meet_the_press-transcripts/t/january-colin-powell-cory -booker-haley-barbour-mike-murphy-andrea-mitchell/#.U2usdWdoK5Q.

40   Powell, appearance on *Meet the Press*.

41   Powell, appearance on *Meet the Press*.

Chapter 1

1   Jacques Derrida, *Writing and Difference*, trans. Alan Bass (Chicago: University of Chicago Press, 1978), 280.

2   Barbara Christian, "The Race for Theory," *Cultural Critique* 6 (1987): 55.

3   Henry Louis Gates Jr., "American Letters, African Voices: History of African American Authors," *New York Times Book Review*, December 1, 1996, ¶12.

4   For a useful elaboration of this term, see Jacques-Alain Miller, "Extimité," in *Lacanian Theory of Discourse*, ed. Mark Bracher et al. (New York: New York University Press, 1994).

5   Jacques Lacan, *The Seminar of Jacques Lacan Book XI: The Four Fundamental Concepts of Psychoanalysis*, trans. Alan Sheridan (New York: Norton, 1998), 149.

6   For more on this, see especially Saussure's "Nature of the Linguistic Sign," in Ferdinand de Saussure, *Course in General Linguistics*, trans. Wade Baskin (New York: McGraw-Hill, 1966).

7   Lacan, *Four Fundamental Concepts*, 20, 46.

8   Derrida, *Writing and Difference*, 292, emphasis in original.

9   Lacan, *Four Fundamental Concepts*, 25.

10   Lacan, *Four Fundamental Concepts*, 22.

11   Judith Butler, *Bodies That Matter: On the Discursive Limits of Sex* (New York: Routledge, 1993), 229.

12   Butler, *Bodies That Matter*, 241.

13   Butler, *Bodies That Matter*, 223.

14   Henry Louis Gates Jr., *Black Literature and Literary Theory* (New York: Routledge, 1984), 285.

15   Gates, *Black Literature and Literary Theory*, 285–86.

16   Derrida, *Writing and Difference*, 285.

17   Henry Louis Gates Jr., *Loose Canons: Notes on the Culture Wars* (New York: Oxford University Press, 1992), 69, 50.

18   Houston A. Baker Jr., *Modernism and the Harlem Renaissance* (Chicago: University of Chicago Press, 1989), 25, emphasis in original; and Houston A. Baker Jr., *Turning South Again: Re-thinking Modernism / Re-reading Booker T.* (Durham, N.C.: Duke University Press, 2001), 5.

19   Lacan, *Encore*, 21.

20   Jacques Lacan, *The Seminar of Jacques Lacan Book XVII: The Other Side of Psycho-analysis*, trans. Russell Grigg (New York: Norton, 2007), 63.

21   Jacques Lacan, "The Instance of the Letter in the Unconscious," in *Écrits: The First Complete Edition in English*, trans. Bruce Fink (New York: Norton, 2006), 430.

22   Lacan, *Four Fundamental Concepts*, 48.

23   Lacan, *Four Fundamental Concepts*, 26–27.

24   Lacan, "Instance of the Letter," 413, 414.

25   Lacan, *Four Fundamental Concepts*, 20, 46, 199.

26   Lacan, *Four Fundamental Concepts*, 218.

27   Lacan, *Four Fundamental Concepts*, 219.

28   Hortense J. Spillers, *Black, White, and in Color: Essays on American Literature and Culture* (Chicago: University of Chicago Press, 2003), 203, 219.

29   Spillers, *Black, White, and in Color*, 209.

30   Spillers, *Black, White, and in Color*, 208, 214, 215, emphasis in original.

31   Spillers, *Black, White, and in Color*, 204, 209, 208.

32   William Wells Brown, "Narrative of the Life and Escape of William Wells Brown," in *Clotel; or The President's Daughter* (New York: Penguin, 2004), 9, emphasis in original.

33   James Olney, " 'I Was Born': Slave Narratives, Their Status as Autobiography and as Literature," in *The Slave's Narrative*, ed. Charles T. Davis and Henry Louis Gates Jr. (New York: Oxford University Press, 1985), 155.

34   Brown, "Narrative," 6.

35   Frederick Douglass, *Narrative of the Life of Frederick Douglass, An American Slave, Written by Himself*, ed. William L. Andrews and William S. McFeely (New York: Norton, 1997), 15.

36   Brown, "Narrative," 20.

37   Lacan, *Four Fundamental Concepts*, 25.

38   Lacan, *Four Fundamental Concepts*, 26.

39   Lacan, *Other Side of Psychoanalysis*, 189.

40   Lacan, *Other Side of Psychoanalysis*, 189.

41   Lacan, *Other Side of Psychoanalysis*, 124, 90.

42   Kalpana Seshadri-Crooks, *Desiring Whiteness: A Lacanian Analysis of Race* (New York: Routledge, 2000), 4.

43   Seshadri-Crooks, *Desiring Whiteness*, 55.

44   Seshadri-Crooks, *Desiring Whiteness*, 3.

45   Lacan, *Other Side of Psychoanalysis*, 108, 175.

46   Karl Marx, *Theories of Surplus Value* (New York: Prometheus Books, 2000), 1:46, emphasis in original.

47   Marx, *Theories of Surplus Value*, 1:46.

48   Lacan, *Other Side of Psychoanalysis*, 53.

49   Jacques Lacan, *The Seminar of Jacques Lacan Book VII: The Ethics of Psychoanalysis*, trans. Dennis Porter (New York: Norton, 1997), 229.

50   Lacan, *Other Side of Psychoanalysis*, 49.

51   Spillers, *Black, White, and in Color*, 225, 215, emphasis in original.

52   Lacan, *Other Side of Psychoanalysis*, 177.

53   Lacan, *Other Side of Psychoanalysis*, 177.

54   Lacan, *Other Side of Psychoanalysis*, 103.

55   Lacan, *Other Side of Psychoanalysis*, 201, 97.

56   Lacan, *Other Side of Psychoanalysis*, 107.

57   Lacan, *Other Side of Psychoanalysis*, 50.

58   Lacan, *Other Side of Psychoanalysis*, 20.

59   Lacan, *Other Side of Psychoanalysis*, 201.

60   Lacan, *Other Side of Psychoanalysis*, 89.

61   Lacan, *Other Side of Psychoanalysis*, 97.

62   Lacan, *Encore*, 95.

63   Jacques Lacan, "Desire and the Interpretation of Desire in *Hamlet*," in "Literature and Psychoanalysis: The Question of Reading Otherwise," special issue, *Yale French Studies*, nos. 55/56 (1977): 15.

64   For more on the importance of the slave to southern society and white identity, see especially Walter Johnson, *Soul by Soul: Life Inside the Antebellum Slave Market* (Cambridge, Mass.: Harvard University Press, 1999), which has influenced my statements in this paragraph.

65   Thomas Jefferson, *Notes on the State of Virginia*, in *Writings* (New York: Library of America, 1984), 270. The uncertainty implied in Jefferson's use of the word "suspicion," along with his statements in other writings that actively assert the intellect of blacks, suggests Jefferson's deeper ambivalence about race. This ambivalence (and the aesthetical focus of his statements above) seems further complicated by Jefferson's love affair with a female slave, Sally Hemings. See especially Annette Gordon-Reed, *The Hemingses of Monticello: An American Family* (New York: Norton, 2008), for more on this history.

66   Jefferson, *Notes*, 264.

67   Jefferson, *Notes*, 264, 265.

68   For more on the relation to slavery of arguments about the slave's ability to feel pain, see especially Robin Bernstein, *Racial Innocence: Performing American Childhood from Slavery to Civil Rights* (New York: New York University Press, 2011); and Saidiya V. Hartman, *Scenes of Subjection: Terror, Slavery, and Self-Making in Nineteenth-Century America* (New York: Oxford University Press, 1997).

69   Jefferson, *Notes*, 265.

70   Lacan, *Ethics of Psychoanalysis*, 184, 198.

71   Lacan, *Other Side of Psychoanalysis*, 50–51; Lacan, *Ethics of Psychoanalysis*, 194; and Lacan, *Encore*, 74. While Lacan's association of *jouissance* with fantasy in *The Other Side of Psychoanalysis* seems to counter his earlier work in the *Ethics* seminar, this notion of a *jouissance* beyond the Symbolic also centers Lacan's reading of feminine sexuality in *Encore*, a seminar given two years after *The Other Side of Psychoanalysis*.

72   Lacan, *Ethics of Psychoanalysis*, 177.

73   Sigmund Freud, *Reflections on War and Death*, trans. Dr. A. A. Brill and Alfred B. Kuttner (New York: Moffat, Yard, 1918), 22, 15–16.

74   Douglass, *Narrative*, 23, 24.

75   Douglass, *Narrative*, 24.

76   Douglass, *Narrative*, 24.

77   Brown, "Narrative," 44.

78   Lacan, *Ethics of Psychoanalysis*, 194.

79   Lacan, *Ethics of Psychoanalysis*, 212.
80   Douglass, *Narrative*, 28, 29.
81   Douglass, *Narrative*, 29.
82   Lacan, *Other Side of Psychoanalysis*, 72.
83   Lacan, *Ethics of Psychoanalysis*, 198.
84   Douglass, *Narrative*, 24.
85   Lacan, *Ethics of Psychoanalysis*, 202.
86   Lacan, *Ethics of Psychoanalysis*, 202.
87   Lacan, *Four Fundamental Concepts*, 84.
88   Jacques Lacan, "Kant with Sade," in *Ècrits: The First Complete Edition in English*, trans. Bruce Fink (New York: Norton, 2006), 662–63.
89   Spillers, *Black, White, and in Color*, 207.
90   Lacan, *Other Side of Psychoanalysis*, 49.
91   Spillers, *Black, White, and in Color*, 206.
92   Lacan, *Other Side of Psychoanalysis*, 49.
93   Lacan, *Other Side of Psychoanalysis*, 77; Lacan, *Ethics of Psychoanalysis*, 184.
94   Lacan, *Four Fundamental Concepts*, 62.
95   Lacan, *Four Fundamental Concepts*, 62.
96   Lacan, *Other Side of Psychoanalysis*, 50.
97   Lacan, *Other Side of Psychoanalysis*, 50.
98   Lacan, *Four Fundamental Concepts*, 63.
99   Lacan, *Other Side of Psychoanalysis*, 77.
100   For more on this, see Melvin Dixon, "Singing Swords: The Literary Legacy of Slavery," in *The Slave's Narrative*, ed. Charles T. Davis and Henry Louis Gates Jr. (New York: Oxford University Press, 1985), 298–318; Lawrence W. Levine, "Slave Songs and Slave Consciousness," in *American Negro Slavery: A Modern Reader*, 3rd ed., ed. Allen Weinstein, Frank Otto Gatell, and David Sarasohn (New York: Oxford University Press, 1979), 143–72; Johnson, *Soul by Soul*; Hartman, *Scenes of Subjection*; and Ron Eyerman, *Cultural Trauma: Slavery and the Formation of African American Identity* (Cambridge: Cambridge University Press, 2001).
101   James Albert Ukawsaw Gronniosaw, "A Narrative of the most Remarkable Particulars in the Life of James Albert Ukawsaw Gronniosaw, An African Prince, As Related by HIMSELF," in *Unchained Voices: An Anthology of Black Authors in the English-Speaking World of the Eighteenth Century*, ed. Vincent Caretta (Lexington: University Press of Kentucky, 1996), 40, 33. This argument, stressed by clergy member Walter Shirley in the preface sold with Gronniosaw's narrative, highlights the deeper implication of Gronniosaw's religious rhetoric throughout the narrative.
102   Gronniosaw, "Narrative," 33.
103   Lacan, *On the Names-of-the-Father*, 65.
104   Lacan, *Encore*, 6.
105   Lacan, *Encore*, 85.
106   Albert J. Raboteau demonstrates that the revivalism of the Great Awakening, beginning in 1740 and surging again in the "closing years of the eighteenth and early decades of the nineteenth centuries," led to "an unprecedented spread of Christianity among Afro-Americans." Albert J. Raboteau, *Slave Religion: The "Invisible Institution" in the Antebellum South* (New York: Oxford University Press, 1980), 152.

107 Levine, "Slave Songs and Slave Consciousness," 153.

108 Gronniosaw, "Narrative," 48.

109 Farhad Dalal, *Race, Colour and the Processes of Racialization: New Perspectives from Group Analysis, Psychoanalysis and Sociology* (New York: Routledge, 2002), 142.

110 Lacan, *Ethics of Psychoanalysis*, 215.

111 Though Eyerman astutely defines the post-Reconstruction period as seminal to establishing the concept of a unique African American identity grounded in slavery, he reads the trauma of slavery as a purely discursive construct produced by African Americans themselves, missing the essential function of the Real within and after slavery. Eyerman, *Cultural Trauma*.

Chapter 2

1 W. E. B. Du Bois, "The Problem of Amusement," *Southern Workman* 27 (1897): 181, 183.

2 W. E. B. Du Bois, "The Religion of the American Negro," *The New World: A Quarterly Review of Religion, Ethics and Theology*m vol. 9, December 1900 (Boston: Houghton, Mifflin, 1900), 623, emphasis in original.

3 W. E. B. Du Bois, "The Conservation of Races," in *Occasional Papers, No. 2* (Washington, D.C.: American Negro Academy, 1897), 12, 14, 13.

4 Du Bois, "Conservation of Races," 15.

5 Lucius Outlaw, *Critical Social Theory in the Interests of Black Folk* (New York: Rowman & Littlefield, 2005), 142.

6 Anthony K. Appiah, *In My Father's House: Africa in the Philosophy of Culture* (New York: Oxford University Press, 1992), 45.

7 Outlaw, *Critical Social Theory*, 144, 145, 152, emphasis in original.

8 Outlaw, *Critical Social Theory*, 157.

9 Outlaw, *Critical Social Theory*, 157.

10 W. E. B. Du Bois, *Dusk of Dawn: An Essay Toward an Autobiography of a Race Concept* (New York: Schocken Books, 1971), 137.

11 Outlaw, *Critical Social Theory*, 145.

12 Outlaw, *Critical Social Theory*, 140.

13 Outlaw, *Critical Social Theory*, 145, 144.

14 Outlaw, *Critical Social Theory*, 159, emphasis in original.

15 Outlaw, *Critical Social Theory*, 140.

16 Outlaw, *Critical Social Theory*, 142, 143.

17 Lacan, *Four Fundamental Concepts*, 51.

18 Lacan, *Four Fundamental Concepts*, 55.

19 Lacan, *Four Fundamental Concepts*, 59.

20 Lacan, *Four Fundamental Concepts*, 59.

21 Lacan, *Four Fundamental Concepts*, 53–54.

22 Lacan, *Four Fundamental Concepts*, 52.

23 Lacan, *Four Fundamental Concepts*, 67, 53, emphasis in original.

24 W. E. B. Du Bois, "Criteria of Negro Art," in *The Crisis: A Record of the Darker Races*, authorized reprint ed., vol. 32, no. 6, October 1926 (New York: Arno Press, 1969), 296.

25 W. E. B. Du Bois, *The Souls of Black Folk*, ed. Henry Louis Gates Jr. and Terri Hume Oliver (New York: Norton, 1999), 11.

26 Lacan, *Four Fundamental Concepts*, 211.

27 Lacan, *Four Fundamental Concepts*, 208, 207, 208, emphasis in original.

28 Lacan, *Four Fundamental Concepts*, 213, 212, emphasis in original.

29 Lacan, *Four Fundamental Concepts*, 211, 212, emphasis in original.

30 Lacan, *Four Fundamental Concepts*, 212.

31 Lacan, *Four Fundamental Concepts*, 141.

32 Lacan, *Four Fundamental Concepts*, 141.

33 Du Bois, "Criteria of Negro Art," 297.

34 W. E. B. Du Bois, "Returning Soldiers," in *The Crisis: A Record of the Darker Races*, authorized reprint ed., vol. 18, no. 1, May 1919 (New York: Arno Press, 1969), 14.

35 Du Bois, *Dusk of Dawn*, 115.

36 Du Bois, *Dusk of Dawn*, 133.

37 Du Bois, *Dusk of Dawn*, 116, 133.

38 Du Bois, *Dusk of Dawn*, 105, 115.

39 Du Bois, *Dusk of Dawn*, 116–17.

40 Appiah, *In My Father's House*, 42, emphasis in original.

41 Appiah, *In My Father's House*, 41.

42 Appiah, *In My Father's House*, 42.

43 Lacan, *Four Fundamental Concepts*, 68.

44 Lacan, *Four Fundamental Concepts*, 68.

45 Lacan, *Four Fundamental Concepts*, 68.

46 Lacan, "Instance of the Letter," 439.

47 Lacan, "Instance of the Letter," 421, 431.

48 Lacan, "Instance of the Letter," 425.

49 Du Bois, *Dusk of Dawn*, 116.

50 Lacan, *Encore*, 71.

51 Lacan, "Instance of the Letter," 422.

52 Lacan, "Instance of the Letter," 422.

53 Lacan, "Instance of the Letter," 422.

54 Jacques Lacan, *The Seminar of Jacques Lacan Book III: The Psychoses*, trans. Russell Grigg (New York: Norton, 1997), 261; Du Bois, *Dusk of Dawn*, 115.

55 Du Bois, *Dusk of Dawn*, 166.

56 Du Bois, *Dusk of Dawn*, 101.

57 Lacan, *Psychoses*, 261; Lacan, "Instance of the Letter," 417.

58 Lacan, *Four Fundamental Concepts*, 64.

59 Lacan, *Four Fundamental Concepts*, 64.

60 Lacan, *Four Fundamental Concepts*, 164, 197.

61 Lacan, *Four Fundamental Concepts*, 176.

62 Lacan, *Four Fundamental Concepts*, 177.

63 Lacan, *Four Fundamental Concepts*, 198.

64 Lacan, *Four Fundamental Concepts*, 180.

65 Lacan, *Psychoses*, 261, 258.

66 Lacan, "Instance of the Letter," 419; Jacques Lacan, "The Subversion of the Subject and the Dialectic of Desire in the Freudian Unconscious," in *Ècrits: The First Complete Edition in English*, trans. Bruce Fink (New York: Norton, 2006), 681.

67 Lacan, *Psychoses*, 268.

68 Lacan, "Instance of the Letter," 422; Lacan, *Psychoses*, 264; Lacan, "Instance of the Letter," 423.

69 Lacan, *Psychoses*, 268.

70 Du Bois, *Dusk of Dawn*, 132.

71 Lacan, *Psychoses*, 268.

72 Lacan, *Psychoses*, 268.

73 Jacques Lacan, "Le Sinthome," trans. Luke Thurston, *Ornicar?* 6–11 (1976–1977): 22.

74 Lacan, *Four Fundamental Concepts*, 106, 107.

75 Lacan, *Four Fundamental Concepts*, 96.

76 Lacan, *Four Fundamental Concepts*, 100.

77 Lacan, "Le Sinthome," 40.

78 Lacan, "Le Sinthome," 14, 55, 18, 19.

79 Lacan, "Le Sinthome," 60, 19.

80 Lacan, *Psychoses*, 269.

81 Du Bois, *Dusk of Dawn*, 100.

82 Du Bois, *Souls of Black Folk*, 10.

83 Du Bois, *Souls of Black Folk*, 10.

84 Jacques Lacan, "The Mirror Stage as Formative of the *I* Function as Revealed in Psychoanalytic Experience," in *Ècrits: The First Complete Edition in English*, trans. Bruce Fink (New York: Norton, 2006), 76.

85 Lacan, "Mirror Stage," 78.

86 Lacan, "Mirror Stage," 76.

87 Lacan, *Four Fundamental Concepts,* 106.

88 Lacan, *Four Fundamental Concepts*, 96.

89 Lacan, "Mirror Stage," 76.

90 Du Bois, *Souls of Black Folk*, 10.

91 Lacan, "Mirror Stage," 79.

92 Lacan, "Mirror Stage," 79.

93 Du Bois, *Dusk of Dawn*, 130.

94 Du Bois, *Dusk of Dawn*, 98, 99.

95 Du Bois, *Dusk of Dawn*, 99.

96 Du Bois, *Dusk of Dawn*, 99.

97 Du Bois, *Dusk of Dawn*, 130.

98 Du Bois, *Dusk of Dawn*, 99.

99 Du Bois, *Dusk of Dawn*, 130.

100 Du Bois, *Dusk of Dawn*, 130.

101 Du Bois, *Dusk of Dawn*, 100, 131.

102 Lacan, *Four Fundamental Concepts*, 97.

103 Lacan, *Four Fundamental Concepts*, 49.

104 Lacan, *Four Fundamental Concepts*, 58.

105 Lacan, *Four Fundamental Concepts*, 55.

106 Lacan, *Four Fundamental Concepts*, 55.

107   Lacan, *Four Fundamental Concepts*, 55, 51, emphasis in original.

108   Kai Erikson, "Notes on Trauma and Community," in *Trauma: Explorations in Memory*, ed. Cathy Caruth (Baltimore: Johns Hopkins University Press, 1995), 185.

109   Louis Althusser, "Ideology and Ideological State Apparatuses," in *Lenin and Philosophy* (New York: Monthly Review Press, 1971), 171.

110   Frantz Fanon, *Black Skin, White Masks*, trans. Charles Lam Markmann (New York: Grove Press, 1967), 110.

111   Fanon, *Black Skin, White Masks*, 113.

112   Fanon, *Black Skin, White Masks*, 111.

113   Lacan, *Four Fundamental Concepts*, 54, emphasis in original.

114   Fanon, *Black Skin, White Masks*, 110.

115   Lacan, *Four Fundamental Concepts*, 53–54.

116   Fanon, *Black Skin, White Masks*, 110.

117   Fanon, *Black Skin, White Masks*, 112.

118   Fanon, *Black Skin, White Masks*, 112.

119   Lacan, *Four Fundamental Concepts*, 52.

120   Fanon, *Black Skin, White Masks*, 113.

121   Fanon, *Black Skin, White Masks*, 112.

122   Althusser, "Ideology and Ideological State Apparatuses," 174.

123   Althusser, "Ideology and Ideological State Apparatuses," 173; Fanon, *Black Skin, White Masks*, 110.

124   Fanon, *Black Skin, White Masks*, 112, 113.

125   Fanon, *Black Skin, White Masks*, 115.

126   Fanon, *Black Skin, White Masks*, 123.

127   Charles Shepherdson, "The Intimate Alterity of the Real," *Postmodern Culture* 6, no. 3 (1996): ¶34, http://jefferson.village.virginia.edu/pmc/text-only/issue.596/shepherdson.596. For more on the two versions of the Real, see also Bruce Fink, *The Lacanian Subject: Between Language and Jouissance* (Princeton, N.J.: Princeton University Press, 1997).

128   Lacan, *Four Fundamental Concepts*, 51.

129   Lacan, *Four Fundamental Concepts*, 69.

130   Lacan, *Four Fundamental Concepts*, 61.

131   Lacan, *Four Fundamental Concepts*, 62, 61, 62.

132   Du Bois, "Conservation of Races," 7.

133   Du Bois, "Conservation of Races," 8.

134   Lacan, *Encore*, 85.

135   Outlaw, *Critical Social Theory*, 158, 141.

136   Lacan, *Four Fundamental Concepts*, 180.

137   Lacan, *Four Fundamental Concepts*, 144.

138   Du Bois, *Souls of Black Folk*, 10, 11, 15.

139   Du Bois, "Conservation of Races," 9.

140   Du Bois, *Souls of Black Folk*, 11.

141   Du Bois, *Souls of Black Folk*, 16, 11.

142   Du Bois, "Conservation of Races," 12.

143   Cathy Caruth, *Trauma: Explorations in Memory* (Baltimore: Johns Hopkins University Press, 1995), vii.

144 Du Bois, *Souls of Black Folk*, 11.

145 Erikson, "Notes on Trauma and Community," 195.

146 Du Bois, *Souls of Black Folk*, 16.

147 Ralph Ellison, "Richard Wright's Blues," in *Shadow and Act* (New York: Vintage Books, 1995), 78.

148 A telling example of Baldwin's reading is his novel *Giovanni's Room*, in which the unnamed protagonist is identified simply as a white man unable to come to terms with the realities of his personal and sexual identity because he is driven by the desire for an Eden-like state of innocence and purity. James Baldwin, *Giovanni's Room* (New York: Delta, 2000).

149 James Baldwin, "The Fire Next Time," in *Baldwin: Collected Essays* (New York: Library of America, 1998), 343.

150 For more on Baldwin and suffering, see Stanley Crouch, "Aunt Medea," in *Notes of a Hanging Judge: Essays and Reviews 1979–1989* (New York: Oxford University Press, 1990), 202–9.

151 Cornel West, *Democracy Matters: Winning the Fight against Imperialism* (New York: Penguin, 2005), 20.

152 Caruth, *Trauma*, vii.

153 Appiah, *In My Father's House*, 178.

154 Anna Stubblefield, *Ethics along the Color Line* (Ithaca, N.Y.: Cornell University Press, 2005), 176, 158, 161, 158.

155 Leroi Jones, *Black Music* (Boston: Da Capo Press, 1998), 190.

156 Lacan, *Encore*, 12; Lacan, *Four Fundamental Concepts*, 273.

157 Lacan, *Ethics of Psychoanalysis*, 132.

158 Lacan, *Four Fundamental Concepts*, 41.

Chapter 3

1 Henry Louis Gates Jr., "Introduction: 'Tell Me Sir, . . . What Is *Black* Literature?,'" *PMLA* 105, no. 1 (1990): 20.

2 Lacan, *Ethics of Psychoanalysis*, 10.

3 Lacan, *Ethics of Psychoanalysis*, 70, 71.

4 Toni Morrison, *Beloved* (New York: Plume, 1988), 36.

5 Morrison, *Beloved*, 36.

6 Morrison, *Beloved*, 35.

7 Morrison, *Beloved*, 36.

8 Morrison, *Beloved*, 5.

9 Lacan, *Ethics of Psychoanalysis*, 112.

10 Lacan, *Ethics of Psychoanalysis*, 261–62.

11 Lacan, *Ethics of Psychoanalysis*, 262.

12 Lacan, *Ethics of Psychoanalysis*, 262.

13 Quoted in Marsha Jean Darling, "In the Realm of Responsibility: A Conversation with Toni Morrison," *Women's Review of Books* 5, no. 6 (1988): 5.

14 Quoted in Darling, "In the Realm of Responsibility," 5.

15 Lacan, *Four Fundamental Concepts*, 276.

16 Lacan, *Ethics of Psychoanalysis*, 309, 265.

17   Lacan, *Ethics of Psychoanalysis*, 323.

18   Slavoj Žižek, *The Plague of Fantasies* (New York: Verso, 1997), 50.

19   Lacan, *Ethics of Psychoanalysis*, 71.

20   Lacan, *Ethics of Psychoanalysis*, 61.

21   Morrison, *Beloved*, 215.

22   Morrison, *Beloved*, 275.

23   Morrison, *Beloved*, 198.

24   Toni Morrison, "Home," in *The House That Race Built*, ed. Wahneema Lubiano (New York: Pantheon Books, 1997), 7.

25   Morrison, "Home," 8.

26   Lacan, *Ethics of Psychoanalysis*, 262.

27   Lacan, *Ethics of Psychoanalysis*, 261, 262.

28   Lacan, *Ethics of Psychoanalysis*, 262.

29   Quoted in Mervyn Rothstein, "Toni Morrison, in Her New Novel, Defends Women," *New York Times*, August 26, 1987, C17.

30   Morrison, *Beloved*, 251.

31   In *Risking Difference*, Jean Wyatt also links Beloved to the Real, stating that specifically the book's "last two pages put the exiled Beloved in the space of the real." Jean Wyatt, *Risking Difference: Identification, Race, and Community in Contemporary Fiction and Feminism* (New York: State University of New York Press, 2004), 182.

32   Morrison, *Beloved*, 42, 46.

33   Morrison, *Beloved*, 182, 193.

34   Morrison, *Beloved*, 163.

35   Lacan, *Four Fundamental Concepts*, 275.

36   Morrison, *Beloved*, 184, 272.

37   Lacan, *Ethics of Psychoanalysis*, 52.

38   Morrison, *Beloved*, 182.

39   Morrison, *Beloved*, 213; Lacan, *Ethics of Psychoanalysis*, 301.

40   Lacan, *Ethics of Psychoanalysis*, 301.

41   Lacan, *Ethics of Psychoanalysis*, 309.

42   Lacan, *Ethics of Psychoanalysis*, 303.

43   Lacan, *Ethics of Psychoanalysis*, 323.

44   Lacan, *Ethics of Psychoanalysis*, 319.

45   Lacan, *Ethics of Psychoanalysis*, 249.

46   Lacan, *Ethics of Psychoanalysis*, 281, 247.

47   Lacan, *Ethics of Psychoanalysis*, 263.

48   Lacan, *Ethics of Psychoanalysis*, 262.

49   Lacan, *Ethics of Psychoanalysis*, 263.

50   Lacan, *Ethics of Psychoanalysis*, 282. What Lacan refers to here as a "desire of death," or a "death instinct," is more fully elaborated as "the drive" in *Four Fundamental Concepts of Psychoanalysis*.

51   Lacan, *Ethics of Psychoanalysis*, 247, 281.

52   Lacan, *Ethics of Psychoanalysis*, 295.

53   Lacan, *Ethics of Psychoanalysis*, 270.

54   Morrison, *Beloved*, 83; Lacan, *Ethics of Psychoanalysis*, 278.

55   Lacan, *Ethics of Psychoanalysis*, 280.

56   Morrison, *Beloved*, 9.
57   Morrison, *Beloved*, 150.
58   Morrison, *Beloved*, 12.
59   Lacan, *Ethics of Psychoanalysis*, 247.
60   Lacan, *Ethics of Psychoanalysis*, 295.
61   Lacan, *Ethics of Psychoanalysis*, 239.
62   Lacan, *Ethics of Psychoanalysis*, 238.
63   Lacan, *Ethics of Psychoanalysis*, 309.
64   Morrison, *Beloved*, 256.
65   Morrison, *Beloved*, 256.
66   Morrison, *Beloved*, 256.
67   Morrison, *Beloved*, 92.
68   Morrison, *Beloved*, 256.
69   Morrison, *Beloved*, 258, 259, 256, 259.
70   Morrison, *Beloved*, 275.
71   Morrison, *Beloved*, 78, 273.
72   Lacan, *Ethics of Psychoanalysis*, 134.
73   Morrison, *Beloved*, 191.
74   Morrison, *Beloved*, 190.
75   Morrison, *Beloved*, 191.
76   Morrison, *Beloved*, 191.
77   Morrison, *Beloved*, 193.
78   In *Quiet as It's Kept*, J. Brooks Bouson reads this moment in the text as emblematic of a traumatic "shaming" to which African Americans are continually submitted. For Bouson, the scene displays the "dirtying power of racist discourse, which constructs white identity as racially and biologically pure and black identity as impure or dirty." J. Brooks Bouson, *Quiet as It's Kept: Shame, Trauma, and Race in the Novels of Toni Morrison* (New York: State University of New York Press, 2000), 146. My own reading suggests that shame, as a source of trauma, should be understood within the larger framework of the relation between the Other's signifier and the subject's lack.
79   Morrison, *Beloved*, 193.
80   Morrison, *Beloved*, 193.
81   Morrison, *Beloved*, 193.
82   Shepherdson, "Intimate Alterity of the Real," ¶46.
83   Shepherdson, "Intimate Alterity of the Real," ¶46.
84   Morrison, *Beloved*, 188.
85   This scene may be read as a moment in which Sethe, through the eyes of schoolteacher, experiences the Lacanian gaze, the look of the Other through which we apprehend ourselves as lack. In *Subversive Voices*, Evelyn Schreiber uses this concept to read *Beloved* as enabling a process wherein "marginalized blacks and women confront the gaze and become the gaze for dominant white males," a process through which "cultural changes can occur." Evelyn Jaffe Schreiber, *Subversive Voices: Eroticizing the Other in William Faulkner and Toni Morrison* (Knoxville: University of Tennessee Press, 2001), 17. My suggestion that Sethe's psyche is here almost shattered by her encounter with schoolteacher's gaze confirms Schreiber's own sense that such change is "extremely difficult" to bring about (16).

86   Morrison, *Beloved*, 162.

87   Morrison, *Beloved*, 163.

88   Morrison, *Beloved*, 162.

89   Morrison, *Beloved*, 163; Lacan, *Ethics of Psychoanalysis*, 134.

90   Morrison, *Beloved*, 162.

91   Morrison, *Beloved*, 162.

92   Morrison, *Beloved*, 268, 270, 162.

93   Lacan, *Four Fundamental Concepts*, 221, 212.

94   Lacan, *Four Fundamental Concepts*, 212.

95   A number of theorists have read Sethe's act as a form of maternal excess, a blurring of the limits between mother and child. Jill Matus, for example, points to an altered "genealogy of mothering under slavery," one that, first, produces in Sethe a "maternal subjectivity," or an "identification" with the mother who leaves her behind while attempting to run away from slavery, and, second, urges Sethe to "replay[]" in the murder "her longing for a mother who would similarly protect and stay with her." Jill Matus, *Toni Morrison: Contemporary World Writers* (Manchester, U.K.: Manchester University Press, 1998), 111. Though compelling, such readings ground Sethe's act primarily in the Imaginary, missing the Lacanian recognition that the mother's absence merely marks the place of that more primal lack, as Real, constituted in subjectivity.

96   Morrison, *Beloved*, 200.

97   Morrison, *Beloved*, 163.

98   Lacan, *Four Fundamental Concepts*, 227, emphasis in original.

99   Lacan, *Four Fundamental Concepts*, 213, emphasis in original.

100   Morrison, *Beloved*, 201.

101   Morrison, *Beloved*, 262.

102   Morrison, *Beloved*, 262.

103   Lacan, *Ethics of Psychoanalysis*, 321.

104   Lacan, *Ethics of Psychoanalysis*, 320.

105   Lacan, *Ethics of Psychoanalysis*, 315.

106   Lacan, *Ethics of Psychoanalysis*, 323, 319.

107   Here I am in agreement with Frances Restuccia's argument in *Amorous Acts* that "recent claims made by Žižek and others in support of an 'ethics of jouissance' [an ethics grounded on the drive, instead of on desire] are based on a misreading of Lacan." Frances Restuccia, *Amorous Acts: Lacanian Ethics in Modernism, Film, and Queer Theory* (Stanford: Stanford University Press, 2006), xiii.

108   My argument here is influenced by Jean Wyatt's reading of Denver's relation to the mirror stage in her essay "Giving Body to the Word: The Maternal Symbolic in Toni Morrison's *Beloved*," *PMLA* 108, no. 3 (1993): 474–88.

109   Morrison, *Beloved*, 209, 12.

110   Morrison, *Beloved*, 206, 205.

111   Morrison, *Beloved*, 205.

112   Morrison, *Beloved*, 209.

113   Morrison, *Beloved*, 208.

114   Morrison, *Beloved*, 208, 121.

115   Lacan, *Ethics of Psychoanalysis*, 321.

116   Morrison, *Beloved*, 4, 205, 14.
117   Morrison, *Beloved*, 207.
118   Lacan, *Ethics of Psychoanalysis*, 319.
119   Lacan, *Four Fundamental Concepts*, 235.
120   Lacan, *Four Fundamental Concepts*, 232, 276.
121   Lacan, *Four Fundamental Concepts*, 276.
122   Lacan, *Ethics of Psychoanalysis*, 300.
123   Lacan, *Ethics of Psychoanalysis*, 195.
124   Morrison, *Beloved*, 243.
125   Morrison, *Beloved*, 243.
126   Morrison, *Beloved*, 242.
127   Morrison, *Beloved*, 243.
128   Morrison, *Beloved*, 242, 243.
129   Morrison, *Beloved*, 243.
130   Wyatt also makes note of Baby Suggs' role in bringing Denver to the Symbolic. But
      Wyatt overvalues the importance of Baby Suggs' gender and reads too literally the
      term "paternal metaphor," using Baby Suggs as further proof for her argument that
      the text presents the radical notion of a "*Maternal Symbolic*" that is distinct from
      Lacan's. Wyatt, "Giving Body to the Word," 475, emphasis in original.
131   Morrison, *Beloved*, 244.
132   Morrison, *Beloved*, 244.
133   Morrison, *Beloved*, 244.
134   Morrison, *Beloved*, 245.
135   Lacan, *Ethics of Psychoanalysis*, 301.
136   Morrison, *Beloved*, 248.
137   Morrison, *Beloved*, 248.
138   Morrison, *Beloved*, 253.
139   Morrison, *Beloved*, 258.
140   Morrison, *Beloved*, 259.
141   Lacan, *Ethics of Psychoanalysis*, 32.
142   Lacan, *Ethics of Psychoanalysis*, 32.
143   Morrison, *Beloved*, 261.
144   Lacan, *Ethics of Psychoanalysis*, 244.
145   Lacan, *Ethics of Psychoanalysis*, 252.
146   Lacan, *Ethics of Psychoanalysis*, 323.
147   Lacan, *Ethics of Psychoanalysis*, 56.
148   Lacan, *Ethics of Psychoanalysis*, 56.
149   Lacan, *Ethics of Psychoanalysis*, 56.
150   Lacan, *Ethics of Psychoanalysis*, 56.
151   Lacan, *Four Fundamental Concepts*, 273.
152   Lacan, *Four Fundamental Concepts*, 270. Though Greg Forter's "Against Melancho-
      lia" urges a strict distinction between historical and constitutive losses, my argument
      suggests that the trauma of slavery is both linked to and extricable from the Real
      lack of subjectivity. Calling for a focus on historical specificity, Forter uses the work
      of Eric Santner and Judith Butler to argue that "to absorb historical losses—which
      are contingent and therefore resistible—into structural losses—which are inevitable

and therefore irresistible—is to vacate the field of ethical choice and political action altogether": it is to make "resistance to the forces impelling those losses impossible." Greg Forter, "Against Melancholia: Contemporary Mourning Theory, Fitzgerald's *The Great Gatsby*, and the Politics of Unfinished Grief," *differences: A Journal of Feminist Cultural Studies* 14 (2003): 137, 143. My reading of *Beloved*, however, presents the process of disarticulating the historical losses of slavery from the ahistorical lack of subjectivity as a political and ethical imperative for African Americans. And as contemporary African Americans have not lived through this past that claims many of them, what is salutary is not their engagement with the historical specificities of slavery but rather an individualized investigation of their current psychic relation to the past.

153   Morrison, *Beloved*, 273.
154   Morrison, *Beloved*, 273.
155   Lacan, *Ethics of Psychoanalysis*, 7.
156   Morrison, *Beloved*, 272–73.

Chapter 4

1   Jacques Lacan, *The Triumph of Religion*, trans. Bruce Fink (Boston: Polity Press, 2013), 22.
2   Lacan, "Desire and the Interpretation of Desire in *Hamlet*," 20, 41.
3   Lacan, "Desire," 45, 46.
4   Lacan, "Desire," 16.
5   Jacques Lacan, "The Neurotic's Individual Myth," *Psychoanalytic Quarterly* 48, no. 3 (1979): 408.
6   Lacan, "Desire," 42.
7   Jacques Lacan, "The Signification of the Phallus," in *Écrits: The First Complete Edition in English*, trans. Bruce Fink (New York: Norton, 2006), 580.
8   Lacan, "Signification of the Phallus," 579.
9   Lacan, "The Signification of the Phallus," 579; Lacan, "Subversion of the Subject," 687; Lacan, "Signification of the Phallus," 579.
10   Lacan, "Signification of the Phallus," 579.
11   Lacan, "Signification of the Phallus," 579.
12   Lacan, "Signification of the Phallus," 580.
13   Lacan, "Subversion of the Subject," 689; Lacan, *Encore*, 14.
14   Lacan, "Subversion of the Subject," 698.
15   Lacan, "Desire," 51.
16   Lacan, "Desire," 28.
17   Lacan, "Desire," 15.
18   Lacan, "Subversion of the Subject," 700.
19   Lacan, "Subversion of the Subject," 700.
20   Lacan, "Desire," 48, 16.
21   Lacan, "Signification of the Phallus," 579; Lacan, *Encore*, 81.
22   Lacan, "Signification of the Phallus," 581.
23   Lacan, "Desire," 51; Lacan, "Subversion of the Subject," 696–97.
24   Lacan, "Desire," 15.

25   Lacan, "Desire," 15.

26   William Shakespeare, *Hamlet*, 2nd ed., ed. Cyrus Hoy (New York: Norton, 1992), Act I Scene V lines 187–88.

27   Lacan, "Desire," 17.

28   Lacan, "Desire," 43.

29   Lacan, "Desire," 40.

30   Lacan, "Desire," 37, 37, 38.

31   Lacan, "Desire," 38.

32   Lacan, "Desire," 38, 39.

33   Ralph Ellison, *Invisible Man* (New York: Vintage International, 1995), 3.

34   Jacques Lacan, *On the Names-of-the-Father*, trans. Bruce Fink (Boston: Polity Press, 2013), 9; Ellison, *Invisible Man*, 3.

35   Ellison, *Invisible Man*, 4.

36   Ellison, *Invisible Man*, 8.

37   Ellison, *Invisible Man*, 8.

38   Ellison, *Invisible Man*, 9.

39   Ellison, *Invisible Man*, 10.

40   Ellison, *Invisible Man*, 10.

41   Ellison, *Invisible Man*, 11.

42   Ellison, *Invisible Man*, 11.

43   Ellison, *Invisible Man*, 11.

44   Ellison, *Invisible Man*, 10.

45   Ellison, *Invisible Man*, 11.

46   Ellison, *Invisible Man*, 13.

47   Ellison, *Invisible Man*, 14, 13, 14.

48   Ellison, *Invisible Man*, 13.

49   Ellison, *Invisible Man*, 5.

50   Ellison, *Invisible Man*, 16.

51   Ellison, *Invisible Man*, 16, 17, 16.

52   Shakespeare, *Hamlet*, Act I Scene V lines 7 (revenge) and 2 (mark); Ellison, *Invisible Man*.

53   Lacan, "Desire," 12, 13.

54   Lacan, "Desire," 31, 29.

55   Ellison, *Invisible Man*, 16.

56   Ellison, *Invisible Man*, 18.

57   Ellison, *Invisible Man*, 17.

58   Ellison, *Invisible Man*, 17.

59   Lacan, "Desire," 30; Ellison, *Invisible Man*, 25.

60   Ellison, *Invisible Man*, 19.

61   Ellison, *Invisible Man*, 19.

62   Lacan, "Signification of the Phallus," 581.

63   Lacan, "Signification of the Phallus," 582.

64   Lacan, "Signification of the Phallus," 582.

65   Ellison, *Invisible Man*, 19.

66   Ellison, *Invisible Man*, 19.

67   Ellison, *Invisible Man*, 19.

68   Ellison, *Invisible Man*, 19.

69   Ellison, *Invisible Man*, 30.

70   Ellison, *Invisible Man*, 33.

71   Ellison, *Invisible Man*, 39. The chapter thus may be read as a response to focuses upon only the social and the economical that extend all the way to Washington's assertion to whites that "in all things that are purely social we can be as separate as the fingers, yet one as the hand in all things essential to mutual progress." Booker T. Washington, *Up from Slavery* (New York: Airmont Books, 1967), 136.

72   Ellison, *Invisible Man*, 41.

73   Ellison, *Invisible Man*, 42.

74   Ellison, *Invisible Man*, 45.

75   Ellison, *Invisible Man*, 43.

76   Ellison, *Invisible Man*, 43.

77   Jacques Lacan, *Television: A Challenge to the Psychoanalytic Establishment*, trans. Denis Hollier, Rosalind Krauss, and Annette Michelson (New York: Norton, 1990), 32.

78   Ellison, *Invisible Man*, 42, 43, 42.

79   Ellison, *Invisible Man*, 50.

80   Ellison, *Invisible Man*, 51.

81   Ellison, *Invisible Man*, 51.

82   Ellison, *Invisible Man*, 49.

83   Lacan, *Encore*, 51.

84   Lacan, *Encore*, 59. This phallic *jouissance* is what I describe as *surplus jouissance* in chapter 1.

85   Lacan, *Encore*, 55, 59, 76, 59.

86   Lacan, *On the Names-of-the-Father*, 74.

87   Lacan, *On the Names-of-the-Father*, 74.

88   See especially section IV of Sigmund Freud's *Totem and Taboo*, trans. James Strachey (New York: Norton, 1989).

89   Jacques Lacan, "Presentation on Transference," in *Ècrits: The First Complete Edition in English*, trans. Bruce Fink (New York: Norton, 2006), 182.

90   Lacan, "Desire," 52.

91   Lacan, *Encore*, 100.

92   Ellison, *Invisible Man*, 76.

93   Lacan, *Encore*, 59.

94   Lacan, *Encore*, 51, 112.

95   Lacan, "Desire," 48.

96   Ellison, *Invisible Man*, 37.

97   Ellison, *Invisible Man*, 42.

98   Ellison, *Invisible Man*, 53.

99   Ellison, *Invisible Man*, 53.

100   Ellison, *Invisible Man*, 54.

101   Ellison, *Invisible Man*, 54.

102   Lacan, *Encore*, 71; Lacan, "Signification of the Phallus," 580.

103   Ellison, *Invisible Man*, 56.

104   Ellison, *Invisible Man*, 56.

105   Ellison, *Invisible Man*, 56.

106   Ellison, *Invisible Man*, 56, 54.

107   Ellison, *Invisible Man*, 57.

108   Ellison, *Invisible Man*, 57, 58.

109   For more on this association, see Ida B. Wells-Barnett, *On Lynching* (Salem, N.H.: Ayer, 1991).

110   Ellison, *Invisible Man*, 59.

111   Ellison, *Invisible Man*, 59, 60, emphasis in original.

112   Ellison, *Invisible Man*, 60.

113   Ellison, *Invisible Man*, 60.

114   Ellison, *Invisible Man*, 60.

115   Ellison, *Invisible Man*, 60.

116   Ellison, *Invisible Man*, 60.

117   Ellison, *Invisible Man*, 66.

118   Ellison, *Invisible Man*, 66.

119   Ellison, *Invisible Man*, 66.

120   Ellison, *Invisible Man*, 55.

121   Ellison, *Invisible Man*, 55, emphasis in original.

122   Ralph Ellison, *Juneteenth* (New York: Vintage International, 2000), 296.

123   Ellison, *Juneteenth*, 292, 290.

124   Ellison, *Juneteenth*, 296–97.

125   Ellison, *Juneteenth*, 289, 288.

126   Ellison, *Juneteenth*, 288, 287.

127   Lacan, "Neurotic's Individual Myth," 422.

128   Lacan, "Neurotic's Individual Myth," 423.

129   Lacan, "Neurotic's Individual Myth," 423.

130   Lacan, "Desire," 51.

131   Lacan, "Desire," 16.

132   Lacan, "Desire," 36.

133   Lacan, "Desire," 36.

134   Lacan, "Subversion of the Subject," 700.

135   Lacan, "Subversion of the Subject," 700.

136   Lacan, "Subversion of the Subject," 700.

137   Lacan, "Subversion of the Subject," 700.

138   Lacan, "Subversion of the Subject," 698.

139   Lacan, "Neurotic's Individual Myth," 424, 423.

140   Lacan, "Neurotic's Individual Myth," 423.

141   Lacan, *On the Names-of-the-Father*, 77.

142   Ellison, *Juneteenth*, 303, 302.

143   Ellison, *Juneteenth*, 308.

144   Ellison, *Juneteenth*, 308.

145   Ellison, *Juneteenth*, 121, 128.

146   Ellison, *Juneteenth*, 129.

147   Ellison, *Juneteenth*, 129.

148   Ellison, *Juneteenth*, 162.

149   Lacan, "Desire," 17; Lacan, *Four Fundamental Concepts*, 183.

150 Ellison, *Juneteenth*, 162.
151 Ellison, *Juneteenth*, 163, 162.
152 Ellison, *Juneteenth*, 162.
153 Ellison, *Juneteenth*, 161, 160.
154 Ellison, *Juneteenth*, 162.
155 Lacan, "Subversion of the Subject," 697.
156 Jacques Lacan, *The Seminar of Jacques Lacan Book I: Freud's Papers on Technique 1953–1954*, trans. John Forrester (New York: Norton, 1991), 221.
157 Lacan, *Four Fundamental Concepts*, 182; Lacan, *Freud's Papers on Technique*, 220.
158 Ellison, *Juneteenth*, 163.
159 Ellison, *Juneteenth*, 163.
160 Lacan, *Four Fundamental Concepts*, 185.
161 Lacan, *Freud's Papers on Technique*, 222.
162 Jacques Lacan, "On a Question Prior to Any Possible Treatment of Psychosis," in *Ècrits: The First Complete Edition in English*, trans. Bruce Fink (New York: Norton, 2006), 463.
163 Lacan, "Question Prior to Treatment of Psychosis," 463; Lacan, *Triumph of Religion*, 25.
164 Lacan, *Freud's Papers on Technique*, 221.
165 Lacan, "Desire," 15; Lacan, *Freud's Papers on Technique*, 221.
166 Lacan, *Freud's Papers on Technique*, 221.
167 Lacan, *Freud's Papers on Technique*, 221, 220, 221.
168 Ellison, *Juneteenth*, 117.
169 Ellison, *Juneteenth*, 153.
170 Ellison, *Juneteenth*, 148, 149.
171 Ellison, *Juneteenth*, 153, 148.
172 Lacan, "Subversion of the Subject," 699. Lacan associates this kind of slippage with homosexuality, which he sees as emerging sometimes as a subcategory of perversion. Lacan, *Freud's Papers on Technique*, 221. For more on homosexuality and the mOther, also see Ellie Ragland, "Lacan and the Hommosexuelle: 'A Love Letter,'" in *Homosexuality and Psychoanalysis*, ed. Tim Dean and Christopher Lane (Chicago: University of Chicago Press, 2001), 98–119.
173 Ellison, *Juneteenth*, 202, 178.
174 Ellison, *Juneteenth*, 256.
175 Ellison, *Juneteenth*, 260.
176 Ellison, *Juneteenth*, 110, 223.
177 Ellison, *Juneteenth*, 233.
178 Ellison, *Juneteenth*, 190, 191.
179 Ellison, *Juneteenth*, 185, 186.
180 Ellison, *Juneteenth*, 191.
181 Lacan, *Freud's Papers on Technique*, 221; Ellison, *Juneteenth*, 191, 192.
182 Lacan, *Freud's Papers on Technique*, 221.
183 Ellison, *Juneteenth*, 193.
184 Ellison, *Juneteenth*, 193.
185 Ellison, *Juneteenth*, 193.
186 Ellison, *Juneteenth*, 162, 6.

187 Ellison, *Juneteenth*, 162.
188 Lacan, *Freud's Papers on Technique*, 221.
189 Ellison, *Juneteenth*, 115, 116.
190 Ellison, *Juneteenth*, 265.
191 Ellison, *Juneteenth*, 201.
192 Ellison, *Juneteenth*, 19, 257.
193 Ellison, *Juneteenth*, 264.
194 Ellison, *Juneteenth*, 257.
195 Ellison, *Juneteenth*, 257.
196 Lacan, "Desire," 12.
197 Ellison, *Juneteenth*, 282.
198 Ellison, *Juneteenth*, 282, 280, 281.
199 Ellison, *Juneteenth*, 280.
200 Lacan, *Triumph of Religion*, 77.
201 Ellison, *Juneteenth*, 268.
202 Ellison, *Juneteenth*, 270.
203 Ellison, *Juneteenth*, 271.
204 Ellison, *Juneteenth*, 283.
205 Ellison, *Juneteenth*, 280.
206 Barack Obama, "Second Inaugural Address," *NBC News*, January 21, 2013, http://www.nbcnews.com/video/nbc-news/50535269.
207 Obama, "Second Inaugural Address."

Conclusion

1 Lacan, *Triumph of Religion*, 74; Lacan, "Subversion of the Subject," 686.
2 Lacan, "Signification of the Phallus," 581.
3 Lacan, *Encore*, 24.
4 Lacan, *Encore*, 32.
5 Lacan, *On the Names-of-the-Father*, 24, emphasis in original.
6 Lacan, *Triumph of Religion*, 16; Lacan, *On the Names-of-the-Father*, 71.
7 Lacan, *Encore*, 99.
8 Lacan, *On the Names-of-the-Father*, 25.
9 Lacan, "Instance of the Letter," 423.
10 Lacan, *Four Fundamental Concepts*, 218.
11 Du Bois, *Souls of Black Folk*, 11.
12 Ralph Ellison, "The World and the Jug," in *Shadow and Act* (New York: Vintage Books, 1995), 140.
13 Ellison, "World and the Jug," 111, 116.
14 Ellison, "World and the Jug," 116.
15 Ellison, "World and the Jug," 140.
16 Ellison, "World and the Jug," 140.
17 Ellison, "World and the Jug," 140.
18 Lacan, "Subversion of the Subject," 699, 689.
19 Lacan, *Four Fundamental Concepts*, 219, 224.

20   Lacan, "Subversion of the Subject," 691; Lacan, *Four Fundamental Concepts*, 298; Lacan, "Subversion of the Subject," 690.
21   Lacan, "Subversion of the Subject," 690.
22   Lacan, *On the Names-of-the-Father*, 46.
23   Lacan, "Le Sinthome," 42.
24   Lacan, "Le Sinthome," 42, 4.
25   Lacan, "Le Sinthome," 6.
26   Lacan, "Le Sinthome," 1, 3.
27   Lacan, "Le Sinthome," 15, 16.
28   Lacan, *Four Fundamental Concepts*, 149.
29   Lacan, "Subversion of the Subject," 693.
30   Lacan, "Subversion of the Subject," 693; Lacan, "Le Sinthome," 42.
31   Lacan, "Le Sinthome," 41.
32   Lacan, *On the Names-of-the-Father*, 70.
33   Lacan, "Le Sinthome," 50.
34   Lacan, *Encore*, 121.
35   Lacan, *Four Fundamental Concepts*, 273, 243.
36   Lacan, *Four Fundamental Concepts*, 274.

Bibliography

Alexander, Michelle. *The New Jim Crow: Mass Incarceration in the Age of Colorblindness*. New York: New Press, 2012.

Althusser, Louis. "Ideology and Ideological State Apparatuses." In *Lenin and Philosophy*, 127–86. New York: Monthly Review Press, 1971.

Appiah, Anthony K. *In My Father's House: Africa in the Philosophy of Culture*. New York: Oxford University Press, 1992.

Baker, Houston A., Jr. *Modernism and the Harlem Renaissance*. Chicago: University of Chicago Press, 1989.

———. *Turning South Again: Re-thinking Modernism / Re-reading Booker T.* Durham, N.C.: Duke University Press, 2001.

Baldwin, James. "The Fire Next Time." In *Baldwin: Collected Essays*. New York: Library of America, 1998.

———. *Giovanni's Room*. New York: Delta, 2000.

Bernstein, Robin. *Racial Innocence: Performing American Childhood from Slavery to Civil Rights*. New York: New York University Press, 2011.

Bonilla-Silva, Eduardo. *Racism without Racists: Color-Blind Racism and the Persistence of Racial Inequality in the United States*. 3rd ed. Lanham, Md.: Rowman & Littlefield, 2009.

Bouson, J. Brooks. *Quiet as It's Kept: Shame, Trauma, and Race in the Novels of Toni Morrison*. New York: State University of New York Press, 2000.

Brown, William Wells. "Narrative of the Life and Escape of William Wells Brown." In *Clotel; or The President's Daughter*. New York: Penguin, 2004.

Butler, Judith. *Bodies That Matter: On the Discursive Limits of Sex*. New York: Routledge, 1993.

Caruth, Cathy. *Trauma: Explorations in Memory*. Baltimore: Johns Hopkins University Press, 1995.

Christian, Barbara. "The Race for Theory." *Cultural Critique* 6 (1987): 51–63.

Corey, Angela. Quoted in "What's Next in the Florida Loud Music Killing Case." *Washington Post*, February 18, 2014. http://www.washingtonpost.com/news/post-nation/wp/2014/02/18/whats-next-in-the-florida-loud-music-killing-case/.

Crouch, Stanley. "Aunt Medea." In *Notes of a Hanging Judge: Essays and Reviews 1979–1989*. New York: Oxford University Press, 1990.

Dalal, Farhad. *Race, Colour and the Processes of Racialization: New Perspectives from Group Analysis, Psychoanalysis and Sociology*. New York: Routledge, 2002.

Darling, Marsha Jean. "In the Realm of Responsibility: A Conversation with Toni Morrison." *Women's Review of Books* 5, no. 6 (1988): 5–6.

Derrida, Jacques. *Writing and Difference*. Translated by Alan Bass. Chicago: University of Chicago Press, 1978.

Dixon, Melvin. "Singing Swords: The Literary Legacy of Slavery." In *The Slave's Narrative*, edited by Charles T. Davis and Henry Louis Gates Jr., 298–318. New York: Oxford University Press, 1985.

Douglass, Frederick. *Narrative of the Life of Frederick Douglass, An American Slave, Written by Himself*. Edited by William L. Andrews and William S. McFeely. New York: Norton, 1997.

Du Bois, W. E. B. "The Conservation of Races." *Occasional Papers, No. 2*, 5–15. Washington, D.C.: American Negro Academy, 1897.

———. "Criteria of Negro Art." In *The Crisis: A Record of the Darker Races*. Authorized reprint ed. Vol. 32, no. 6. October 1926, 290–97. New York: Arno Press, 1969.

———. *Dusk of Dawn: An Essay Toward an Autobiography of a Race Concept*. New York: Schocken Books, 1971.

————. "Of Our Spiritual Strivings." In Du Bois, *The Souls of Black Folk*. Edited by Henry Louis Gates Jr. and Terri Hume Oliver. New York: Norton, 1999.

————. "The Problem of Amusement." *Southern Workman* 27 (1897): 181–84.

————. "The Religion of the American Negro." In *The New World: A Quarterly Review of Religion, Ethics and Theology*. Vol. 9. December 1900. Boston: Houghton, Mifflin, 1900.

————. "Returning Soldiers." In *The Crisis: A Record of the Darker Races*. Authorized reprint ed. Vol. 18, no. 1. May 1919, 13–14. New York: Arno Press, 1969.

————. *The Souls of Black Folk*. Edited by Henry Louis Gates Jr. and Terri Hume Oliver. New York: Norton, 1999.

Dunn, Michael. Michael Dunn Trial—Day 5—Part 2 (Dunn Testifies). http://topic.ibnlive.in.com/ajit-pawar/videos/michael-dunn-trial-day -5-part-2-dunn-testifies-TLdjAJiOqoE-1881933.html.

————. Web Extra: Letters written by Michael Dunn from jail. http://www .firstcoastnews.com/story/news/local/michael-dunn-trial/2014/01/ 24/michael-dunn-jail-letters-jordan-davis/4836401/.

Ellison, Ralph. *Invisible Man*. New York: Vintage International, 1995.

————. *Juneteenth*. New York: Vintage International, 2000.

————. "Richard Wright's Blues." In *Shadow and Act*, 77–94. New York: Vintage Books, 1995.

————. *Shadow and Act*. New York: Vintage Books, 1995.

————. "The World and the Jug." In *Shadow and Act*, 107–43. New York: Vintage Books, 1995.

Erikson, Kai. "Notes on Trauma and Community." In *Trauma: Explorations in Memory*, edited by Cathy Caruth, 183–99. Baltimore: Johns Hopkins University Press, 1995.

Eyerman, Ron. *Cultural Trauma: Slavery and the Formation of African American Identity*. Cambridge: Cambridge University Press, 2001.

Fanon, Frantz. *Black Skin, White Masks*. Translated by Charles Lam Markmann. New York: Grove Press, 1967.

Fink, Bruce. *The Lacanian Subject: Between Language and Jouissance*. Princeton, N.J.: Princeton University Press, 1997.

Forter, Greg. "Against Melancholia: Contemporary Mourning Theory, Fitzgerald's *The Great Gatsby*, and the Politics of Unfinished Grief." *differences: A Journal of Feminist Cultural Studies* 14 (2003): 134–70.

Freud, Sigmund. *Reflections on War and Death*. Translated by Dr. A. A. Brill and Alfred B. Kuttner. New York: Moffat, Yard, 1918.

———. *Totem and Taboo*. Translated by James Strachey. New York: Norton, 1989.

Gates, Henry Louis, Jr. "American Letters, African Voices: History of African American Authors." *New York Times Book Review*, December 1, 1996.

———. *Black Literature and Literary Theory*. New York: Routledge, 1984.

———. "Introduction: 'Tell Me Sir, . . . What Is *Black* Literature?' " *PMLA* 105, no. 1 (1990): 11–22.

———. *Loose Canons: Notes on the Culture Wars*. New York: Oxford University Press, 1992.

Gordon-Reed, Annette. *The Hemingses of Monticello: An American Family*. New York: Norton, 2008.

Gronniosaw, James Albert Ukawsaw. "A Narrative of the most Remarkable Particulars in the Life of James Albert Ukawsaw Gronniosaw, An African Prince, As Related by HIMSELF." In *Unchained Voices: An Anthology of Black Authors in the English-Speaking World of the Eighteenth Century*, edited by Vincent Caretta, 32–58. Lexington: University Press of Kentucky, 1996.

Hartigan, John, Jr. *What Can You Say? America's National Conversation on Race*. Stanford, Calif.: Stanford University Press, 2010.

Hartman, Saidiya V. *Scenes of Subjection: Terror, Slavery, and Self-Making in Nineteenth-Century America*. New York: Oxford University Press, 1997.

Holder, Eric. "Attorney General Eric Holder's Remarks on Trayvon Martin at NAACP Convention (full text)." *Washington Post*, July 16, 2013. http://www.washingtonpost.com/politics/attorney-general-eric -holders-remarks-on-trayvon-martin-at-naacp-convention-full -text/2013/07/16/dec82f88-ee5a-11e2-a1f9-ea873b7e0424_story .html.

Jefferson, Thomas. *Notes on the State of Virginia*. In *Writings*, 123–325. New York: Library of America, 1984.

Johnson, Walter. *Soul by Soul: Life Inside the Antebellum Slave Market*. Cambridge, Mass.: Harvard University Press, 1999.

Jones, Leroi. *Black Music*. Boston: Da Capo Press, 1998.

Kennedy, Randall. *The Persistence of the Color Line: Racial Politics and the Obama Presidency*. New York: Vintage Books, 2011.

Lacan, Jacques. "Desire and the Interpretation of Desire in *Hamlet*." In "Literature and Psychoanalysis: The Question of Reading Otherwise." Special issue, *Yale French Studies*, nos. 55/56 (1977): 11–52.

———. "The Instance of the Letter in the Unconscious." In *Ècrits: The First Complete Edition in English*, translated by Bruce Fink, 412–41. New York: Norton, 2006.

———. "Kant with Sade." In *Ècrits: The First Complete Edition in English*, translated by Bruce Fink, 645–68. New York: Norton, 2006.

———. "The Mirror Stage as Formative of the *I* Function as Revealed in Psychoanalytic Experience." In *Ècrits: The First Complete Edition in English*, translated by Bruce Fink, 75–81. New York: Norton, 2006.

———. "The Neurotic's Individual Myth." *Psychoanalytic Quarterly* 48, no. 3 (1979): 405–25.

———. "On a Question Prior to Any Possible Treatment of Psychosis." In *Ècrits: The First Complete Edition in English*, translated by Bruce Fink, 445–88. New York: Norton, 2006.

———. *On the Names-of-the-Father*. Translated by Bruce Fink. Boston: Polity Press, 2013.

———. "Presentation on Transference." In *Ècrits: The First Complete Edition in English*, translated by Bruce Fink, 176–85. New York: Norton, 2006.

———. *The Seminar of Jacques Lacan Book I: Freud's Papers on Technique 1953–1954*. Translated by John Forrester. New York: Norton, 1991.

———. *The Seminar of Jacques Lacan Book III: The Psychoses*. Translated by Russell Grigg. New York: Norton, 1997.

———. *The Seminar of Jacques Lacan Book VII: The Ethics of Psychoanalysis*. Translated by Dennis Porter. New York: Norton, 1997.

———. *The Seminar of Jacques Lacan Book XI: The Four Fundamental Concepts of Psychoanalysis*. Translated by Alan Sheridan. New York: Norton, 1998.

———. *The Seminar of Jacques Lacan Book XVII: The Other Side of Psychoanalysis*. Translated by Russell Grigg. New York: Norton, 2007.

———. *The Seminar of Jacques Lacan Book XX: Encore*. Translated by Bruce Fink. New York: Norton, 1998.

———. "The Signification of the Phallus." In *Ècrits: The First Complete Edition in English*, translated by Bruce Fink, 575–84. New York: Norton, 2006.

———. "Le Sinthome." Translated by Luke Thurston. *Ornicar?* 6–11 (1976–1977): 1–65.

———. "The Subversion of the Subject and the Dialectic of Desire in the Freudian Unconscious." In *Ècrits: The First Complete Edition in English*, translated by Bruce Fink, 671–702. New York: Norton, 2006.

———. *Television: A Challenge to the Psychoanalytic Establishment*. Translated by Denis Hollier, Rosalind Krauss, and Annette Michelson. New York: Norton, 1990.

———. *The Triumph of Religion*. Translated by Bruce Fink. Boston: Polity Press, 2013.

Levine, Lawrence W. "Slave Songs and Slave Consciousness." In *American Negro Slavery: A Modern Reader*, 3rd ed., edited by Allen Weinstein, Frank Otto Gatell, and David Sarasohn, 143–72. New York: Oxford University Press, 1979.

Li, Stephanie. *Signifying without Specifying: Racial Discourse in the Age of Obama*. New Brunswick, N.J.: Rutgers University Press, 2012.

Marx, Karl. *Theories of Surplus Value*. Vols. 1–3. New York: Prometheus Books, 2000.

Massey, Douglas S., and Nancy A. Denton. *American Apartheid: Segregation and the Making of the Underclass*. Cambridge, Mass.: Harvard University Press, 1993.

Matus, Jill. *Toni Morrison: Contemporary World Writers*. Manchester, U.K.: Manchester University Press, 1998.

Miller, Jacques-Alain. "Extimité." In *Lacanian Theory of Discourse*, edited by Mark Bracher, Marshall W. Alcorn, Ronald J. Corthell, and Françoise Massardier-Kenney, 74–87. New York: New York University Press, 1994.

Morrison, Toni. *Beloved*. New York: Plume, 1988.

———. "Home." In *The House That Race Built*, edited by Wahneema Lubiano, 3–12. New York: Pantheon Books, 1997.

Obama, Barack. Quoted in "Obama: 'If I Had a Son, He'd Look Like Trayvon': President Obama Addresses the Trayvon Martin Shooting from a White House Rose Garden Event." *NBC News*, March 23, 2012. http://www.nbcnews.com/video/nbc-news/46834310#46834310.

———. "Remarks by the President on Trayvon Martin." WhiteHouse
.gov. July 19, 2013. http://www.whitehouse.gov/the-press-office/2013/
07/19/remarks-president-trayvon-martin.

———. "Second Inaugural Address." *NBC News*, January 21, 2013.
http://www.nbcnews.com/video/nbc-news/50535269.

Olney, James. " 'I Was Born': Slave Narratives, Their Status as Autobiography and as Literature." In *The Slave's Narrative*, edited by Charles T.
Davis and Henry Louis Gates Jr., 148–74. New York: Oxford University Press, 1985.

Outlaw, Lucius. *Critical Social Theory in the Interests of Black Folk.* New
York: Rowman & Littlefield, 2005.

Powell, Colin. Appearance on *Meet the Press.* January 13, 2013. http://
www.nbcnews.com/id/50447941/ns/meet_the_press-transcripts/t/
january-colin-powell-cory-booker-haley-barbour-mike-murphy
-andrea-mitchell/#.U2usdWdoK5Q.

Raboteau, Albert J. *Slave Religion: The "Invisible Institution" in the Antebellum South.* New York: Oxford University Press, 1980.

Ragland, Ellie. "Lacan and the Hommosexuelle: 'A Love Letter.' " In
Homosexuality and Psychoanalysis, edited by Tim Dean and Christopher Lane, 98–119. Chicago: University of Chicago Press, 2001.

Restuccia, Frances. *Amorous Acts: Lacanian Ethics in Modernism, Film, and
Queer Theory.* Stanford: Stanford University Press, 2006.

Rothstein, Mervyn. "Toni Morrison, in Her New Novel, Defends Women."
New York Times, August 26, 1987, C17.

Saussure, Ferdinand de. *Course in General Linguistics.* Translated by Wade
Baskin. New York: McGraw-Hill, 1966.

Schreiber, Evelyn Jaffe. *Subversive Voices: Eroticizing the Other in William
Faulkner and Toni Morrison.* Knoxville: University of Tennessee Press,
2001.

Seshadri-Crooks, Kalpana. *Desiring Whiteness: A Lacanian Analysis of Race.*
New York: Routledge, 2000.

Shakespeare, William. *Hamlet.* 2nd ed. Edited by Cyrus Hoy. New York:
Norton, 1992.

Shepherdson, Charles. "The Intimate Alterity of the Real." *Postmodern
Culture* 6, no. 3 (1996). Accessed February 13, 2015, http://jefferson
.village.virginia.edu/pmc/text-only/issue.596/shepherdson.596.

Spillers, Hortense J. *Black, White, and in Color: Essays on American Literature and Culture*. Chicago: University of Chicago Press, 2003.

Strolla, Cory. Quoted in "Attorney: Dunn 'Overcharged' due to Trayvon Killing." *USA Today*, February 13, 2014. http://www.usatoday.com/story/news/2014/02/13/attorney-says-michael-dunn-overcharged-due-to--trayvon-martin-death/5457507/.

Stubblefield, Anna. *Ethics along the Color Line*. Ithaca, N.Y.: Cornell University Press, 2005.

Washington, Booker T. *Up from Slavery*. New York: Airmont Books, 1967.

Wells-Barnett, Ida B. *On Lynching*. Salem, N.H.: Ayer, 1991.

West, Cornel. *Democracy Matters: Winning the Fight against Imperialism*. New York: Penguin, 2005.

Wyatt, Jean. "Giving Body to the Word: The Maternal Symbolic in Toni Morrison's Beloved." *PMLA* 108, no. 3 (1993): 474–88.

———. *Risking Difference: Identification, Race, and Community in Contemporary Fiction and Feminism*. New York: State University of New York Press, 2004.

Žižek, Slavoj. *The Plague of Fantasies*. New York: Verso, 1997.

INDEX